Bridging Science and Religion

edited by
Ted Peters
Gaymon Bennett

**THEOLOGY
AND THE
SCIENCES**

FORTRESS PRESS
Minneapolis

**Published under the auspices of the Center for Theology
and the Natural Sciences**

ISBN 0-8006-3625-2

Printed in the U.S.A.

07   06   05   04   03   1   2   3   4   5   6   7   8   9   10

Contents

Part One
Methodology: How Bridges Are Built

Part Two
Constructing Scientific Spans

Part Three
Constructing Religious Spans

Acknowledgments

We at the Center for Theology and the Natural Sciences (CTNS) at the Graduate Theological Union (GTU) are deeply indebted to Sir John Templeton. It is with a spirit of gratitude that we recognize the generous financial support he has tendered through grants from the John Templeton Foundation for our work in the CTNS Science and Religion Course Program (SRCP) from 1998 to 2002. It has been our mission at SRCP to introduce teaching faculty in colleges, universities, and seminaries all over the world to the dialogue between natural science and religious reflection. The editing and publishing of this book provides a basic resource for use in classrooms in Asia, Australia, Europe, Africa, and the Americas. We thank Sir John Templeton for underwriting this and many other similar projects within SRCP. It is our hope that this book represents a fulfillment of his vision for future dialogue between science and religion.

We want to honor our colleague in Hong Kong, Kang Phee Seng, who in January 2001 collaborated with us in planning what would become the first draft of this book, an abbreviated version published in Chinese characters by the Chinese Academy of Social Sciences in Beijing. Phee Seng along with Liang Yuanyuan and Carla Jimenez provided invaluable organizational planning and support for what would become our multi-city lecture tour in the People's Republic of China, Taiwan, and Hong Kong during May 2002. Thanks are due the tour faculty and participants: Francisco Ayala, Mary Anne Cooney, David Karoly, Christin Quissell, Charlotte Russell, and Robert Russell. This lecture tour in combination with the Chinese publication prompted lively engagement, and helped to shape the final draft of *Bridging Science and Religion*.

Hilary Regan, our SRCP workshop director in Australia, has represented CTNS well in the United Kingdom, Brazil, and Indonesia. He has cheerfully borne the burden of negotiating publishing contracts in English, Portugese, and Bahasa. For his cosmopolitan vision for the interaction of science and religion, we thank Hilary.

We thank as well Kristin Johnston for impeccable work helping to prepare the English language manuscript.

We remind ourselves and our readers of the indispensable contributions made by our friends and colleagues here at CTNS. Particular gratitude is due to the Berkeley SRCP staff who daily share their intelligence, humor and chicken sandwiches with us: Anne Bade, Ceciley Bauman, Whitney Bauman, Nathan Hallanger, Peter Hess, Carla Jimenez, Stan Lanier, Melissa Moritz, Christin Quissell and Kathryn Smith.

Finally, we recognize the work of CTNS Founder and Director Robert John Russell. It was Bob's original conception of the *creative mutual interaction of science and theology* that gave birth to the Center in 1981; it is Bob's continued intellectual leadership that guides CTNS in the current decade. To Bob and to all of our CTNS colleagues, we offer thanks.

Ted Peters
Gaymon Bennett
Berkeley, California

Contributors

Gaymon Bennett, Communications Coordinator, Science and Religion Course Program of the Center for Theology and the Natural Sciences, Berkeley, California, USA.

Philip Clayton, Professor of Philosophy, California State University at Sonoma; Principal Investigator, Science and the Spiritual Quest, the Center for Theology and the Natural Sciences, Berkeley, California, USA.

Eduardo Cruz, Professor of Religious Studies at the Pontifical Catholic University of São Paulo, Brazil.

Peter M. J. Hess, Associate Program Director of the Science and Religion Course Program of the Center for Theology and the Natural Sciences, Berkeley, California, and adjunct faculty, University of San Francisco, San Francisco, California, USA.

Martinez J. Hewlett, Professor, Department of Molecular and Cellular Biology, University of Arizona, Tucson, USA.

Muzaffar Iqbal, Founder and President of the Center for Islam and Science, Islamabad, Pakistan.

George L. Murphy, Pastoral Associate, St Paul's Episcopal Church, Akron, Ohio, and adjunct faculty, Trinity Lutheran Seminary, Columbus, Ohio, USA.

Nancey Murphy, Professor of Christian Philosophy, Fuller Theological Seminary, Pasadena, California, USA.

Richard K. Payne, Dean and Associate Professor of Japanese Buddhism, Institute of Buddhist Studies at the Graduate Theological Union, Berkeley, California, USA.

Ted Peters, Professor of Systematic Theology, Pacific Lutheran Theological Seminary and the Graduate Theological Union, and Program Director of the Science and Religion Course

Program of the Center for Theology and the Natural Sciences, Berkeley, California, USA.

Varadaraja V. Raman, Professor of Physics, Rochester Institute of Technology, Rochester, New York, USA.

Robert John Russell, Professor of Theology and Science in Residence, Graduate Theological Union, and Founder and Director of the Center for Theology and the Natural Sciences, Berkeley, California, USA.

Kirk Wegter-McNelly, Doctoral Candidate in Theology at the Graduate Theological Union and Editing Coordinator of the Center for Theology and the Natural Sciences, Berkeley, California, USA.

Laurie Zoloth, Professor of Social Ethics and Jewish Philosophy, and Director of the Program in Jewish Studies at San Francisco State University, San Francisco, California, USA.

Foreword

This is an extraordinary book. Its resources are an "open door" welcoming new voices to enter into the discussions of the past forty years and to begin to contribute to them. The goal is to bring about a fruitful interaction between the profound discoveries of the natural sciences and the venerable and living wisdoms of the world religions.

The book bears on its cover a striking image, the Golden Gate Bridge. I am honored that this image was chosen, since it is one dear to my heart, one that I have used often since founding CTNS in 1981. To me the image of the bridge conveys much that is of great value about the nature of the interdisciplinary field of science and religion.

First, when a bridge is under construction, all our attention is focused on its actual structure and composition and the people specialized in and dedicated to the enormous challenge of building it. Similarly, for the first decades of science and religion, starting with the pioneering contributions by Ian Barbour in the early 1960s, most of the scholarly attention was focused on methodology: how to actually bring together into a fruitful exchange such apparently distant, even conflicting, fields as science and religion. The idea was to draw upon the combined secular resources of the philosophy of science and the philosophy of religion to argue against reductionism and to argue for a systematic analogy between the rationality of theory construction and testing in science and in religion (the "internal" perspective), as well as between the effects on such rationality as it is carried out by the community of scholars in each field (the "externalist" perspective). The result, called "critical realism" by Barbour and adopted in various forms by most scholars in the field, is a methodology by which the discoveries of the sciences and their philosophical interpretation can be brought carefully and critically into the ongoing work in theology and, at least in principle, the insights of theology and philosophy can prove beneficial to scientists as they, in turn, pursue their own theoretical work. Thus the methodology of critical realism serves as a "two-way" bridge between science and religion. Moreover, since the bridge is built without explicitly using the actual theories of either field ("the bridge is not the territory"), it is not "confessionally bound up" or prejudiced by the particular points of view embodied in, say, Christian theology, or evolutionary biology. In short, the bridge can be used by anyone interested in the interaction between a given religious community (e.g., Buddhism, Taoism, etc.) and a given scientific community ("Western" or not).

Secondly, once the bridge is in place, attention turns from the bridge itself to the traffic it bears between the two now-linked communities, and the effects and changes and innovations this traffic produces in both of them. Over the past two or three decades, I have seen an ever-widening ripple spread through my discipline – Christian theology – as it has been increasingly influenced, at least in some communities, by the discoveries and methods of science and their philosophical interpretation. Big Bang and inflationary cosmology, relativity, quantum physics, irreversible thermodynamics, chaos and complexity theory, molecular and evolutionary biology, human genetics, the cognitive sciences, the neurosciences, computer science and many other scientific fields have been carefully and systematically brought across the bridge and introduced into discussions of God as creator, as an actor in history and nature who does not "break" the laws of nature but acts through and with them, of theodicy in nature, the *imago dei*, human sin and even the meaning and scope of redemption. Likewise, theologians from Judaism, Islam, and more recently Buddhist and Confucian scholars, have entered into conversations with science, particularly as science has served as a fruitful template for interreligious discussion. Conversely, scholars have explored the philosophical and theological dimensions lying within and under contemporary natural science. For example, in very recent years, some Christian scholars have begun to explore possible implications for research science arising from the idea of Jesus' resurrection and of a divine transformation that encompasses the universe as a whole. So, although uneven and still patchy in places, traffic is now flowing in both directions across this amazingly resilient bridge.

Curiously, the 'bridge' image has sometimes been criticized as suggesting that the communities it links are static and fixed; in reality, of course, science and religion are ever in flux. However, the structural supports for the bridge – the steel pillars that support the suspension cable and, in turn, carry the weight of the actual bridge – are firmly grounded in bedrock below each community. In this way the bridge structures remain reliable even as the communities it links experience dynamic change. Without bedrock, the communities themselves would be vulnerable to each new wave of discovery and revelation that arises in history. It is their bedrock that allows the communities to retain their identity over time while being alive with vitality and dynamic growth. The bedrock of science involves the assumptions about the world which underlie its methods and give rise to the empirical method, including the contingent rationality and intelligibility of nature, the value of honesty in reporting and sharing data, the thirst to know the world and joy in the mathematical beauty of physical laws. The religious bedrock varies depending on the tradition in question. In the traditions of Western monotheism for example, the bedrock would consist of the reality of God, the love and wisdom of God, the world as God's free and loving creation, the normative revelation of God through sacred texts and distinct historical events, and God as the ground, redemption and consummation of all that is. It is clear that these bedrock foundations of each community will not change as new scientific and theological research is pursued, but the way they are represented by these research programs in science and in theology will vary enormously, especially in light of the interactions between them.

For the particular interaction between Western monotheisms and science the bridge image works well for a third reason: take away the waters which the bridge spans and one finds an underlying common foundation from which the mountains of science, on the one side, and of Western monotheism on the other, extend upwards, making the land on which the two communities are built. This foundation is best expressed by the philosophical category of contingency, shared by both science and theology: since nature is God's creation it will be contingent, and since it is contingent it will require science to discover its empirical secrets. "Do not put God into my equations!" is thus the scientific version of the theological command against idolatry.

As this book will be read by scholars and students from a plurality of traditions and scientific disciplines, discussions may focus on a further profound question: whether a similar bridge can be built between cosmology, physics, biology and genetics on the one side and on the other side the religious traditions that grow strong throughout the diverse cultures of the world. Perhaps other materials will be needed, other architectural visions will be tried, before a reliable bridge takes shape here. Only then will we learn whether nature and human spiritualities as seen through different philosophical and theological lenses will still allow the familiar bridge to span the gulf and connect religion with the natural sciences or whether it will lead to their reconstruction along new lines. But build we must, for we are answerable not only to the foundational human questions which both science and religion address, but also to the growing international and intercultural crises in population, food, medicine, technology and the environment which call out for new solutions and a new global vision of the future.

These are challenging questions that only the future can decide. Today, however, this wonderful book is available to facilitate the process of dialogue and interaction. May its elegance and integrity be a gracious gift for all those who use it to cross over to the other side and discover the joy of new communities.

Robert John Russell

Introduction

GAYMON BENNETT

I heard the voice of a desperate mother on the radio today. Through the tangled wires of her telephone line, across the media infrastructure of National Public Radio, and into my car our worlds were spanned. The religious, social, political, and economic contexts of her life are largely foreign to me. At the time of the interview, she was locked in an apartment in Bethlehem, held hostage with her terrified and uncomprehending children by the crossfire centered on the Church of the Nativity just outside her home. Her days were marked by repetitions of prayer: prayer that the siege at the church would come to an end without massacre; prayer that when she left her apartment to find bread for her family she would not be shot by snipers; prayer that the religiously rooted war between the Israelis and the Palestinians would finally come to an end. Meanwhile, I sat in my car in Berkeley, California, hurrying off to work in an anxiety-induced rush. My anxiety was not created by guns and dying children, but by the relatively inconsequential fact that chapters of this very volume remained as yet unedited. The contrast of contexts informing our lives at that moment was clear. Nevertheless, for three minutes, reaching halfway around the world, our lives were bridged.

Perhaps because of the state of my concerns at the time, I found myself struck by two particular aspects of this contrast-of-contexts, aspects that likely would have otherwise remained unnoted in quotidian invisibility. First, I was struck by this familiar, yet extraordinary, bridging of worlds. Global media markets and worldwide telecommunications are such a usual part of our lives. We are rarely, if ever, impressed with this potential for such immediate and intimate contact with otherwise strange and distant worlds. This woman, whose concerns and struggles would likely not, in other historical times, have affected me so directly, was able to speak to me, an anonymous other, halfway around the globe.

I was struck by this experience in a second way: my response to this woman's struggles was imbued with science and religion. One example: informed by theological and humanitarian commitments, I found myself wondering about the biological roots of that violent behavior. I asked myself: does this latest example of human evil merely evince latent animal instincts not yet "selected out" of human nature by evolution? If so, at the end of the day, can moral condemnation, informed by religious vision, make a substantive difference for peace?

In short, given my state of preoccupation with the preparation of this book – a collection of essays emphasizing the global breadth and contextual relevance of building bridges between science and religion – I noted what often remains unnoted. Our everyday world is indeed global; there are no unaffected corners in which we can hide from the influence of global affairs. Moreover, that global world with its wide range of influence is indelibly marked by science and by religion.

Here is the thesis, the organizing principle, that finds itself elaborated in the collected pages of this book: faced by the reality of a global world, scholars from widely varying religious, cultural, scientific, and geographical contexts are engaging in the shared task of building two-way bridges of dialogue between science and religion; this shared engagement justifies and necessitates the mutual exchange of bridge-building resources – designs, processes, materials, and tools. The essays in this book have been collected together to facilitate that exchange, enabling scholars and students to construct and traverse new bridges between science and religion.

It is instructive to note what this thesis assumes. First, it assumes that scholars and students from varying contexts around the world are, will be, and ought to be building bridges of dialogue between science and religion. Second, it assumes that, though variegated contexts present scholars and students with varying and often unique bridge-building challenges, these challenges, and the solutions to them, are often trans-contextual. Scholars and students from varying cultural, religious, and scientific contexts benefit from one another's work. Hence, while chapters in this book address concerns that arise within the engagement of particular religious traditions with particular areas of the natural sciences, they less often take as a primary concern the justification of either bridge-building as such, or the idea that scholars from differing cultural and religious contexts can and do benefit from the insights of one another's work. This book is concerned with a constructive task; its payoff is the building of bridges. It is intended to be a forum for scholars, experienced in bridge-building, to let us in on their building projects, to let a global community of scholars and students share in the designs, processes, materials, and tools they have found useful in their work.

Global Dialogue and Contextual Concerns

The thesis for this book found its formulation in concern for teaching. Over the past several years Ted Peters and I, co-editors of this volume, have been working for the Science and Religion Course Program at the Center for Theology and the Natural Sciences at the Graduate Theological Union in Berkeley, California. The mission of the Center is to support the creative mutual interaction between contemporary theology and the natural sciences. The Center is committed to drawing theologians, philosophers, historians, religious studies scholars, ethicists, and other scholars in the humanities into conversation with scientists on questions of mutual concern. Since its inception in 1981, the Center for Theology and the Natural Sciences has asked: What are the best means of facilitating the long-term success of this mission? Answers to this question have fallen into three categories: research, public service, and teaching. It was in response to this third, teaching, that in 1998, CTNS inherited and expanded the Science and Religion Course Program.

The Science and Religion Course Program was designed to support faculty addressing science–religion questions through teaching at institutions of higher learning throughout the world. The form this support has taken has depended on our ability to determine, in conversation with colleagues from several continents, how well, and in what way, existing resources in science and religion meet the needs of scholars and students in various cultural and religious contexts. The dialectic between global sharing and contextual creativity led to the formulation of our thesis mentioned above.

The content of this book is shaped by the distinction between the global nature of dialogue and the meaningfulness of contextual concerns. The differing directions taken by the contributing authors find a unifying orientation in their attentiveness to that distinction. These scientists, theologians, philosophers, and ethicists engage in dialogue for varying reasons. As a result, they build dialogue bridges that serve differing purposes, accomplish differing ends, and require the use of differing designs, materials, tools, and techniques. The authors are engaged in a globe-wide dialogue, constructing bridges from a common warehouse of intellectual materials yet spanning local divides.

Global Dialogue

What does it mean to say that dialogue between science and religion is global in character? Is this simply an acknowledgement of the self-evident fact that science and religion affect and are affected by people from every corner of the globe, or does it suggest a more substantive insight?

The phrase "science and religion dialogue" is shorthand for a diverse, complex, and rapidly expanding series of questions, issues, and insights, which in many ways resist simple and corporate designation. Dialogue between science and religion is necessarily multidisciplinary and interdisciplinary. It necessarily involves multiple religious traditions and, at times, is interreligious. From the nature of nature, to questions of consciousness, to the moral status of the embryo, the numerous tasks involved in dialogue between science and religion require a range of resources. Does this multiplicity of tasks serve as counter-evidence to the claim that dialogue between science and religion is by nature global? Or worse, is the global character of dialogue the result of intellectual colonialism, expansion of a dialogue indigenous only to the Western academy now inflicted onto peoples of the non-Western world?

Despite the multiplicity of intellectual tasks, questions, and issues invoked by the designation "science and religion," these tasks, questions, and issues do, at points, coincide. These points of coincidence suggest that dialogue between science and religion is genuinely global in scope, in concern, in nature. It bears noting that, as both Muslim chemist Muzaffar Iqbal and Buddhist scholar Richard Payne note in their chapters, much early work done in science and religion took place within a recognizably Christian and English-language context. Nevertheless, the resources developed from this work have been shared and, at times, found to be effective in addressing concerns beyond those considered by the original authors of those resources. As demonstrated by the contributing authors in this volume, this early work has been received, critiqued, revised, and expanded. Scholars around the world have transformed this work and pressed it into the service of local constructions. In turn, insights gained from these local constructions are being reinvested in new collaborative projects: the building of global bridges, multidirectional spans covering distance not simply between science and religion, but between the concerns and interests of local and global contexts.

The modifier "global" has become culturally iconic. In addition to describing specific, concrete instances of global exchange, this term brings to mind a spectrum of phenomena characterized by the fundamental interconnectedness of world affairs – political, cultural, military, and particularly economic affairs. In applying the modifier "global" to the idea of dialogue between science and religion, we intend to invoke the general iconic sense of the term. The term global used in this way implies that the relationship between science and religion bears on the lives, concerns, and well-being of all peoples and institutions worldwide. Both those who try to sequester science, sheltering it from the perceived corruptions of religion, and those who try to reject science as the imposition of secularism on religion, live a naive existence. Science and religion are ubiquitous in human society; they permeate human existence; and they interpenetrate one another. The relationship between them, in its historically and dynamic relevance, serves to frame and shape human life, providing the intellectual raw materials out of which we fashion our lenses for viewing human and non-human nature. It is first of all in this sense of worldwide interconnectedness that science and religion is a global concern.

While granting the intellectual integrity of religion, we should be honest about the fact that the global nature of dialogue between science and religion is, in large part, the result of the global nature of science itself. Science is characterized by an uncanny cultural mobility. This is true for at least three reasons. First, science has played, and will continue to play, a greater and greater role in the phenomenon of globalization generally, and in the expansion of global markets and international telecommunications more specifically.

Thomas Friedman, Pulitzer Prize-winning author, has suggested that in the early part of the twenty-first century we find ourselves in the middle of the second great movement of globalization in world history. In the late nineteenth and early twentieth centuries, driven primarily by military, political, and industrial expansion, enabled in part by advances in technology, globalization took the world from a size large to a size medium. Yet, if this first chapter of globalization drew much of the world into tighter quarters, its ability to make Laplanders and Creoles global neighbors was insignificant by comparison to the second chapter of globalization which we are currently experiencing. With the fall of the Berlin wall, globalization became the ideological name-of-the-game in world affairs. In a few short years the new globalization, driven not by military, but by economic expansion, quickly shrank the world from a size medium to a size small. If the first chapter was enabled in part by technology, this one is fundamentally dependent on it. The knife-edge of expanding global markets is sharpened by complex, evolving, science-based technologies.

What is the net effect of these trends in globalization for dialogue between science and religion? Economic globalization has woven together, more tightly than ever before, the corporate future of individuals and institutions. This weave is restructuring the internal and external lives of nation states. Where political status was once determined by military might, it is now largely determined by participation in multinational economic structures. How do nation states equip themselves to participate in these structures? One way is the development of technology. How do nation states develop technology? They develop it through science, or, more precisely, science education. Those who fear globalization also fear big science and big technology, because these seem to threaten local self-determination. Yet, forces of local self-determination frequently arm themselves with their own science and technology to prevent being overrun by globalization.

Science and science education is an integral part of both globalization and resistance to globalization. However, in order to effect scientific change, many countries experience a concurrent revival and revision of cultural and religious values. For better or worse, this global culture is informed by a largely Western scientific worldview. Biologist Martinez Hewlett, in his chapter, reminds us of the ways in which the Darwinian model of natural history has impacted areas of cultural life far beyond the science in which it's embedded. Physicist V. V. Raman in his chapter describes a challenging juxtaposition: the Hindu tradition, which has shaped his spiritual existence, presumes that, in some respects, the spiritual realm is more real than the phenomenal realm, while the science which has expanded his intellectual horizons is committed to the reality of the latter.

Science is not simply one cultural artifact among many, and its cultural mobility does not only depend on current trends in globalization. The second reason that science is consistently able to penetrate a range of cultural and religious traditions because of its effectively transcontextual methods, tools, and assumptions. While work in the philosophy of science has reminded us that the scientific enterprise often progresses with haphazardness and a serendipity that belie idealized portrayals of science, that progress is marked by certain consistencies. Experimental results, for example, must be repeatable in Britain and Bangladesh. The tools of quantification and the language of mathematics regularly bridge the distances of varying cultural assumptions. Perhaps most importantly, science assumes that nature is open to investigation, and that principles derived from the workings of nature are regular and reliable. This constancy allows scientists to make universal claims. As Brazilian theologian Eduardo Cruz notes in his chapter, unlike certain schools of philosophical and theological thought which edge toward relativism in their assessment of the nature of truth claims, science makes claims that, in their universal articulation, apply to all people. Either $e = mc^2$ is applicable to both you and me, or it is not applicable at all.

Lastly, and perhaps most importantly, science is so culturally mobile because of the compelling claims it makes about the nature of the world we live in and from the technological benefits that accrue as a result of those claims. The second chapter by physicist/theologians Robert Russell and Kirk Wetger-McNelly explores the implications of contemporary cosmology for theological understandings of the far future of the universe. Do Christian theological claims about the transformation of the cosmos into a new creation make sense in a universe that, according to much current evidence, will die in the ice-death of dissipated energy? Science calls into question the tenability of certain core theological claims.

In his review of the genetic sciences, theologian Ted Peters notes the challenges for theological anthropology raised by genetic research, such as genetic reductionism, genetic determinism, and Neo-Darwinian evolution. And yet, as Peters reminds us, the genetic sciences promise medical revolution, a revolution which might serve as a means of fulfilling religious commitments to addressing sickness and suffering.

Why is it important to recognize, even to emphasize, that dialogue between science and religion is global in character? Simply, dialogue is not a culturally idiosyncratic concern. If it were, scholars in varying contexts would not need to take seriously one another's work and insights. Religious and cultural traditions must face the fact of globalization. They must face the fact that science and technology will inevitably be a component of that encounter. Science and religion co-inhabit a single global world. Because that cohabitation is enabled if not enforced by the global interconnectedness of institutions and peoples, the task of navigating the science–religion relationship cannot simply be a matter of local concern. An engagement of global breadth requires the concerted efforts of scholars from around the world. Significantly, scholars from around the world recognize that they are indeed asking interrelated questions, and that they, like the contributors to this volume, must work together to construct global bridges both between science and religion and between their respective contexts.

The claim that dialogue between science and religion is global in nature carries with it certain sociological, economic, and political implications. Many of these important implications will not be directly addressed in this volume. In particular this book will not take up the causes and relative merits of globalization. It will not address the question of whether or not the global character of science, and the science–religion dialogue with it, is hegemonic. The book does not attempt to answer the question of whether the natural sciences, as developed in Europe and America, are genuinely universal. That is, we do not address the question, Are there one or many sciences? Generally speaking, the chapters in the book recognize the phenomenon of global dialogue as a significant given, and work out their theses accordingly. In short, our intention in recognizing the global nature of dialogue between science and religion was simply to instill in the volume a sense of realism with regard to how science and religion is being done, and needs to be done around the world. This realism informs our commitment to bring existing resources in science and religion which have been largely developed in Christian and English-speaking contexts into a single volume with resources for dialogue being developed in contexts which are largely non-Christian and non-English. In organizing the book, we have attempted to face squarely what we've experienced in our collaborations with scholars and students: science and religion is a global concern, and as such its nature is necessarily global. Scholars from varying cultural, religious, and scientific contexts face similar challenges in constructing bridges between science and religion and will benefit from access to one another's work.

Contextual Concerns

Globalization affects but by no means extinguishes the concerns, interests, and commitments of specific cultural and religious traditions. Hence, while dialogue between science and religion is indeed global, it is no less shaped and sharpened by contextual concerns. The recognition that dialogue is invaluable may be shared; the relative meaningfulness of that dialogue, and the particular directions the dialogue takes, however, are often dependent upon concerns inspired by specific contexts.

In August 1999, with Peter Hess, a colleague here at CTNS, I met with doctoral students at INAOE, the National Institute of Astrophysics, Optics and Electronics in Tonantzintla, Mexico, to discuss the relationship between science and religion in Latin America. The teaching of courses in religion is outlawed in Mexico's publicly funded universities. Yet the students at INAOE were anxious to discuss the implications of dialogue between science and religion. Why? These students frame science, and technology with it, in social justice terms. Mexico is burdened by a 30-plus percent poverty rate. These students are committed to the idea that science and technology, if made more widely available, will reverse trends of political injustice in their country. The assumption at work here is that science, as science, has the ethical traction needed to contribute to the cause of justice. As our discussion progressed, it became clear that the students' vision for justice was not necessarily native to science, but was inspired by religious and philosophical commitments. Certainly science contributed to that vision. Nevertheless, religious and philosophical articulations of justice could not be disentangled from what the students saw as the cultural significance of science. Inevitably, the areas of dialogue with religion that the students found most compelling and were most willing to pursue were those areas that dealt with questions of justice, from eschatology to theological anthropology.

A little over a year later in March 2001, Ted Peters and I met with a group of scientists, philosophers, and Buddhist monks from Thailand. For many this meeting represented creative new beginnings, a first formal assessment of the value of science–religion discourse for science, for Buddhism, for Thailand. For these Thai colleagues, science–religion dialogue increased in relevance as the conversation bore more or less directly on primary commitments within Buddhism and on issues of pressing social concern within Thailand. For example, while all seemed to agree that questions of hermeneutics and methodology were keys to facilitating dialogue, the interest in dialogue increased when it centered on genetics.

Hunger in Thailand is spreading. Buddhist monks and laity feel a tremendous responsibility for halting this scourge. Genetics, for these Buddhists, is crucial to successfully taking responsibility insofar as it allows for the development of strains of rice that will grow in the nutrition-depleted soils of certain areas of their country. Many believe that religious commitment alone may be inadequate to the task of adequately addressing pressing social concerns. Scientific insights supplement this effort. In the words of one Buddhist monk present: compassion is not enough to feed the poor; we need understanding.

Early in 2002, Ted Peters and I met with a select group of Roman Catholic bioethicists, philosophers, and theologians, to address the question, How ought work in embryology and developmental biology contribute to a theological assessment of the beginning of life? The Roman Catholic tradition of natural law, with its thoughtful history of relating "the book of God" and "the book of nature," is particularly well equipped to address this question. Reflecting the methodological sophistication of this intellectual tradition, the participants pressed into their inquiry with systematic care. What is the proper relationship between theology and science? What theological doctrines – theology of creation, theological anthropology, eschatology – provide commitments that might inform how that relationship should be navigated? How ought theology relate to philosophy, philosophy to science, science to ethics, and ethics to theology? This careful commitment to philosophical foundations provided solid footing for new traffic between embryology and theology. New knowledge gained from embryology and genetic research reveals the scientific naivety of presuming that active embryos can only be formed through the merger of sperm DNA and egg DNA. With techniques such as cloning and parthenogenesis, traditional ways of envisioning the beginning of life are challenged. Participants asked: how ought natural law respond to these new understandings of nature?

The contextual nature of concerns has a practical effect on the way in which bridges between science and religion are currently being built. Scholars and students, depending on their interests and intellectual commitments, give certain issues particular weight, ask questions differently, ask different questions. Jewish theologian and bioethicist Laurie Zoloth suggests in her chapter that because Judaism holds the healing of the sick to be a fundamental religious obligation, Jewish scholars and students of science and religion may be first attracted to interactions with the biomedical sciences. A Christian scholar, such as George Murphy, may pay particularly careful attention to the suffering in nature poignantly revealed by evolutionary biology, sparking new inquiry into the nature and possibility of God's suffering. A Muslim scholar, according to Iqbal, may find it valuable to answer the question of how the sciences and their investigation of nature fits within a single framework of knowledge organized according to Qur'anic commitments. Context, in the end, shapes the way in which dialogue between science and religion takes place.

It is crucial to recognize that certain questions within the science and religion dialogue would simply not be raised without the influence of prompting from within these contexts. The impulses of certain religious traditions will push scholars to explore certain questions more deeply than others. This push provides an invaluable opportunity for the wider community of scholarship: the discovery and development of insights into the nature of the relationship between science and religion that in other contexts may have been left undiscovered and underdeveloped.

The way in which one builds bridges between science and religion is largely determined by how one answers the question: Why build bridges at all? Individual scientists, theologians, historians, ethicists, and philosophers often answer this question differently. And while recognizing the relevance of one another's answers, the practical result is that they build bridges for different reasons. Because they build bridges for different reasons they build bridges differently. The bridges are intended to span different kinds of cultural, intellectual, political divides, forcing scholars to contend with differing intellectual terrain. In short, the tools, techniques, and materials appropriate for scholars engaged in one bridge-building project are not always the appropriate tools for another.

Our emphasis upon the contextual concerns that shape dialogue between science and religion, much like our emphasis upon the global nature of that dialogue, carries with it several questions that are not directly taken up in this volume. Though most chapters make reference to it, no single chapter is devoted to addressing the question of the contextual nature of truth claims. Again, generally speaking, the authors accept the premise that differing cultural and religious traditions will address dialogue between science and religion differently, though only a few explore the cumulative effect of these differences. This book, for example, does not address directly the question of how the development of the preponderance of materials in science and religion within a largely Christian and English-speaking context benefits or adversely affects the work of scholars in non-Christian and non-English-speaking contexts. Rather the book assumes that intellectual traffic flows between Christian and non-Christian scholars, between English and non-English readers. This book does not address directly the question of cultural relativism, although the unique needs of specific traditions are clearly recognized.

It is in light of these varying needs that we have tried to collect together essays by scholars representing different religious and cultural traditions, and different academic disciplines. While our representation is by no means exhaustive, and is necessarily restrictive given the limitations of a single volume, the chapters included bear witness to the need for students and scholars within particular contexts to develop intellectual tools appropriate for science and religion dialogue within those contexts.

Bridge-Building and Hypothetical Consonance

The aim of this book is constructive in character; that is, its success will be measured by the bridges between science and religion it helps to construct. In providing scholars and students with a forum for sharing bridge-building resources, the book implicitly poses a constructive question: How might science and religion contribute – through rigorous examination, mutual critique, and creative idea-sharing – to one another's internal concerns as well as to areas of shared interest? The value of the book ultimately lies in the value of the answers given to this question. It is our intent that these provisional answers be educational. That, by exploring various models of how the bridging of science and religion can be done, scholars and students of science and religion will increase in their own ability to build bridges.

The question posed above presupposes a particular kind of co-operative partnership between science and religion, what Ted Peters has referred to elsewhere as *hypothetical consonance*. As historian Peter Hess notes in his chapter, the popular image of an alleged warfare between science and religion somewhat misrepresents the intellectual commerce being exchanged between scholars in the sciences and the humanities. A growing number of scientists and theologians are finding points of shared interest and mutual concern. Hypothetical consonance is one constructive form this shared interest has taken.

The term *consonance* suggests that there are areas of correspondence, connection, or relevance between the understandings of nature as conceived by the natural sciences and as developed through the discernments of various religious traditions. Consonance, as Peters has noted, comes in various forms. In its "committed" form consonance implies virtual accord or harmony. To portray the relationship between science and religion in this sense would be misleading. At many points, the insights of science and religion are dissonant. Consonance can also be conceived of in a "provisional" form. This rendition of consonance more accurately portrays the current relationship between science and religion. The provisional form of consonance functions as a hypothesis, thus, hypothetical consonance.

Hypothetical consonance begins with the assumption that science and religion are trying to make sense of a single – even if complex or multi-faceted – reality. Working from this assumption hypothetical consonance asks a question: Is it reasonable to assume that, if science and religion are making claims about the same reality, those claims, at points, will reinforce, critique, or illuminate one another? The shorthand version goes like this: Science and religion both pursue truth about the same reality; though their methods and routes may vary, shouldn't we expect that, in the end, they would be valuable traveling companions?

In committing to hypothetical consonance both science and religion are taking risks. Religion agrees to subject its presuppositions to scientific scrutiny, and to assume that a scientific description of the natural world might be fruitful for religious insight. Science agrees to subject its presuppositions to religious scrutiny, and to assume that religious insights about the nature of reality might prove to be scientifically fruitful. The risks taken, however, are not without an intellectual safety net. By raising assumptions to the level of a hypothesis, science and religion can engage in common research programs, confirm and disconfirm claims together. Hypothetical consonance is a disposition toward dialogue. More specifically, it is a commitment to the inherent fruitfulness of dialogue. It is this disposition, this commitment, that, in the end, makes hypothetical consonance attractive.

Because hypothetical consonance seeks the fruitfulness of dialogue, note what it avoids. First, hypothetical consonance is not an attempt by either science or religion to prove or disprove one another's claims. Dialogue with science, for example, may challenge one's conception of the transcendent, but it is not engaged in it as an effort to prove or disprove God. Second, hypothetical consonance does not require either science or religion to give up their intellectual integrity. Science need never work the notion of Brahman into its equations. Theologians need not swap their criteria for truth with those native to science. Third, it avoids the hubris of presuming that either science or religion has a lock on truth. Often so-called warfare between science and religion is the result of exclusive claims of access to truth made by some reductionists or fundamentalists. Fourth, hypothetical consonance keeps the relationship between science and religion from devolving into turf war. While science and religion may, from time to time, make mutually exclusive claims about the nature of nature, these claims need not result in the cessation of conversation. Finally, note that hypothetical consonance does not shy away from conflict. Science and religion will have points of disagreement. Hypothetical consonance, however, treats conflict as a means to more fruitful engagement. If dialogue as such is the aim, then conflict can lead to new insight.

Hypothetical consonance supports the constructive task of bridge-building. Often the lane of traffic moving from the scientific toward the religious end of the bridge is the first to be completed. Nevertheless, as suggested in several chapters in this volume, bridges built with the materials of hypothetical consonance can allow intellectual traffic to move from the religious to scientific end as well. As colleagues here at CTNS have reminded us, the divides between science and religion in our contemporary global society are real. In order for them to be bridged, constructive work must be done. This work requires the intellectual humility implied by hypothetical consonance.

Bridges

What we have found, working with students and scholars from various countries, various cultural, scientific, political, and religious contexts, are attempts to build different types of bridges, for often differing reasons, between science and religion. And yet, the common task of bridge-building provides coherence of conversation between variegated endeavors. Bridge-builders in these contexts are interested in sharing insights with one another. They are interested in looking at one another's plans, trying out one another's tools, testing one another's materials, and assessing one another's techniques. While interested in resources that have already been tried and found reliable, they are also interested in critiquing and revising those resources, and in developing materials appropriate for their particular projects.

Perhaps most importantly these students and scholars are interested in collaboration. Beyond the invaluable work of building local bridges they are committed to designing and building transcontinental, transcontextual bridges, global spans. These spans are intended to carry two-way traffic. Science must inform religion. Religion must inform science. These two-way spans are intended to move not only between science and religion, but between cultural and religious contexts as well. Scholars from various traditions will not complete these transcontextual spans if they fail to recognize their mutual dependence on one another's contributions

This book is intended to contribute to these resource-sharing efforts. As editors working in an English-speaking context, trained in Christian theology and philosophy, we inevitably left our intellectual fingerprints both on the book's table of contents and on its chapters. Yet in the end we accomplished what we set out to accomplish – to put together a collection of essays that provided basic materials and techniques for the building of bridges between science and religion. In selecting these essays we considered the global nature of dialogue between science and religion. In light of this consideration, we selected authors and materials that have shown themselves to be particularly fruitful in the contemporary academic study of science and religion. At the same time, in selecting these essays, we've considered the contextual concerns that bring relevance and meaningfulness to the dialogue between science and religion. For this reason we have interspersed the work of more familiar science and religion scholars with that of scholars contributing in new ways to science–religion dialogue – critiquing, revising, and redirecting that dialogue. The chapters selected are instructive on many levels, confirming the unique character of questions being asked in different traditions, exemplifying the transcontextual relevance of all work in science and religion.

Part One
Methodology: How Bridges Are Built

Science and Theology: Mutual Interaction

ROBERT JOHN RUSSELL and
KIRK WEGTER-MCNELLY

In 1996, Elizabeth A. Johnson, then President of the Catholic Theological Society of America, called for a theological and philosophical re-engagement with the sciences, entailing a "return to cosmology, in order to restore fullness of vision and get theology back on the track from which it fell off a few hundred years ago."[1] This essay examines such a "re-engagement" by surveying the methodological foundations of the rapidly growing interdisciplinary field of "theology and science." The immediate historical groundings of this field can be found in the 1960s. Major movements in the secular disciplines of philosophy of science and philosophy of religion, and new theories and discoveries in the natural sciences, as well as complex shifts in the Christian theological landscape, made possible constructive interaction between otherwise separate and even hostile intellectual communities. If these movements cleared the ground for constructive engagement, work in methodology provided the structural supports upon which the traffic of mutual interaction has moved.

This survey is divided into sections on methodological typologies, critical realism, methodological developments, anti-reductionism, and the role of philosophy in dialogue. We conclude the chapter with an examination of the most pressing challenges within the field, and a brief assessment of future directions the field should and probably will take. As is customary in "theology and science," this chapter focuses primarily on theoretical, philosophical, and foundational issues. While acknowledging their pertinence to the field, it is not focused on either ethical or spiritual concerns. Throughout this chapter, we refer to "theology" as the intellectual reflection upon religious tradition. By "science," we refer to the natural sciences, especially physics, cosmology, biology (with attention to evolutionary biology and genetics), and neuroscience. Lastly, it should be noted that this chapter focuses on the interaction between the natural sciences and the diversity of Christian theologies, where most of the material in the field to date has been developed.[2]

Methodology in Theology and Science

Dialogue between science and theology most often begins with the question of methodology: how should we relate theology and science? The past four decades have seen a variety of important proposals on methodology. Although they differ significantly on key questions, they still form a somewhat continuous developmental path. This path leads from early insights to a wide variety of current research proposals.[3] Before exploring this continuously developing path – often called "critical realism" – we will spend a brief time on how to classify approaches to theology and science.

Methodological Typologies

A number of typologies have been suggested to classify the relations between science and religion. They bring to light underlying assumptions that strongly shape both public and scholarly conversations.

Physicist Ian Barbour's typology remains the most widely used in the field. Barbour lists four types of relations between science and religion, each with subtypes:

1. *Conflict* includes scientific materialism and biblical literalism. Scientific materialists claim that the world is made up of matter alone; there is no room for mind, spirit, or God. Moreover, they claim science is the only way to obtain true knowledge; religion tells us nothing of real value about the world or humanity. Biblical literalists believe that the Bible should be read literally, requiring no interpretation, and that it alone gives us true knowledge about the world, humanity, and God; they often view science as a challenge to biblical faith.
2. *Independence* asserts that science and religion employ contrasting methods and differing languages. Here science and religion are kept totally isolated from each other. Thus, there is no conflict, but neither is there any interaction or even dialogue. Some argue that science and religion use totally different methods of inquiry, such

as reason versus faith, and that science is based on facts, and religion on values. Science is objective; religion is subjective. Science can be falsified but not religion. Scientific language refers to the way things are in the world, but religion uses language to describe our emotions, hopes, and beliefs.

3. *Dialogue*, as a model of relating science and religion, includes boundary questions and methodological parallels. While science can tell us a great deal about the world, there are some questions that lie at the edge or limits of science, questions that science raises but can never answer. If the universe had a beginning, what happened before it? Why do we feel compassion or altruism? Why does the universe exist? Others claim that ways in which science tests its theories are not entirely different from those of theology: both use data (empirical facts for science; sacred texts, religious experience, liturgy for religion), both involve communities of scholars which work together to find out what is true, both use reason as well as aesthetic values to choose between competing theories (in theology, theories are called "doctrines"), and so on.

4. *Integration* includes natural theology, theology of nature, and systematic synthesis. Natural theology is the attempt to start with the world and to discover something about God: that God exists, the nature of God, God's will and purpose, and so on. A theology of nature starts with theology and seeks to incorporate into it the discoveries of science; it involves a reformulation of theology in light of these discoveries. The goal of systematic synthesis is a combination of both theology and science into a single framework. It often combines them by using a single metaphysical system, such as a process metaphysic as derived from the philosophy of Alfred North Whitehead, or a Thomistic metaphysics. In this way, concepts such as space, time, matter, causality, mind, spirit, and even God, are used in similar ways in both theological and scientific theories and research.

Through the 1980s and 1990s, a variety of additional typologies appeared, many responding directly to and augmenting Barbour's work. Theologian and biochemist Arthur Peacocke published a typology listing differences and similarities in the realms, approaches, languages, and attitudes of theology and science. Georgetown theologian John Haught includes conflict, contrast, contact, and confirmation. The first three are similar to Barbour's first three types. "Confirmation," however, identifies a different type of relationship between science and religion than those identified by Barbour. Haught draws this type of relationship from work in the philosophy of science. By confirmation Haught means that there are important philosophical assumptions underlying science that have their roots in theology. One such philosophical assumption is that the universe is contingent: its fundamental properties and laws might have been different from what they are. This means that if we are to know what's "out there" we must make observations and take data. Thus the empirical method on which science is based rests on the assumption that nature is contingent. This assumption, historically, is based on the doctrine of creation in Christian theology: God created the universe as a free act, and God presumably could have created it different than it is. Thus in this "second order" way, Christian theology underlies the philosophy of science and, in turn, the view of nature out of which science works.

Ted Peters has also developed an expanded typology, providing additional nuance to Barbour's fourfold typology. For example, his treatment of "conflict" distinguishes between atheistic scientific materialists, who reject the idea of God, and scientific imperialists, for whom science alone produces genuine knowledge, even Knowledge of God. Peters also includes ethical issues that overlap science and theology, New Age spirituality, which draws on science to form new models of "integration," and what Peters refers to as "hypothetical consonance," in which the discovery of common themes in theology and science encourage us to explore further such themes.

Mark Richardson has illuminated the broad differences in the genre of literature in theology and science. He identifies works which focus narrowly on intellectual and rational concerns, others which stress the romantic, aesthetic and mystical function of texts, and, finally, works within well-developed religious traditions in their appropriation of science.[4]

Critical Realism

In his groundbreaking publication *Issues in Science and Religion*, Barbour develops a framework for viewing science, which he calls "critical realism." This framework includes a series of arguments involving epistemology (What kind of knowledge is involved?), language (How is it expressed?), and methodology (How is knowledge obtained and justified?). Together these arguments provided the initial "bridge" between science and religion. Barbour understands critical realism as an alternative to three predominant philosophical views of science. (1) According to classical or "naive" realism, scientific theories provide a "photographic" representation of the world.

(2) To instrumentalists, scientific theories are mere calculative devices. (3) Idealists view scientific theories as depicting reality as mental or ideational. For Barber, by contrast, scientific theories yield partial, revisable, and abstract knowledge of the world. According to critical realism, scientific theories are expressed through "metaphors." These are open-ended analogies whose meanings cannot be reduced to a set of literal statements. Metaphors, in turn, are developed into models in science.

For methodology, Barbour turns to contemporary philosophers of science. According to philosopher Carl Hempel, theories and data form a "hypothetico-deductive" loop in which theories are discovered by imaginative analogies and models based on data, and theories in turn lead to widening domains of predictions that can be used in testing them. However, philosophers such as Thomas Kuhn have pointed to what is called the historicist and social/contextual nature of science. This means that science evolves in a particular historical context, and that both personal and social factors influence those at work in scientific research. Data is not entirely pristine and neutral to the observer; instead what we take as relevant data, and how we incorporate data into our theories and their tests is a crucial factor, often referred to as the "theory-ladenness of data." Scientific knowledge is the shared knowledge of a community; it is intersubjective rather than strictly objective. Scientific theories operate within broader systems of assumptions called paradigms. Here, idealized experiments or insights influence the way researchers search for new data and broader applications of their theories.

Scientific advance includes both a normal development of a given paradigm, such as Newtonian mechanics, and its radical replacement during a revolution of paradigms, as when quantum mechanics arose. Paradigms include metaphysical assumptions about nature: whether nature is continuous or discrete, static or dynamic, purely physical or both physical and mental, etc. Aesthetics and values function within the process of theory choice. When two or more theories are available to explain the same data, scientists often choose the one that they consider more beautiful or simple. Moreover, scientists value truth-telling: the reporting of false data is abhorred.

In all, Barbour offered four criteria by which theories are chosen: (1) they must be in agreement with the known data, (2) they must be coherent with other accepted theories, (3) they must be increasingly broad in scope, and (4) they must be fertile, leading to new insights and applications. At the same time he offered a critical realist theory of truth. First, we say a statement is true if it refers to processes and things in the world. Second, we decide whether a statement is true if it corresponds with such processes. If, however, we cannot verify correspondence, then we say it is true if it coheres with other true statements and if it can be used pragmatically. In Barbour's view, our confidence that a theory actually refers to and describes the world is based on more than just that its predictions are correct. We have even more reasons for confidence if a theory increases our understanding (i.e., the intelligibility) of the world and our ability to explain natural processes.

Barbour's crucial "bridging" insight between science and religion is that these arguments in philosophy of science are parallel to arguments in the philosophy of religion: both science and religion make cognitive claims about the world using a hypothetico-deductive method within a contextualist and historicist framework.[5] Both communities organize observation and experience through models that are analogical, extensible, coherent, symbolic, and expressed through metaphors. He also notes, however, important differences between them. The type of "data" found in religion differs from that found in science. Religion serves non-cognitive functions missing in science, such as eliciting attitudes, personal involvement, and transformation. It also contains elements not found in science including story, ritual, and historical revelation. Conversely, science contains both higher-level laws, such as general relativity or quantum mechanics, and lower-level laws, such as Kepler's laws in astronomy and Boyle's law in thermodynamics, which are not found in religion. More importantly, consensus is formed in religion very differently from how it is formed in science. In the end, it is the dynamic tension between these similarities and differences that makes Barbour's approach so fruitful.

Even while Barbour was developing his position, scientific realism was being challenged in a number of other ways. Though philosopher of science Thomas Kuhn has focused primarily on factors *internal* to the scientific community, sociologists in the 1970s explored the social construction of science. These *externalist* accounts emphasized social, political, and economic influences on science.[6] Barbour's recent assessment is that externalist accounts provide a valuable corrective to the internalist view, particularly regarding the factors such as personal interests that are involved during the discovery of new theories (or what is called the "context of discovery"). However, the appeal to interests underestimates the degree to which these social factors or "distortions" are erased, or filtered out, as a theory is tested and deployed by a community of scientists.

Barbour's arguments concerning critical realism have been developed by a variety of scholars. While acknowledging that there are a diversity of views, which claim to be forms of scientific realism,[7] Arthur Peacocke argues that there is a "common core" which these diverse views share. The core has two features: one is that scientific developments are progressive, and the other is that the aim of science is to depict reality. Peacocke makes a similar case for critical realism in theology. Like science, theology is ultimately realist in character: it makes claims about reality. Also like science, however, theological "theories" can yield only partial, revisable, and abstract knowledge of the world and its relationship to the divine or sacred. Religious beliefs, much like scientific theories, are expressed through "metaphor," open-ended analogies whose meaning cannot be reduced to a set of literal statements.

The emphasis upon models and metaphors in critical realism is reflected in the work of theologian Sallie McFague, who describes both similar and different roles played by models in theology and in science. For McFague, in theology, models provide order, while in science they stimulate new discoveries. Similarly, in her study of metaphor in religious and scientific language, Janet Soskice empha sizes the distinction between metaphor and model, and vigorously defends theological realism, while stressing the social and contextual nature of scientific realism.

Barbour's work on critical realism was on the front edge of a widespread reexamination of the way in which science and theology ought to relate to one another. In 1981, Ernan McMullin introduced the theme of "consonance" between theology and science. According to McMullin, science and theology should form a coherent but evershifting worldview to which all kinds of human knowing can make tentative and revisable contributions. Robert John Russell later combined McMullin's idea of consonance with McFague's epistemic claim about the "is and is not" structure of metaphor to discuss the way in which scientific and theological theories can exhibit both consonance and dissonance in relation to one another. As we have noted, Ted Peters advocates a "hypothetical" view of consonance: given theology's commitment to God as creator of this universe, theologians should expect a certain degree of consonance between scientific and theological claims.

Methodological Developments

According to German theologian Wolfhart Pannenberg, the truth of Christianity is intimately tied to the claim that theology is a science

(*Wissenschaft*). Pannenberg brings into theology philosopher of science Karl Popper's view that scientific theories are hypotheses, which are always open to revision. He rejects Popper's idea that to be "scientific" a theory must be falsifiable by evidence. Instead, he argues that theories in the natural and human sciences are to be judged by the criteria of coherence, parsimony, and accuracy. The most adequate theory, for Pannenberg, is not simply one that lends itself to falsification, but the one that can account for and incorporate competing theories.

Philosopher Nancey Murphy criticizes Pannenberg's methodology. Murphy points out that David Hume and Pannenberg offer "incommensurable" theories of rationality, that is, competing theories that are diametrically opposed. Hume's theory cannot be incorporated into Pannenberg's theory. In this way, then, Pannenberg's theory fails by Pannenberg's own criterion. As an alternative, Murphy recommends Imre Lakatos's methodology of scientific research programs as a more accurate, and ultimately more fruitful, account of how scientific theories work. According to Lakatos, scientific theories consist of a central core idea, such as Isaac Newton's famous equation, "$f = ma$," or his theory of gravity. This core is surrounded by a "belt" or "ring" of auxiliary hypotheses that explain how to apply the theory to specific situations, such as how to apply Newton's law to the motion of planets. According to Lakatos, we should judge the relative progress or degeneration of research programs by their ability to predict and corroborate novel facts. Murphy provides a crucial modification of Lakatos's conception of a "novel fact" so that his method can be used in theology to help us decide which theological programs are empirically progressive. Her approach has been implemented in her own discussion of cosmological fine-tuning, and by other theologians to discuss theological anthropology, evaluate religion, and interpret cosmology.[8]

Philosopher Philip Clayton also urges theologians to use Lakatosian methodology. Clayton views "explanation" as the key concept embracing the natural sciences, the social sciences, and theology. In the natural sciences, where one interprets physical data, the truth of an explanation is pivotal. In the social sciences, however, where one interprets the actions of subjects who are themselves engaged in interpreting the world (or what is called the "double hermeneutic"), explanation means "understanding" (*Verstehen*). Theological explanations, then, are tested not only by verifying them directly against evidence, but also by weighing them against the combined experience and knowledge of a community. Such theories are neither "completely objective" nor "purely subjective" but "inter-subjective," and he claims that scientific theories are intersubjective, too.

Anti-Reductionism

Constructive interaction between science and theology has been facilitated by critiques of reductionistic assumptions at work in scientific materialism.

Francisco Ayala has distinguished three types of reductionism operative in science. (1) Methodological reductionism is a research strategy for studying wholes in terms of their parts, and a process for applying theories successful in one area to others. (2) Epistemological reduction is the claim that processes, properties, laws, or theories at higher levels of complexity can be derived entirely from those at lower levels. (3) Ontological reductionism is the view that higher-level entities are nothing but complex organizations of simpler entities. In a recent essay, Nancey Murphy has added two additional types. (4) Causal reductionism asserts that all causes are "bottom-up," i.e., the characteristics and processes of the parts entirely determine those of the whole. (5) Reductive materialism insists that "[only] the entities at the lowest level are *really* real." Murphy rejects reductive materialism by arguing that higher-level entities are "as real as" the entities that compose them, but she accepts ontological reductionism's rejection of vitalism and other ontological dualisms.

A Non-Reducible Hierarchy of the Sciences

Most scholars in theology and science accept methodological reductionism. However, they view other forms of reductionism as undercutting the credibility of higher-level disciplines. To counter this, they typically argue that the academic disciplines form a non-reducible hierarchy. It starts with physics at the bottom and moves upwards through chemistry, biology, physiology, and the neurosciences, to the behavioral, psychological, and social sciences.[9] Lower levels place *constraints* on upper levels while allowing for genuine *emergence* of upper-level laws, processes, and properties. Arthur Peacocke developed this hierarchy in two dimensions, vertically and horizontally. Vertically, it contains levels of increasing complexity (the physical world, living organisms, their behavior, and human culture). Horizontally, it orders systems by part-to-whole hierarchies (e.g. in biology: macromolecules, organelles, cells, organs, individual organisms, populations, ecosystems).

Peacocke's analysis reflects the broad consensus of the scientific community regarding the way in which various scientific disciplines relate to and rely upon one another. A key addition in Peacocke's work, though, is the place and role of theology in the hierarchy of sciences. Peacocke places it at the top, since theology seeks to integrate the totality of knowledge, and since it must be constrained by them all. This gives theology an essential role in the system: it completes all the lower levels by offering answers to fundamental questions raised by them.[10]

Ontological Implications

We now face the most challenging question: What is an appropriate ontology for these epistemic schemes? That is, what is the nature of reality if this epistemic hierarchy is correct? Most writers in theology and science avoid two extreme positions: monism, which reduces all reality to physical material (or, conversely, reducing physical phenomena to expressions of the spiritual) and dualism, which treats both matter and spirit as separate substances.

A prominent mediating position between these two extremes is *emergentist monism.* Emergentist monism holds that within the natural world, genuinely new properties and processes emerge at higher levels of organization. Complex, or spiritual phenomena are composed of no separate substance beyond the material from which they emerge. This ontology accounts for the complexity of reality, overcoming ontological reductionism, without positing the existence of a separate spiritual substance.

The Role of Philosophy in Dialogue

Philosophy typically functions in one of two ways in conversations between theology and science. (1) It can provide an overarching metaphysical framework for all fields of knowledge. Examples include Neo-Thomism and Whiteheadian (process) philosophy. The advantage is that terms such as causality or purpose ordinarily have very different meanings in different disciplines. When these disciplines are gathered together within a single metaphysical framework, differences in meaning can be overcome and the terms can be brought together into a common conceptuality. Moreover, the most general issues facing theology and science, such as God's relation to humanity and nature, can be more adequately addressed within a single metaphysical system than they can without one. The difficulty comes when science changes and requires an adjustment in the philosophical system; such adjustments are very hard to accomplish. Another difficulty is that a given philosophical system may not be adequate or appropriate to a particular theology. Process philosophy has a hard time, for example, accommodating the Judeo-Christian doctrine that God created the world out of nothing (*creatio ex nihilo*).

(2) Philosophy can also serve a more limited goal. It can provide definitions of specific terms and concepts shared by differing disciplines without forcing them into a larger, metaphysical framework. Examples include the terms "law" and "chance" which occur in biological evolution and in the doctrine of creation, or the term "open" which occurs in discussing quantum mechanics and in discussing divine action. The difficulty here is that without a single metaphysical framework to unify these disciplines, it is hard to address other, broader questions underlying the entire relationship between theology and science. For example, how do we understand God as acting both within human experience and in the natural world?

Summary

Over the past four decades, the predominant school of thought among scholars in theology and science, with regard to methodology, has been "critical realism." It has provided the crucial "bridge" between theology and science, making possible real dialogue and growing integration between theology and science. It continues to be presupposed by most working scientists and many theologians, and is operative in much of the public discourse about science and religion.

During these four decades, however, elements of this approach have come under criticism. It is very difficult to give a realist interpretation of many scientific theories, especially quantum mechanics. It is even more difficult to defend a realist interpretation of key theological concepts such as "God." Realism itself is subject to a growing diversity of interpretations; which then should we choose and defend? Another challenge to realism comes from sociologists of knowledge, who view knowledge more as a human construct or convention than as a genuine discovery about the world. How we interpret the relative realism of either science or religion affects the way in which we construct the relationship between them.

While discussion of critical realism remains strong, there is a growing diversity of methodological models used to support mutual interaction between science and religion. This diversity consists of a growing concern for what constitutes rationality and the role an understanding of rationality plays in theology and science. Others have concerned themselves with the import of nonfoundationalist epistemologies. Foundationalists since the Enlightenment have believed that all of our knowledge rests on indisputable foundations. These foundations could be sense experience and scientific data or self-evident concepts, such as mathematics provides. Today, some scholars believe that no such foundations exist; moreover, they are not really needed. We can have reasons to believe that our system of thought is valid and rational without absolutely certain foundations. Instead, such "nonfoundationalists" appeal to the overall coherence of a system of thought, its fruitfulness, its compelling power, and so on, to warrant its acceptance.

Finally, some scholars place themselves at increasing distances from critical realism. Some draw on feminist critiques of both science and theology, arguing that science is biased by the presuppositions of its predominantly male practitioners and that such gender bias is carried into and colors the "theology and science" conversation. Others draw on continental and postmodernist philosophies, often rejecting the attempt to form a "metanarrative" or single worldview, as is done in science and, often, in theology.

On balance, though, critical realism remains enduringly important to theology and science, both for its crucial role in the historical developments of the past decades and as a foundational support upon which much current research is being constructed. Whatever directions are taken in the future, critical realism constitutes the key contribution by the "first generation" to the ongoing discussion.

Challenges and Future Directions

Having surveyed the methodological foundations of the growing field of science and theology, we now turn to an examination of challenges and future directions.

Feminist Critiques of Science and of Theology and Science

In the introduction to their anthology *Feminism and Science*, Evelyn Fox Keller and Helen E. Longino pose a watershed question: Are the sciences neutral to social values and does the harm they can do come only from their misuse, or is there a more innate relation at work here? According to their analysis, the roots of this question lie in the 1960s revolution in the philosophy of science. Feminist theory since that time has had a profound effect on our view of science, particularly through its novel concept of "gender" as the social constitution of masculinity and femininity. Early feminists sought a "gender-free" science by urging greater access for women in science education and research, and by retrieving the stories of outstanding women scientists. More recently, feminists have used gender analysis on the content and practice of science, many advocating a rooting-out of sexist distortions in epistemology, metaphysics, methodology, and the philosophy of science.[11]

Feminist theology emerged in roughly the same period as the feminist critique of science and, today, is a crucial voice in the community of religious scholars. Despite feminist criticisms of science and the prominence of feminist theologians in theological circles, when we turn to the field of theology and science, we find that feminist issues have not yet been widely discussed. As Ann Pederson and Mary Solberg have stressed, very few women are active today in "theology and science," the number of feminist women (or men) is even fewer, and gender issues clearly continue to affect the field. Others argue that since participants in science and religion tend to be white, male, and socially privileged, they carry the same biases into the science–theology dialogue that feminists have illuminated in science. They urge scholars to more actively engage "voices from the margins," to turn to postmodernist views of knowledge, to honor the importance of diversity within intellectual community, and to adhere to participatory values.

Historical studies on gender bias in science are also leading to a clearer understanding of gender bias in science and theology. David Noble notes that the clerical ascetic culture that first came to dominance in the High Middle Ages was an exclusively male society. When women entered the academic world in the nineteenth century, they were confronted by "a male scientific professionalism that betrayed the same misogynistic . . . habits of the clerical culture it superseded." Margaret Wertheim explores the relation between the marginalization of women in religion and the marginalization of women in physics. "The struggle women have faced to gain entry into science parallels the struggle they have faced to gain entry into the clergy."[12]

We believe that a sustained focus on issues surrounding gender will mark an important new development in science and theology. The inclusion of womanist, *mujerista*, and other women's voices in this conversation is crucial. This is particularly important since ecofeminist concerns about technology and the environment help relate theoretical issues to issues of practical concern.[13]

Postmodern Challenges to Science and to Theology and Science

According to Princeton theologian Wentzel van Huyssteen, certain strains of postmodern[14] thought threaten to undercut advances in theology and science. Issues such as pluralism and relativism undercut reliance upon the presumed university of reason in the natural sciences. Van Huyssteen's response is twofold. First, we should understand postmodernity as a movement within modernity, rather than as modern thought coming to its end; and second, we should recognize that cosmology and evolutionary biology provide the resources for interdisciplinary knowledge without forcing an ideological metanarrative, or all-embracing interpretive story. Danish theologian Niels Gregersen also supports the search for a fruitful interdisciplinary dialogue in the context of postmodern pluralism. He argues that what he calls a "contextual coherence theory" has operated throughout Christian history and can now provide a middle ground between critical realism and a radical pluralism.

Interreligious Dialogue, World Spiritualities, and Science

Most of the literature in theology and science has focused on Christian theology. However, a rapidly growing diversity of religious voices is entering the conversation. Religious scholars such as Norbert Samuelson and Daniel Matt, and scientists such as Joel Primack in cosmology, Carl Feit in biology, and Ken Kendler in genetics and psychiatry, have embarked on serious explorations of the relation between Judaism and science. Muslim dialogue with science is developing through the work of religious scholars such as S. H. Nasr, Noman Haq, and Z. Sardar, and scientists such as Muzaffar Iqbal in chemistry, Mehdi Golshani in physics, and Bruno Guiderdoni in astronomy.[15] Buddhist dialogue with science now includes religious scholars such as Rusei Tanaka, Mark Unno, and Jensine Andresen.[16] Native American scholars such as theologian George Tink Tinker and biologist Dawn Adams are contributing to the field, as are colleagues in the American Indian Science and Engineering Society.[17] Scholars from the Hindu tradition have also made important new contributions to the field.

History of Science and Religion

Although there is a widespread assumption that science and religion are at war with each other, this is proving to be less of a challenge than expected. Careful historical research has thoroughly discredited the claim that the relation between science and religion throughout the nineteenth and twentieth centuries was solely one of "warfare."[18] Historian and theologian Claude Welch shows that there were at least three kinds of response to science in the nineteenth century: in addition to "opposition" there was "cautious mediation" or "accommodation" and the "exaltation of evolution" or "assimilation". Oxford historian John Brooke has argued in great detail that historical research into the religious origins of modern science has disclosed a complex interplay of factors in the historical relations between science and religion. Numerous scholars, notably David Lindberg, Ron Numbers, and Peter Hess, have taken up the broad portrayal of the positive significance of religion for the rise of science.

An Interaction Model of Theology and Science

A major challenge continues to be whether science and theology can genuinely *inter*-act in a mutually constructive way, each offering something of intellectual value to the other.[19] Robert Russell has identified eight distinct ways in which genuine interaction can take place, five involving the influence of science on theology and three the influence of theology on science. He illustrates his claim by discussing the relations of physics and cosmology to theology. The first five ways are: (1) Physical theories can act as data that place constraints on theology. For example, a theology of divine action should not violate special relativity. (2) Physical theories can act as data to be incorporated into theology. For example, the beginning of time, or, $t = 0$ in Big Bang cosmology may be explained via creation *ex nihilo*; the explanation, though, is part of theology and not of science. (3) Theories in physics, after philosophical analysis, can act indirectly as data in theology. For example, $t = 0$ can be interpreted philosophically as evidence of contingency in the Big Bang universe, and thus suggestive of the existence of God. (4) Theories in physics can also act indirectly as theological data when they are incorporated into a fully articulated philosophy of nature. Finally, (5) theories in physics can function heuristically in the theological context of discovery by providing conceptual, experiential, moral, or aesthetic inspiration. Russell then discusses the three paths by which theology can influence physics:

(6) Theology has provided key historical assumptions that underlay the development of science, such as the contingency and rationality of nature.[20] These deserve a renewed appraisal. (7) Theological theories can act as sources of inspiration in the scientific "context of discovery." An example is the influence of religious ideas on the pioneers of quantum theory, including Planck, Einstein, Bohr, and Schrödinger.[21] Finally, (8) theological theories could provide criteria, alongside empirical adequacy, coherence, scope, and fertility, for theory choice in physics.

Conclusion

In the past few decades ongoing work in methodology has provided structural support for the bridge scientists and theologians are building between their respective fields. Though this work is sound, allowing for the weight of regular traffic, points of instability are still being discovered. But even where science and theology falls under criticism, it gains strength in the effort scholars are making to responsibly address challenges raised by feminist, postmodern, multi-religious, and other critiques.

Science at its best, and theology at its best, both pursue truth. Both science and theology are self-critical when they fall short of truth. Both are humble and persistent in the face of mystery. If it be true, as theologians claim, that the God of Israel is the creator of this magnificent universe, then every truth about this universe discovered by science only enhances appreciation for God's creative handiwork.

2

Bridging Theology and Science in a Postmodern Age

NANCEY MURPHY

Relating theology and science is a growing concern today. Biochemist and Anglican priest A. R. Peacocke, United Church of Christ minister and physicist Robert Russell, and professor of religious studies and physics Ian Barbour are but three of a growing list of noteworthy scholars concentrating on this task, while an increasing number of institutions and events are dedicated to this goal. At the same time, other theologians claim to have found a "postmodern" way of think-ing that casts fresh light on the theological task. This topic, too, has attracted growing interest. Are these two movements compatible, or does postmodern thinking undermine the theology and science project? Is the attempt to relate theology to the natural sciences a *modern* preoccupation whose day has passed with the publication of George Lindbeck's *Nature of Doctrine*[1] and other postmodern theo-logical works?

In this chapter I shall examine two proposals for relating theology and science. One is the *critical realism* of Peacocke and Barbour.[2] The other is the comparative study of the *methods* of science and theology. I shall argue that critical realism is a doctrine at home only in a modern worldview. However, this doctrine may be abandoned with-out loss, in favor of an investigation of the similarities in method between theology and science. Postmodern philosophy of science will turn out to be just the bridge needed for relating the two disciplines. Before discussing critical realism, however, it will be necessary to examine modern thought and propose a means for distinguishing that which is genuinely postmodern.

What is Modern Thought?

Mine is not the first attempt at a brief characterization of modern thought as it developed in Western Europe. I shall concentrate here on philosophical theses, assuming that philosophy itself attempts to come to terms with the patterns of thought current in any age and *exemplified* in other disciplines such as theology and the sciences.

The beginning of the modern period has been characterized as the "turn to the subject." It was the era in which epistemology became the center of philosophy, replacing cosmology and metaphysics – at least until philosophy took the (still modern) "linguistic turn." It was the age of skepticism, reductionism, individualism, and the "flight from [traditional] authority." These truisms point to three central philosophical theses dominating modern thought. The first was epistemological foundationalism – the view that knowledge can only be justified by finding indubitable "foundational" beliefs upon which the rest of knowledge is constructed. The second was the representational–expressivist theory of language – the view that language must gain its primary meaning by representing the objects or facts to which it refers; otherwise it merely expresses the attitudes of the speaker. The third pillar of modern thought was individualism – an approach to ethics and political philosophy that saw the individual as prior to the community, and the community as merely a collection of like individuals.

Epistemological Foundationalism

The foundationalist doctrine, a legacy from René Descartes, assumed that it was the philosopher's job to justify the knowledge claims of other disciplines by finding indubitable beliefs upon which they depend. The reasoning behind the search for foundations is this: In the attempt to justify a given belief, the chain of supporting beliefs must not be circular or form an infinite regress. Therefore, the chain must at some point reach a belief that needs no further justification – it must be something that cannot fail to be believed.

Modern epistemology has been much concerned with skepticism, and it is clear why this should be the case. If the foundation fails or construction breaks down, knowledge fails to find its justification and skepticism follows. Thus, skepticism is correlative with foundationalism. Modern skeptics and foundationalists held the same view of knowledge, and one became a skeptic insofar as one became aware of difficulties in the foundationalist program.[3] Therefore, modern epistemological thought might be conceived as falling along an *axis* with optimistic foundationalism at one end, and pessimism (skepticism) at the other.

For Descartes, the foundations of knowledge were intuitions (clear and distinct ideas), and the means of construction demonstrative reasoning. Descartes should be placed at the optimistic end of the axis because, for him, God guarantees that ideas represent a real world. David Hume continued Descartes's foundationalism but turned to sense knowledge ("impressions") for the foundation, and realized that deductive reasoning was no longer an appropriate means of construction.

The concern with foundations of knowledge continued into the twentieth century, exemplified clearly, for example, in positivist philosophy of science with its search for the indubitable facts upon which scientific knowledge was supposed to be based.

The Representational–Expressivist Theory of Language

Modern philosophy of language has by and large sought the meaning of language among the objects in the world to which it refers. Language was thought to work by naming objects and by reflecting or representing facts about those objects. Unfortunately, a number of sentences seem not to refer to objects – one such area of discourse being that of ethics. Hence, a second theory of meaning was usually appended to the representational theory. The expressivist or emotivist theory of meaning holds that ethical discourse merely expresses the attitudes or emotions of the speaker. Like foundationalism and skepticism, these two theories of meaning are *correlative* since the importance attached to the expressivist theory will vary according to one's optimism regarding the ability of the representational theory to account for all significant discourse. Thus, modern philosophers of language can be imagined to fall along a second axis whose poles are emphases on representation or expression.

There is a close link between modern epistemology and modern philosophy of language in the idea of *representation*. For Aristotle, knowledge consisted in the intellect's grasping the substantial forms; the forms themselves got into the intellect in the same way they inhered in objects. But for Descartes, knowledge was by means of *ideas* that merely represented the objects. This change shaped the whole of subsequent modern epistemology, which has been concerned in one way or another with whether the ideas (impressions, sense data, etc.) represent, and how accurately they do so. By the end of the modern period the problem of accurate representation had been taken up in philosophy of language. The main concern was no longer with ideas (mental entities) that represent the world more or less accurately, but now with propositions or sentences.

Ludwig Wittgenstein's *Tractatus Logico-philosophicus*[4] is perhaps the most elegant exposition of the representational theory of language. Propositions, he said, are "pictures" of facts. Words name objects and relations, and the order of the words in the sentence represents the order of the objects in the world. Because of the integral connection between theories of language and knowledge, the linguistic and epistemological axes may be used to define a two-dimensional "space" in which modern philosophers may be located.

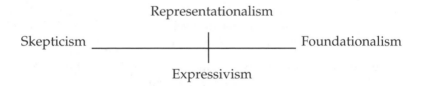

Optimistic proponents of the modern program, such as Descartes and Wittgenstein, will be located in the upper right-hand quadrant. Hume, who held the representational theory of language but saw more clearly the difficulties with foundationalism, would fall in the upper left-hand quadrant. Theorists who dedicated themselves to development of an expressivist theory of meaning without questioning epistemological foundations would fall in the lower right-hand quadrant.[5] Modern reactions against the positive programs of modern writers have taken more than one form, but the existentialists are perhaps the most important in this regard; they should be located in the lower left-hand quadrant.

Individualism and the Generic View of Community

The rise to prominence of the individual in modern European thought was not unconnected with the epistemological changes instigated by Descartes. In the Middle Ages *authority* had been a central epistemological category. Thought in the modern period might be characterized as flight from traditional authority (the Bible, the Church, the Philosopher), and relocation of authority within the individual.[6] Thus, epistemological authority was granted to the individual's foundational beliefs, be they Descartes's clear and distinct ideas or the empiricists' sense data. Likewise, political authority was based upon the consent of individuals, and moral authority was ceded to the individual rational will.

Individualism appeared in modern political thought in the form of the social contract theory of government, which asserts the equality and integrity of individuals before (or apart from) their agreement to enter into society. Society is merely a collection of individuals united for their own mutual benefits. We might call this the generic view of community. Marxism, wherein the economic class replaces the individual as the primary unit of social interaction, is the best-known reaction against Enlightenment individualism. However, while according higher value to the class than to the individual, Marx takes for granted the modern (generic) view of the relation of the individual to society. Thus, his collectivism is *correlative* with individualism and we find that he shares an axis with the individualists, who we may designate as the third axis of modernity.

Thus, we see that three philosophical stances central to modern thought each admit of development as axes – position versus counterposition – and that the three axes can be meaningfully related to one another in order to define a three-dimensional space in which modern thinkers can be located.

Emerging Postmodern Thought

I propose that we define as postmodern any mode of thought that departs from two or more of the three modern axes described above. Some philosophers and theologians have moved beyond modern thought in one area but not in others. However, there are connections among positions that transcend modern assumptions, just as there were among the modern axes themselves. Here we shall consider two important postmodern philosophical positions: holism in epistemology and the theory of meaning as use in philosophy of language.

Willard V. O. Quine deserves the title of postmodern epistemologist because of his explicit rejection of foundationalism, replacing it with a holist account. In his "Two Dogmas of Empiricism" he traced the fate of the "reductionist dogma" – the view that all meaningful discourse can be translated into language about immediate experience. For Hume, individual terms were supposed to be so reducible, while Wittgenstein tried instead to translate whole statements. It was Quine's judgment that even statements are still too small a unit to be reducible to experience; rather the whole fabric of our knowledge "faces the tribunal of experience."

The totality of our so-called knowledge or beliefs, from the most casual matters of geography and history to the profoundest laws of atomic physics or even of pure mathematics and logic, is a man-made fabric which impinges on experience only along the edges. Or, to change the figure, total science is like a field of force whose boundary conditions are experience. A conflict with experience at the periphery occasions readjustments in the interior of the field, but the total field is so underdetermined by its boundary conditions, experience, that there is much latitude of choice as to what statements to re-evaluate in the light of any single contrary experience. No particular experiences are linked with any particular statements in the interior of the field, except indirectly through considerations of equilibrium affecting the field as a whole.[7] The particular changes made in the face of "recalcitrant experience" will be governed by pragmatic considerations such as conservatism and simplicity.

In philosophy of science the change from foundationalism to holism was more gradual. The first crack in the positivists' foundations came in Karl Popper's *Logik der Forschung*,[8] where he stated that the facts upon which science is based are not indubitable, but may be called into question if they fail to square with accepted theory. Popper replaced the foundation metaphor with that of piles driven into a swamp. Factual statements are provisionally accepted, but if questioned can be subjected to test – driven deeper. The scientific community decides which facts are to be considered solid; thus an element of conventionalism enters science even at its most basic level.

Thomas Kuhn is probably the most widely read philosopher of science today. He argued in a much more radical way for the theory-dependence and community-dependence of facts, claiming that the very meaning of terms in a factual statement is a function of theoretical assumptions. Kuhn's view is holistic in that a paradigm is accepted or rejected as a whole. The scientific community makes such decisions on the basis of "maxims" such as the injunctions to seek simplicity and empirical fit.[9] So here we see a philosophy-of-science version of Quine's view of knowledge as a fabric in which changes are made on the basis of pragmatic considerations. A major difference between Kuhn and Quine is Kuhn's interest in revolutions – those episodes in which large swatches of fabric are torn out at once and replaced with a new scientific paradigm.

Postmodern Philosophy of Language

Ludwig Wittgenstein, writing in the late 1930s and 1940s at Cambridge, produced nothing short of a revolution in philosophy of language. He is a particularly interesting philosopher for the purposes of this chapter, since his earlier and later writings respectively provide exemplars of modern and postmodern philosophy of language. In his later *Philosophical Investigations*[10] he did not state a new theory of language, but rather attempted to *show* what language is like and how it works. Here he focused on the uses of language and on how language contributes to the whole of life. Languages *are* "forms of life." To study language is to examine the "language games" in which speakers participate. There is no one way in which language relates to the world; there is no one account of the conditions of the meaningfulness of an utterance, except to say that the meaning will be found in the use. Thus, he called into question the assumption that the proposition, the assertion of a fact, is the paradigm for all language, and with it the entire representational theory.

Wittgenstein made a second contribution to postmodern philosophy by showing that there could be no language that merely expresses private sensations. Earlier theorists had imagined that individual speakers "look within" to perceive a sensation – blueness, or pain – then name it "blue" or "pain" in order to be able to communicate it to others. Wittgenstein argued that language conceived on this model is impossible because naming something requires that one be able to recognize it again when it reappears. But if the object is entirely private there can be no criterion for sameness – no way to distinguish it from something that only seems the same. Thus, language must be public from the very start or it is not *language* at all. Thanks to Wittgenstein's arguments the modern account of language as naming or expressing ideas has also been rejected.

Emerging Unity in Postmodern Thought

Space does not permit exploration of postmodern ethics.[11] However, a non-individualist or "corporate" view of community is built into holist epistemology and the postmodern understanding of language. Moderns assumed that any individual (given the basic sensory and intellectual equipment) was as competent as any other to form justified beliefs and speak the language. Society's knowledge and language were merely the collection of the individuals'. However, in postmodern thought the community itself plays an indispensable role. It is the community of scientists who decide when to take anomalous facts seriously. The community must decide where to make changes in the Quinian net of beliefs. The conventions, the language games, in which one participates precede individual speech and determine what can and cannot be said. In short, language and the search for knowledge are *practices*, dependent upon *tradition* – they are communal achievements. Thus, escape from either of the modern epistemological or linguistic axes calls for a corresponding detachment from the individualist axis as well.[12]

The Critical Realist Approach to Relating Theology and Science

Critical realism is a philosophical theory regarding the ontological status of the referents of theoretical terms in science. It has recently been employed by A. R. Peacocke and Ian Barbour as a device for showing the comparability and compatibility of religious and scientific views of reality. They claim that both theology and science yield *partial, tentative* views of what there is – or put the other way around, to the theoretical language of both theology and science there correspond entities *something like* those described by the theories.

The critical realist thesis has stirred lively debate and some confusion. I believe that the understanding of modern and postmodern thought developed here will allow for a diagnosis of the confusion. We shall see that the opponents talk past one another because advocates of critical realism use modern epistemological and linguistic categories, while opponents use postmodern categories. This diagnosis will not settle the issue; there is no court of appeal to which we may turn to rule in favor of postmodern over modern thought. However, the association of critical realism with modern thought warrants a practical caution. Conceptual changes once begun seldom (if ever) reverse. Therefore, it may be wise to use a postmodern basis for dialogue between science and religion lest we build our house upon sand.

The term "critical realism" has a longer history outside philosophy of science, but here it is a successor to the realism opposed to an instrumentalist account of scientific theories. This earlier position, now called naive realism, maintained that scientific theories were not mere calculating devices but rather gave literal descriptions of unobservable aspects of the real world. Naive realism is generally seen as untenable today, especially in light of emphasis by Kuhn and other philosophers of science on the provisionality of scientific theorizing, and on the fact that strong claims can often be made for each of two or more conflicting scientific accounts.

Based in part on Thomas Kuhn's (postmodern) view of science, the "strong program" in sociology of science has been developed by David Bloor, Barry Barnes, and others,[13] who point out that the under-determination of theory by experience allows room for causal (socio-logical) explanation of true, or accepted, science as well as of false theories. They regard all products of science as social constructions. Critical realists such as Peacocke regard their own position as a middle way between naive realism and what they regard as a purely relativistic, irrationalist sociological account.

I spoke above of confusion in debates regarding critical realism, and claimed that its source could be found by attending to the inter-play of modern and postmodern presuppositions. The sociologists of science are clearly operating with a postmodern conception of knowledge. Consistent with Quine's "Two Dogmas," Bloor sees all knowledge as determined by the "boundary conditions" of experi-ence and (socially transmitted) prior belief. In fact, Bloor's and Quine's descriptions of knowledge could be profitably combined. Along with the pragmatic criteria Quine mentions (conservatism and simplicity), Bloor's research shows the influence of sociological forces on the decisions scientists make when rearranging their web of beliefs.

Bloor continues to speak of true and false beliefs, noting that our everyday understanding of truth is in terms of correspondence. However, he notes, this is a vague idea; no-one has been able to make clear what exactly is meant by "picturing," or "fitting," or "match-ing," or, for that matter, "the world." Without some direct access to the hidden aspects of reality to which our theories are supposed to correspond, there is nothing more to be said about the truth of a theory than to display the justification for holding that theory. Thus, Bloor suggests attending to actual uses of the word "true" rather than invoking the old correspondence theory of truth.

The confusing or puzzling aspect of the critical realist debate is the fact that critical realists accept the same facts about science as do the sociologists: the underdetermination of theory by data; the theory-ladenness of data; the effect on perception of prior belief; the influence in theory construction of ideals of natural order, of tacit assumptions embedded in paradigms; the shift in conceptual frameworks from one era to another. The sociologists go on to demonstrate by means of historical examples the value of sociological factors for explaining the decisions scientists make within the area permitted by rational constraints. The critical realists reject this move, and represent the sociologists as having "firmly barred the way of science to reality."[14]

Notice that the critical realist position is modern, only modern and not postmodern. It is governed by the metaphor of knowledge as a picture or representation of reality. Yet unlike naive realism, it does not occupy the extreme foundationalist position on the epistemological axis but rather has moved some distance toward skepticism in response to the historians' and sociologists' accounts of the underdetermination and changeability of scientific knowledge. Likewise, critical realists have pulled back from the extreme representational position on the linguistic axis; they highlight the metaphorical nature of scientific language; they see scientific models not as literal pictures of reality but as partial, tentative representations of what there is.

Proponents of the strong program, on the other hand, have entirely rejected the modern representational view of knowledge. Confusion enters the discussion when critical realists interpret sociologists' positions in terms of their own modern axes – because the sociologists do not hold the foundationalist–representational view of knowledge and language they place them in the skeptical–expressivist quadrant of modern conceptual space. For example, Bloor notes that the naturalistic account of scientific theories must be applicable to theories in the sociology of scientific knowledge or else those very theories would provide a counterexample to its own theses. Peacocke, commenting on this self-reference, suggests that it is a case of sawing off the branch one is sitting upon. What for Bloor is evidence of the universal applicability of his approach is for Peacocke a reduction to absurdity. A second, related, source of confusion is the claim that critical realism is a *middle* position between naive realism and the sociologists' position. However, there can be no midpoint between positions that are not located in the same space.

What then of the relations between theology and science? I pointed out above that the function served by critical realism for Peacocke and Barbour is to provide a basis for asserting the comparability and compatibility of scientific and religious views of reality. Is there some other basis, compatible with postmodern thought, upon which science and theology can be brought into dialogue as equals? I believe there is, and the seeds of this new approach are already to be found in the works of the critical realists. Both Peacocke and Barbour argue for similarities in method between science and theology. In fact, methodological similarity with science is the very ground used to support the critical realist view of religious knowledge. In the following section I shall sketch a postmodern view of the relation between theology and science.

Relating Science and Religion in a Postmodern Age

It has become common during the modern period to question theology's claims to provide knowledge of a reality external to the religious subject. However, as sociologist Martin Rudwick points out:

> [t]he strong program, by its own axioms, requires us to speak not of "religious beliefs" but of "religious knowledge," impartially with "scientific knowledge," as soon as certain claims about the effects of God or gods become collectively shared by a social group, as of course they are in any actual religious tradition.[15]

In other words, for any culture wherein a reasonable amount of agreement exists to the effect that shared experiences require description or interpretation in theistic terms, that description or interpretation has a claim to be counted as knowledge. To use Quine's imagery again, a region within a culture's web of beliefs that employs a concept of God should be subject only to the same sorts of constraints as are the scientific theories making up other parts of the web.

I have argued elsewhere that Imre Lakatos's theory of scientific method provides a valuable refinement of postmodern epistemology, which is as applicable to theology as to science.[16] He considers limited regions within the scientific web – "research programs" consisting of an abstract "core" theory, and a "surrounding belt" of auxiliary hypotheses – lower-level theories that relate the core theory to its data "at the edges." He argues that an important criterion for assessing theoretical modifications is the prohibition of ad hoc theorizing, that is, of theoretical changes that are merely devices for reconciling the system with anomalous facts but do not add to our knowledge. He expresses the prohibition against ad hoc theorizing by requiring that theoretical modifications in the face of an anomaly also allow for the prediction of some new fact. In this way conceptual changes within the system can be evaluated on the basis of their contribution to the growth of knowledge.[17]

Postmodern theologians such as Lindbeck and Ronald Thiemann[18] claim that the facts to which religious language is connected are the practices of the religious community – its worship, its moral life, its forms of speech, etc. They insist that theological beliefs be governed by the demand for consistency with one another and with these communal practices (and Lakatos's methodology leads us to add here a demand for empirical growth). However, the Quinian picture of knowledge suggests that theological thought would also have to be constrained by demands for consistency with beliefs in neighboring regions of the total web of knowledge. Thus relations between theology and science are built into postmodern epistemology.

Conclusions

In this chapter I have suggested a means for distinguishing between modern and postmodern thought. I proposed that modern thought be viewed as inhabiting a three-dimensional space created by the intersection of three conceptual axes, and defined postmodern thought abstractly as departure from this space. Concretely, I suggested that holism in epistemology and philosophy of science, and meaning as use in philosophy of language, along with their entailed views on the priority of the community, will provide the conceptual framework for developing postmodern thought.

I then addressed the issue of the relation between theology and science, showing that my distinction between modern and postmodern frameworks serves to diagnose confusions in the debate over critical realism, and further sketching in barest outlines an alternative postmodern approach to this issue.[19]

Part Two
Constructing Scientific Spans

3

Natural Law and Divine Action

ROBERT JOHN RUSSELL and
KIRK WEGTER-MCNELLY

As described in our chapter "Science and Theology: Mutual Interaction," the structural supports for the bridge being built between science and theology in recent decades consist largely of work done in methodology. This work was made possible in large part by major movements in the secular disciplines of philosophy of science and philosophy of religion. The increased interactive traffic that the bridge of methodology has supported, however, has been driven by new theories in the natural sciences and complex shifts in the theology. The interaction resulting from these theories and shifts has provided the substantive content of the interdisciplinary field of science and theology.

This chapter surveys these changes in the natural sciences and the accompanying changes in theology. It is divided into sections on God and Nature; Creation and Cosmology; Creation and Evolution; Redemption, Evolution, and Cosmology; and Eschatology. This chapter will focus primarily on theoretical, philosophical, and foundational issues. While acknowledging their pertinence to the field, it is not focused on either ethical or spiritual concerns. Here, as in our first chapter, the term "theology" refers to the intellectual reflection upon religious tradition, the term "science" to the natural sciences, especially physics, cosmology, biology (with attention to evolutionary biology and genetics), and neuroscience. Finally, it should be noted that this chapter focuses primarily on the interaction between new theories in the natural sciences and the diverse shifts within Christian theology, where most of the material in the field to date has been developed.[1]

God and Nature

The diversity of views within contemporary theology regarding the relationship between God and nature is reflected in the past four decades of discussions about theology and science. This diversity ranges from theologians working within traditional theological categories to theologians stressing both temporal and eternal in God. Some point to God as self-emptying, kenotic love, while others attend to the effects of science and technology on society and the environment. Many scholars find traditional philosophical categories, when appropriately modified, helpful for the conversation with science. Theologians who start with God as Trinity take categories such as the future and hope as key to the interaction with science. Some scholars challenge atheists, such as Richard Dawkins or Steven Weinberg, who want to co-opt science as a weapon to attack religion, or those like Carl Sagan, who seek to construct a new "science-based" religion. Some introduce specific scientific issues into constructive theology by using science as a resource for new metaphors in theology, such as the metaphor that the world is God's body. Still others introduce specific scientific theories into the theological discussion, such as quantum mechanics, chaos theory, evolution, or ecology.

Given the vast breadth of literature treating the issue of God's relationship to nature, a more narrow focus on two central issues will illustrate the subtle way in which twentieth-century science both challenges and reshapes the way we view God's relation to nature.

Time and Eternity

Most theologians work with a view of time that emerges out of our ordinary human experience and is often called "flowing time." According to this view, the present moment is fleeting. What was present is now a part of the past while a new moment comes from the future and takes its place. Thus future is potentially but not actually real, the present is actually real, and the past is real but inaccessible. How does this view of time relate to the concept of the eternity of God?

Many contemporary theologians view the divine eternity as even more fully temporal than our experience of time. Eternity is the whole of time without the sense of the past as lost or the future as merely potential that characterizes the "flow" of time for us. To do so, they reject two simpler notions of eternity: eternity as a timeless "now" in which all moments of time are fused into a single moment, and eternity as an infinitely flowing time that is like our time, just more of it. Instead, God is the source of all time, and God experiences the world in time. For theologians who draw on the Christian belief in a triune God as a source for their view of God's relationship to time, God as eternal is the "supra-temporal" source of the world's temporality. This means that the eternity of God is infinitely temporal without times that are lost or unrealized. Eternity is before, above, and after the time of the universe. It embraces all of time even if the universe is infinitely old and continues forever. God here is envisioned as the eschatological future of the universe, the future destination toward which the universe moves.

Theologians drawing on the process philosophy of Alfred North Whitehead argue that God experiences the world at every moment and in this way participates in the world's temporality. British natural theologians stress that God is eternally transcendent to the world and yet immanent or present to the world at every moment. According to some scholars, the view of time as flowing means that even for God the future does not yet exist. Instead God creates each instant of physical time.

All of these views, while differing in important ways theologically, presuppose the notion of flowing time. The notion of flowing time was partially incorporated into science in the sixteenth and seventeenth centuries. Classical physics assumes that time is linear and refers to past, present, and future. The direction of flow, however, or what is popularly called the "arrow of time," was left out of the scientific picture. In this sense classical physics (with very few possible exceptions) is "time reversible"; its fundamental equations do not tell us how to tell the past from the future. Albert Einstein's theory of special relativity directly challenges the notion of flowing time by undercutting two assumptions: one, that the present moment is universally shared by all observers, and two, that the rate at which time flows from future to past is the same for all observers.[2] Instead of a universal present moment, special relativity views the future and the past of each event "P" as separated by the "elsewhen," a domain of events surrounding each moment and consisting of other events which cannot be affected by "P." Because of these and other challenges posed by special relativity, some have argued that the flow of time is an illusion. Instead they propose what is called the "block universe" interpretation of special relativity. According to this interpretation, all events in time are equally real, equally "present," whether we view them as past, present, or future. Theologian Charles Hartshorne found this interpretation deeply antithetical to theology. He wrote that special relativity poses "the most puzzling [challenge] of all" to the classical theistic notion of a universal flowing present.

To some scholars, however, the theological implications of special relativity do not come directly from the scientific theory itself, but from the way it is interpreted philosophically. Theologian/physicist John Polkinghorne has defended a subtle "flowing time" interpretation of special relativity. He argues that the implications of special relativity concern the way we coordinate our observations and reconstruct our picture of the world. They do not directly concern the nature of reality. Moreover, special relativity does not commit us to a deterministic view of the future that leaves no room for the unpredictable and the novel, nor does it force us to accept a timeless view of nature. Other scholars who defend a "flowing time" view believe that if we cannot interpret special relativity in flowing-time terms, we may need to challenge special relativity itself. Still other scholars defend a "block universe" view as the correct interpretation of special relativity. Physicist Ian Barbour stresses that special relativity points to a universe both "dynamic and interconnected." To him the "elsewhen" suggests "a new form of separateness and isolation." Robert Russell suggests we integrate an "event/worldline" interpretation of special relativity into a trinitarian understanding of eternity that might in turn have empirical implications for science. Hence, the issue of "time and eternity" lies at the cutting edge of research in theology and science.

Divine Action

The relation between divine and natural causality also highlights the challenge twentieth-century science poses for the relation of God and nature. "Divine action"[3] is an issue in philosophical theology that underlies the entire scope of systematic theology and surfaces explicitly in science–theology discussions.

According to the Judeo-Christian doctrine of creation, God brings the world into being from nothing (*creatio ex nihilo*), giving the world a rational and intelligible structure. We discover this structure through science and describe it in terms of the laws of nature. God also continues to create the structures of the world in time (*creatio continua*). God's "general providence" directs all processes and events toward their consummation in the eschaton, the end and fulfillment of the world. Although God is the creator of every event, theology holds that God sometimes works through particular events and processes with special intentions, acts of "special providence" often thought of as miracles. Miracles are events which cohere with an overall theological understanding of God's intentions but which seem to fall outside what nature can do on its own.

Following the rise of modern science and the Enlightenment, theological conservatives and liberals split over the meaning of "special providence." Newtonian physics led to a mechanistic philosophy of nature: the universe was seen as a closed system of cause and effect. According to this deterministic view of nature, the future could be predicted completely, at least in principle. If the world is causally closed, it is difficult to conceive of divine action: for God to act in particular events God would have to intervene in the causal order by either breaking or suspending the laws of nature. Conservative theologians maintained that God does act in this way, and accepted the idea of divine intervention. Liberal theologians rejected the idea of interventionism since this seemed to conflict with science. They also argued that God is the ultimate cause behind everything that happens, including those events we describe by the laws of nature. Thus if God were to break the laws of nature God would, in effect, be acting "against God." However, the liberal response undercut the original meaning of special providence. Instead it came to mean merely our subjective response to an ordinary natural event.[4] Twentieth-century theology struggled to overcome this deep divide convincingly.[5]

Remarkably, even as science played a key role in creating this division, it may now play a pivotal role in overcoming it. Wide-ranging developments from quantum physics to evolutionary biology may move us beyond Newtonian mechanism and point to an indeterministic view of nature. If nature is causally indeterministic and the future is genuinely open, it makes possible new approaches to both human freedom and divine action. Such approaches seek to recombine crucial elements of liberal and conservative positions, yielding a non-interventionist, objective view of special divine acts. These approaches divide into three strategies – top-down, whole–part constraint, and bottom-up – with most scholars insisting that a combination of these approaches will eventually be needed for an adequate account of non-interventionist, objective, special divine action.[6]

In "top-down" approaches, processes at higher levels of complexity affect those at lower levels. Theologian and biochemist Arthur Peacocke explores models involving top-down causality in light of Big Bang cosmology with God acting on the "world-as-a-whole." Philosophers Nancey Murphy and Philip Clayton discuss divine action in light of the neurosciences. The assumption here is that at the level of consciousness we experience genuine causal openness, that is, our experience of free will is a genuine experience. The challenge for this approach is to show how God's action at higher levels can bring about actual changes in the processes at lower levels, if those lower-level processes are still governed by classical, deterministic physics.

The "whole–part constraint" approach stays within one level of complexity and focuses on the effects a system as a whole has on its parts. Drawing on non-equilibrium thermodynamics,[7] Peacocke views God as bringing about special events by interacting with thermodynamic systems open to their environment. John Polking-horne interprets chaos theory,[8] pointing to its unpredictability, as sug-gesting that nature is causally open and thus open to the possibility of God acting on it without having to suspend or break natural law. There is a subtle problem here, however. Both thermodynamics and chaos theory are part of classical physics and are thus fully determin-istic; it is therefore extremely difficult to see how this approach will accomplish its goal of accounting for special providence. One possi-bility is that chaotic systems may one day be more accurately described by more complex theories and these could, in turn, point to ontological indeterminism.

In the "bottom-up" approach, God acts at a lower level of com-plexity to influence the processes and properties at a higher level. A number of scholars, such as physicist George Ellis and theologian Robert Russell, have interpreted quantum mechanics[9] as supporting an indeterministic view of reality at the subatomic level.[10] This would allow God to act without disrupting or suspending natural processes. It is possible that a satisfying connection will be found between chaos and quantum mechanics, suggesting that the uncertainty driving chaotic behavior is at least partially due to quantum indeterminism. The challenge here is that quantum physics can also be interpreted in terms of ontological determinism, and this raises tremendously com-plex, and as yet unresolved, philosophical and scientific problems.[11]

Alternative models of divine agency draw on the analogy of embodi-ment – God as world or mind or body. Theologian Sallie McFague combines metaphors of agency and organism in light of evolution to view the world as an emanation of God's body. In theologian Grace Jantzen's view, God is immediately aware of all events in nature (God's body) and acts both universally throughout nature, and par-ticularly in unique events.

Other approaches to divine agency rely on fully developed meta-physical systems. Process theologians such as John Cobb and John

Haught contend that every event in nature, what they call an "actual occasion," comes to existence in light of three factors. One, God "lures" the event toward its best possible future. Two, the event experiences the past as a cause on it by "prehension," that is, prehending that past cause. Three, each event includes an element of spontaneous, intrinsic novelty – every event is genuinely new. Process theology thus offers a robust non-interventionist view. God participates intrinsically in every event in nature without entirely determining the outcome of any event.

Others, such as physicist William Stoeger or theologian Elizabeth Johnson, use a Neo-Thomist metaphysic to understand God's relationship to nature. Here God is held to be the primary cause of the world and science is understood as limited to studying subsequent secondary causes.

Drawing on evolution, physics, and cosmology, Trinitarian theologians, such as Wolfhart Pannenberg and Ted Peters, use the identity of the Immanent Trinity (God in Godself) and Economic Trinity (God as disclosed through the history of revelation) to discuss God's work in nature and history.

The challenge to all these approaches is to show how God brings about novelty where science describes nature deterministically. Moreover, all proponents of divine action must respond to special relativity's challenge to the idea of a universal present tense (i.e., what do we mean by the phrase, the "universe-as-a-whole" when there is no universal present?) and to the theological challenge of theodicy (i.e., if God can act in specific events, why doesn't God act to relieve suffering, cure diseases, and save creatures from death and species from extinction?).

Creation and Cosmology

The Judeo-Christian doctrine of creation has been explored fruitfully in light of contemporary physical cosmology in various ways over the past four decades. In this section we focus on the relation of contemporary cosmology to *creatio ex nihilo* (creation out of nothing), leaving *creatio continua* (continuous creation) to the discussion of biological evolution.

The Big Bang

Creatio ex nihilo has been discussed in relation to two particular features of the standard Big Bang cosmology:[12] "t=0" (time equals zero), which represents the beginning of time, and the anthropic principle, which points to the striking correspondence between the fundamental physical constants and laws of nature and the evolution of life. First we focus on the discussion of $t=0$.

According to various models in what is called "standard Big Bang cosmology," the universe began at a point back in time referred to as "$t=0$" or the beginning of time. In all these models, the universe is currently expanding in size and has an age of about 12–15 billion years. In some models, called "closed," the universe is finite in size. It will expand to a maximum size in the future and then begin to re-collapse back into itself in a fiery ending. In other models, called "open," the universe is infinite in size and it will expand forever, end-lessly cooling. So both "freeze and fry" models see the universe as having a finite past, a specific age, and beginning in a point of infinite temperature and density called $t=0$.

Is $t=0$ directly relevant to the doctrine of creation *ex nihilo*? Some say "yes" while others say "no." To some scholars, the scientific dis-covery of an absolute beginning of all things, including time itself, is empirical confirmation, or even proof, of divine creation. If science tells us that the universe has a finite age, a limited past, a beginning event called $t=0$, this scientific discovery supports the doctrine of creation out of nothing. Pope Pius XII made a claim like this in 1951, as did astronomer Robert Jastrow. Some scholars have developed sophisticated arguments concerning God and creation based on $t=0$. Others say No to these attempts to find theological significance in the Big Bang concept of $t=0$. These hold that *creatio ex nihilo* is a strict-ly philosophical issue regarding the contingency of the universe. According to this view, the idea of God as the creator is meant to explain why the universe exists at all, regardless of its age or how long it will continue to exist in the future. Even if the universe is infinitely old, or if it will go on forever, these facts are irrelevant to the philo-sophical notion of divine creation. No amount of empirical evidence about the characteristics of our universe, including its finite past age, is relevant to the doctrine of creation.

Still other scholars take a middle ground, arguing for the indirect relevance of $t=0$ to *creatio ex nihilo*. Discoveries such as $t=0$ give con-crete empirical content to the more philosophical notion of contin-gency at work in the theology of creation without playing a direct role in supporting it. Robert Russell uses a legal metaphor to suggest that $t=0$ acts as a "character witness," but not an "eyewitness," to the claim that God created the universe. It is important to remember, however, that the infinite future predicted by the open Big Bang model challenges Christian eschatology, as we will see below.

The "anthropic principle" begins by considering the values of the fundamental constants of nature (e.g., the speed of light, Planck's constant) and the specific form of the fundamental physical laws, such as relativity and quantum mechanics. We know that these laws and constants characterize, or apply to, the universe as a whole. What is surprising is that these constants and laws are precisely what are needed for the possibility that life will evolve in the universe, whether on earth as it has, or perhaps on many other planets in the universe. The anthropic principle underscores the fact that if these values had differed from their actual values by as little as one part per million, life could never have evolved anywhere in the universe. Why then do the natural constants and the fundamental laws of nature meet the requirements for the evolution of life?

To some, this remarkable fact suggests that the universe is "fine-tuned" for life, and thus designed by God. Thus over a century since Charles Darwin overthrew the biological basis for a "design argument" (the idea that nature's orderliness displayed evidence of divine design), cosmology suggests a new form of design – that of the universe as a whole. To many scholars, the anthropic principle reopens the case for natural theology and an argument for God's existence. Opponents of design, however, typically appeal to philosopher David Hume's criticisms of design: for example, do you really get "God" from such an argument, or just a "super designer?" And why is there so much suffering in nature if God designed the world? Moreover, they propose that our universe is only one of many universes, each with a different value of the natural constants and perhaps even different physical laws.[13] There are several ways science can be used in support of a "many universes" approach. These approaches were developed to address various technical problems in standard Big Bang cosmology, but they also bear on the anthropic principle. One approach, called "inflationary Big Bang cosmology," suggests that the very early universe expanded at a much, much higher rate than as depicted in standard Big Bang cosmology. During this time, the actual universe was segregated into many different "domains," with the laws and constants taking different form and value in them. Another more speculative approach is "quantum gravity," which denotes the ongoing attempt by scientists to treat the force of gravity in terms of quantum mechanics. Cosmology, according to some theorists in quantum gravity, involves an endless series of universes that branch off from one another, what cosmologist Andre Linde calls "endless inflation." But are we warranted in assuming that these abstract mathematical arguments for "many universes" actually point to their existence? As some have suggested, while the multiple worlds hypothesis is scientifically fruitful and mathematically consistent, it does not render the idea of God non-viable.

Others have joined in the dispute. Some scholars are concerned that we not reify such mathematical projects of many universes. Others ask whether the anthropic principle is really a valid "explanation" of our universe. Theologians such as Mark Worthing caution that evidence of cosmic design could lead not to the God of the biblical tradition but a divine demiurge, suggesting that the anthropic principle is not ultimately helpful for Christian theology. Physicist George Ellis, on the other hand, has indeed developed a "Christian Anthropic Principle," combining design perspectives with a theology drawn from William Temple. For Ellis, fine-tuning is a consequence of, not a proof of, what we mean by God as the creator of life. Robert Russell takes a middle position, stressing that contingency and necessity occur on both sides of the design vs. many-worlds debate. If a many-worlds argument is used to undercut the design of the values of the constants, why are the laws just what is needed for life? If all possible laws as well as constants are real, governing many "many-worlds" scenarios, why are the rules of logic the same for them all? And so, one can point out, the argument may continue indefinitely.

The anthropic principle is at best, then, an ambiguous argument for God. It can, however, illuminate constructive theology's inner meaning, and suggest otherwise unrecognized connections between theological topics such as creation and theological anthropology.

Inflationary Big Bang and Quantum Cosmologies

As already mentioned, since the 1970s a variety of technical problems in the standard Big Bang model have led scientists to pursue inflationary Big Bang models, and beyond that, quantum cosmology.[14] Given their speculative status, the theological focus has, for the most part, remained on Big Bang cosmology. Some scholars, though, have asked what effects quantum cosmology might have on their theology of creation.

Theologians have continued to defend the idea of the temporality of God against the difficulties raised by quantum cosmology. Ted Peters in particular recognizes the "anti-theological" implications of Stephen Hawking's quantum cosmology, since it gets rid of t=0. Peters draws on physicist Christopher Isham's argument that even without an initial singularity, God is present to and active in all events in the universe. Robert Russell has argued that the Hawking/

Hartle model reminds us that the concept of finitude, curiously, need not entail a boundary. Even an unbounded surface, such as the surface of a ball, can be finite. This insight leads to new ways to describe the universe as God's creation.[15]

The idea of an endless infinity of quantum universes is often called "cosmic Darwinism." If valid, it threatens to strip the anthropic principle-design argument of its force. Still, defenders of the anthropic principle stress the technical and philosophical problems with inflation and quantum cosmology while appealing to Occam's Razor (i.e., when possible, choose the simplest explanation) in support of the Big Bang, and in turn God, as the simplest explanation of fine-tuning.

Perhaps the most important result to emerge from shifts in cosmology over the past decades is the recognition that the Big Bang is a "permanent" description of *our* universe from the Planck time $(t=10^{-43}$ s.) some 12–15 billion years ago to the present. Regardless of its origin – in a blinding moment, $t=0$, or out of a prior quantum universe – new cosmologies will probably not overthrow what we now know about the existence and characteristics of our universe. Thus, the time is ripe for a renewed theological focus on the universe in which we have evolved, its 15-billion-year history, the evolution of life on planet Earth, and perhaps on countless other planetary systems as well.

Creation and Evolution

Charles Darwin's theory of evolution represents one of the most significant scientific challenges to theology over the past 140 years. Darwin's theory of natural selection excludes from its explanation divine causation and even inherent purpose of design. This challenge, however, has produced a diversity of positive responses from Christian theologians.[16] These responses by and large assume that what science describes in terms of evolutionary biology[17] is what theology understands to be God's action in the world. Simply put, evolution is God's way of creating life, a view frequently called "theistic evolution." Scholars taking this approach typically employ concepts such as continuous creation (*creatio continua*) and panentheism (i.e., the world is in God but God transcends the world).

Since the 1970s, Arthur Peacocke has argued that chance events, from genetic variation to environmental alterations, do not mitigate against God's creative purposes. The pervasive character of chance in evolution does not point to a fundamental irrationality in the world, as Jacques Monod argued. Instead, God is the ground and source of both chance and law, which together serve as God's means of continuously creating physical, chemical, and biological complexity in a world. Such a world is characterized by continuity and the emergence of the genuinely new, by temporality and by open-endedness. Peacocke likens God to an improviser of unsurpassed ingenuity who gives birth to the world "within herself."

From the perspective of Whiteheadian process metaphysics as developed by Ian Barbour and John Haught, God is an immanent source of order and novelty within nature, acting within each physical and biological system as a top-down cause. God is continuously and preeminently active in nature, though God does not all-powerfully determine everything that happens in the world. God is thus active in evolution, influencing events through persuasive love but not controlling them unilaterally. According to theologians Charles Birch and John Cobb, God is immanent in the world as the "life-giving principle" and "the supreme and perfect exemplification of the ecological model of life." Moreover, life is purposeful, not sheer blind "ongoingness," but demonstrating "the cosmic aim for value."

Evolution and ecology provide the primary context for Sallie McFague's panentheistic and feminist theology. Her metaphors of the world as God's body, and God as mother, lover, and friend, emphasize mutuality, interdependence, caring, and responsiveness within a procreational-emanationist perspective. Others, following similar lines to McFague, propose we replace Darwin's metaphor of "natural selection" with that of nature as a mother giving birth. This metaphor brings into dynamic tension the reproductive, evolutionary character of nature and the biblical doctrine of God as creator.

Trinitarian theologians have also found rich resources in biological evolution and ecology. According to Ted Peters, the interrelationality and interconnection of all life on earth are grounded in God the creator, since God is best seen as "divine-persons-in-relation." German theologian Jürgen Moltmann places evolution within a trinitarian account of continuous creation, and argues that "the 'crown of creation' is God's Sabbath still to come." Robert Russell starts with the fact that genetic mutations are a key to biological evolution. Genetic mutations, in turn, involve quantum processes. He argues, as we already have seen, that quantum mechanics can be interpreted in terms of indeterminism. Thus it points to a view of nature as open to God's special providence. Taken together, this means that God can be thought of as acting within evolution without breaking God's own laws.[18]

Evolutionary biology presents yet another domain for the debate between reductionism and holism mentioned in our earlier chapter. As Ian Barbour and others stress, population genetics and ecology deal with organisms as a whole, though they admit that methodological reductionism has been fruitful in molecular biology. Nevertheless, as evolutionary biologist Francisco Ayala points out, there are biological functions and concepts, including "fitness," "adaptation," and "organ," which cannot be defined in purely chemical and physical terms.

Evolutionary biology also reopens the question of teleology or final purpose. Clearly the chance character of evolution rules out the idea that the whole sweep of life on earth can be seen as governed by a single pre-existent plan or design. But does this rule out any form of teleology? Can nature be given a more limited teleological explanation while avoiding both the view of nature as purposelessness on the one hand, and nature as obeying a grand, detailed, and preconceived overall design on the other? According to Ayala's functionalist interpretation, biological structures, organs, and behaviors are teleological if they are adaptations that increase reproductive success. Such teleological explanations are fully compatible with efficient causal explanations, and in some cases, both are required. Wesley Wildman, however, draws attention to the significant challenges facing teleological arguments that move from functional or apparent ends in nature to a metaphysical system that manifests genuine teleological principles.

Theological Anthropology, Evolution, and Neuroscience

How are we to think about human nature and human origins, including the Judeo-Christian concept *imago dei* (that humans were created in God's image) and sin, in light of evolutionary biology, sociobiology, behavioral genetics, and neuroscience?[19] In 1996 Pope John Paul II questioned the traditional, dualist split between body and soul; instead, he referred to the "spiritual" aspects of humanity, including self-awareness, moral conscience, and freedom. Commenting on the Pope's view, astronomer George Coyne proposed thinking of God as participating through love in the process of evolution, an approach that can preserve what is special about the emergence of spirit without resorting to God's intervention in nature. Theologian Karl Rahner has systematically developed the concept of spirit in light of evolution as self-consciousness and consciousness of God. Evolution is a development of matter towards spirit. This development is through God's continuous, immanent, and creative impulse in nature. In this development, nature becomes conscious of itself in humanity.

Another approach to theological anthropology starts with the biblical concept of the human person in terms developed by St Paul in such places as the New Testament Book of Corinthians, where humans are described as a "psychosomatic unity."[20] According to many theologians, Christian anthropology assumes that the psychosomatic unity of the person is "rooted in materiality;" the sciences shed increasing light on the multileveled character and evolutionary history of this unity. Arthur Peacocke has proposed an account of the personal as an emergent level above the purely biological level of complexity. He attributes mental properties to the "human-brain-in-the-body-in-social-relations." He stresses that we have much to learn from sociobiology. He is, however, sharply critical of its incipient reductionism, especially regarding moral reasoning. Human behavior is both a product of evolution and a system of feedback that shapes human evolution by shaping our environment.

According to evolutionary philosopher Michael Ruse, however, altruism in humans neither has an objective reference nor can be justified rationally. Instead, it is a biological adaptation rooted in our genes to help our species compete. One response is that the content of moral reasoning cannot be determined by evolution, even if it is shaped in accordance with evolutionary history.

Theologian Philip Hefner has contributed significantly to theological anthropology, interpreting human nature through evolution as well as the *imago dei*, describing the human as a "created co-creator." What Hefner means here is that our purpose as humans is to help birth the future that is most wholesome for all of nature. Hefner understands *Homo sapiens* as a symbiosis of genes and culture, a creature comprised of two "co-evolving organisms." Though the genetic organism makes culture possible, culture is crucial since myth, ritual, and religion offer guidance for the future.

Nancey Murphy has developed an approach to the psychosomatic unity of the person based on nonreductive physicalism. She employs both emergence and top-down causation to mitigate against reductive materialism, arguing that supervenient properties, such as mental states, are often influenced by their context.

Others also have discussed mental states as having supervenient influence on brain-states in ways that guard the integrity of neurobiological causality while maintaining a distinctive causal role for mentality. In other words, our decisions as conscious persons determine the physiology of our brains even as our brains affect our conscious states of personhood. Still others have focused on the challenge posed by the neurosciences to the claim that ultimacy is a causal source of religious experience. That is, they have responded to the claim that experiences of the divine or sacred are merely brain states and have no necessary correspondence to a reality beyond the brain itself. Responses to this challenge have included more nuanced interpretations of experiences of the ultimate providing guidelines for characterizing authentic religious experiences. These responses also argued that theological and neurological explanations of religious experience are complementary, not contradictory.

Yet another approach to theological anthropology comes from process theology. Ian Barbour rejects both substance dualism (the idea that humans are made of two distinct metaphysical substances, a material body and an immaterial soul) and reductive materialism (the idea that humans are nothing but a compilation of basic physical parts), opting instead for multilevel theories of the person. The process view is congenial to the biblical perspective, in which humanity is rooted in nature, finitude, creatureliness, and mortality, in an evolutionary context thus symbolizing the universal human journey from innocence to responsibility and sin.

Theological anthropology also has much to gain from genetics research.[21] Ted Peters discusses eight issues relating genetics to theological assumptions about God, evolution, and the human person. These include genetic discrimination, an intensification of the abortion controversy, patenting and cloning, genetic determinism and human freedom, the "gay gene," somatic vs. germ-line intervention, and "playing God." The issue of genetic determinism actually involves a contradiction between "puppet determinism," in which genes are thought to determine all of our behavior, and "Promethean determinism," in which we assume we can guide our evolutionary future armed with genetic knowledge. Both belong to what Peters calls the "gene myth," and both are dangerously misleading in linking genes, crime, class, and race. As for "playing God," Peters argues against viewing the DNA, or any part of creation, as sacred. With Philip Hefner, he understands humanity as a "created co-creator." As humans, we cannot *not* be creative. The ethical challenge comes in aligning our creative efforts with the future God is creating.

One final area to mention is the rapidly growing discussion between theologians and the artificial intelligence[22] community. Anne Foerst has described the construction of Cog, a humanoid robot at MIT, and its implications for the *imago dei*. As an example of embodied artificial intelligence, discussions of Cog lead us to consider a symbolic interpretation of the *imago dei* as performative and relational, and enrich our perception and appreciation of human reality. Noreen Herzfeld extends these insights, arguing that the history of failure in symbolic artificial intelligence, which was built on a substantialist understanding of personhood, supports a relational understanding of the *imago dei*.

Redemption, Evolution, and Cosmology

The point of departure for most Christian theologies of redemption is that God saves us from sin through the life, death, and resurrection of Jesus Christ, and we are transformed by the Holy Spirit. God's power to save us is the power of suffering love found in the cross of Christ. Through the suffering of Christ, our broken humanity is taken up into the life of God. Though we too shall die, we are given hope of resurrection to eternal life through the resurrection of Jesus. How, though, are we to interpret this hope when we expand the scope of redemption beyond the human species to the multi-billion-year evolution of life on earth? What is the relation, if any, between sin and death if death is a "natural part" of the evolution of life? More generally, what is the relation between human sin (or "moral evil") and "natural evil": natural disasters, disease, suffering, the death of organisms and the extinction of species? Does God redeem the entire biological world, including humanity, from natural evil as well as the human family, in particular, from moral evil? Alternatively, if we assume that God works through the processes of evolution, as most scholars in theology and science do, why did God create a world in which there is natural evil? This question can be reframed in terms of "theodicy": if God *can* act in nature, why *does* God allow these natural evils to persist? And when we expand our scope further to include the universe and the possibility of extraterrestrial life, what effect will this have on our theology of redemption? If there is life throughout the universe, is all life to be redeemed by God as suggested by the concept of the "cosmic Christ?"[23]

Let us start with the question of human sin. Generally there are two approaches to the relation of sin and evolution. Some view sin as a radically new phenomenon with no roots in our evolutionary past. Others view sin as emerging within human evolution from a variety of preconditions that fade back indefinitely into the past.

In the first view, sin has an entirely human context: it occurs within personal, social, economic, and political contexts. The evolution of life on earth, and with it biological death and the extinction of species, is seen as unequivocally good, the creation of a loving God. But this position minimizes the problem of "natural evil" by denying that pain, suffering, death, or extinction challenge nature's unequivocal goodness. It also offers no explanation for the occurrence of sin in the human species, leaving us radically distinct from an otherwise benign universe, and yet intimately connected to it through a common evolutionary history. Moreover, the scope of redemption, including the hope for eternal life, is limited to the human species and not all of life.

In the second view, the preconditions entailed by sin can be found in our evolutionary past, even though sin is restricted to the human species. Some of these preconditions can be traced back further to the fundamental character of the physical laws of nature. Creation's "groaning" (as it is described in the New Testament Book of Romans) suggests that suffering and death are to be overcome in an eschatological transformation of the cosmos.

Questions arise with this approach as well. If human sin has roots in the evolutionary and cosmological past, how do we avoid the problem of theodicy – that is, blaming God as the creator of the universe and the laws of nature? And what do we mean by the transformation of the universe into the "new creation," given scientific cosmology?

The relevance of Christology to evolution also depends on whether nature needs redemption. Philosopher Holmes Rolston suggests that whatever is in travail needs redemption, whether or not there is any sin to be dealt with. Ian Barbour claims that the human and divine aspects of Jesus are continuous with pre-human evolution *and* yet both are genuinely new in nature. Christ is the product of God's immanent activity in all of evolutionary history, and yet he is a radically new revelation of God's nature. Similarly, Arthur Peacocke views evolution in terms of the "paradox" of emergence – that is, the rise of the genuinely new within the continuity of natural processes.

Scholars such as Juan Luis Segundo have used evolutionary categories to understand the significance of Jesus of Nazareth in "this-worldly" terms. Jesus preserved the supreme evolutionary quality, flexibility. In him evolution bends back on itself to become conscious, and thus human. Theologian Rosemary Radford Ruether proposes a "this-worldly" view of redemption commensurate with her understanding of mortality as natural. Redemption is the fullness of life within finite limits. Nevertheless, she retains a view of Christ as the *cosmic* manifestation of God as both creator and redeemer.[24]

This raises three key questions as pointed out by Gerd Theissen: Is Jesus a variant (or "mutation") of human existence? Is Jesus the consummation of the prophetic protest against selection? Is Jesus a permanently valid "structure of adaptation"? His response makes Jesus "the central reality to which all life must adapt itself."

Eschatology

A defining theme for Christian theology is the resurrection of Jesus of Nazareth from the dead. How is this miracle, fundamental to the Christian faith, to be put in relation to science? Many theologians agree that the resurrection, if it is to be theologically consistent with the Christian hope for the redemption of the creation, must be more than mere psychology, that is, significant beyond the mere psychology of the believer. The resurrection of Jesus bears on the question of life after death and the general resurrection of all creation. According to Ted Peters, the resurrection is not the reunion of resurrected body with an "immortal soul" – a primarily Greek concept – or a personal psyche. Rather, it is the eschatological transformation of the complete person as a psychosomatic unity, a transformation of all dimensions of creation. Issues of resurrection bring us to the significant challenges at the interface of science and theological doctrines of last, or ultimate things, that is, eschatology.

Some scholars, such as Ruether and Segundo, discuss eschatology primarily in the context of ecology and liberation. According to Ruether, the biblical view of eschatology, with its incorporation of the Jewish-Hebraic view of earthly blessedness, was replaced in Hellenistic Christianity by earthly power in the early church. Ruether develops an "ecofeminist theocosmology" which includes "the transience of selves, the living interdependency of all things, and the value of the personal in communion." For Segundo, the "new earth" suggests a new existence in which all the things that seemed to negate our values and our efforts are done away with. The new earth is the new heaven in which God is identified with the culmination of the human struggle for meaning.

However, as our awareness of the vast size and complexity of the cosmos grows, limiting the scope of our eschatological reflections and hope for our own species, or even our own planet, appears less and less justifiable. Should our hope for redemption then be expanded to include the cosmos as a whole? If the universe is the creation of God, should not all of it participate in the new creation? Such a move to enlarge the scope of eschatology to include the entire universe immediately runs into severe challenges from science. According to Big Bang cosmology, the future of the universe is far from anything like a "new creation." Instead it is freeze or fry, endless expansion or violent re-collapse. Moreover, all life will be extinguished from the universe long before either far-future scenario arrives. Can Christian eschatology be made consistent with either of these scenarios and, in both cases, the universal extinction of life? At first glance, the answer would seem to be an alarming "No!" Several theologians have noted that if it were shown that the universe is indeed headed for an all-enveloping death, this could be taken to falsify Christian faith and abolish Christian hope. Is this conclusion avoidable?

Not easily, if we agree to play by the methodological rules adopted so far. Recall that we are pursuing a twofold strategy that avoids both reductionism and "two-worlds" isolationism: lower epistemic levels (e.g., physics, biology, etc.) constrain the claims of upper levels (e.g., psychology, theology), even while the upper levels cannot be reduced to the lower ones. The problem is then clear: Big Bang cosmology is part of physics, the lowest level. Therefore the "freeze or fry" predictions of Big Bang cosmology must constrain what theology can claim eschatologically – just as the role of death in evolutionary biology undercuts the traditional connection between sin and death. No easy appeal to contingency, novelty, unpredictability, emergence, or philosophical cosmology will solve the problem of eschatology and science.

Some, however, have suggested that the scenario for the future of life in the universe may not be quite so grim as it seems. Freeman Dyson shows how life could survive forever in the open/"freeze" scenario. Similarly, physicists Frank Tipler and John Barrow have applied Dyson's work to the "fry" scenario of a closed universe. In both cases, however, these scientists reduce life to mere "information processing," and "eternal life" to the endless processing of new information. In his more recent writings, Tipler claims to treat a variety of theological concerns, including God, resurrection, and immortality, in terms of his "Omega point theory." Yet Tipler's scientific claims have been attacked aggressively by other scientists, while both Dyson's and Tipler's theological proposals and their reductionist philosophies have been criticized by theological and philosophical scholars.

What then might theologians say about eschatology and cosmology? Theologian Mark Worthing has proposed that we take up Wolfhart Pannenberg's distinction between theological and scientific apocalyptic visions. He also employs Pannenberg's concept of "prolepsis": what we find in Christ is the appearance in time of the events of the eschatological end-time. Worthing suggests that the *parousia* should not be equated with the remote future end of the universe. Instead we should understand it as the ongoing transformation of the universe.

According to Ted Peters, in this transformation, time is taken up into God's eternity. This involves what Peters calls "temporal holism" or the cosmos as a unity of time and space. The cosmos is created proleptically from the future and it is redeemed eschatologically by God's future initiative, which we know in Jesus Christ. To his credit, Peters is ruthlessly honest about the challenge from science, "Should the final future as forecasted by [scientific cosmology] come to pass . . . then we would have proof that our faith has been in vain. It would turn out to be that there is no God, at least not the God in whom followers of Jesus have put their faith."

Conclusion

New developments in science, and shifts internal to theology, have opened up new avenues of interaction between the two disciplines. This bridging, for all its difficulties, is time well invested. Science at its best, and theology at its best, both pursue truth. Both science and theology are capable of self-criticism and self-repair, and this self-revision is enhanced respectively by their interaction. Both yield to new truth; and the theologian is confident that new truths discovered within the universe serve to glorify the God who created it.

4

Biological Evolution in Science and Theology

MARTINEZ J. HEWLETT

One of the most influential, challenging, and significant scientific ideas of the nineteenth century was Charles Darwin's theory that all current life forms on this planet descended from a common ancestor by the survival of variants through a process called natural selection. The immediate impact of this new biological paradigm was felt in many segments of European and American society. The long-range effects of the incorporation of the Darwinian model into global thought is still being experienced, as we see what was initially an explanation for botanical and zoological observations being applied to human behavior, economics, cosmology, history, and even the arts. Perhaps no aspect of cultural life has experienced the effects of this incorporation as strongly as the relationship between science and religion. Despite over a century of controversy – perpetuated in large part by fundamentalist and reductionist thinking in particular religious and philosophical communities – popular misunderstanding of Darwinian evolution and its relationship to religion persists.

To appreciate the broad significance of the Darwinian model, three central questions must be answered. First, exactly what is this theory that Darwin expounded in *Origin of the Species*? Second, how has this model itself developed over time, such that it has become the cornerstone of the modern biological organization? And third, what are the philosophical and theological responses that have resulted from our intellectual encounter with Darwin's thesis? Each of these questions will be explored in this chapter.

What Is Darwinian Evolution?

With the publication of *On the Origin of Species by Means of Natural Selection* in November 1859, Charles Darwin finished a project that had begun some thirty years earlier. His famous voyage on the HMS *Beagle* brought him into a new biological domain, one in which he could observe with fresh eyes the features of the natural world, uncluttered by his European suppositions about nature.

As with the development of any scientific theory, there were data to be collected and a hypothesis to be formulated. His data included the correlation of certain features of the animals he found, such as the Galapagos finches, with aspects of the environment in which they were found, such as the type of food they had available. His hypothesis was crafted from these data and under the influence of the thinking of his grandfather, Erasmus Darwin, the great naturalist. In fact, Erasmus' work *Zoonomia* (1794–6) to some extent anticipated his grandson's thesis.

Modern evolutionary biologist John Maynard Smith has succinctly summarized the Darwinian hypothesis:

1. There exists a population of entities (units of evolution) with three properties:
   - multiplication (one can give rise to two)
   - variation (not all entities are alike)
   - heredity (like usually begets like during multiplication).
2. Differences between entities will influence the likelihood of surviving and reproducing. That is, the differences will influence their fitness.
3. The population will change over time (evolve) in the presence of selective forces.
4. The entities will come to possess traits that increase their fitness.

These four principles of Darwin's hypothesis are often summarized as "descent with modification through natural selection." The idea of survival of the fittest often incorporates ideas of direct competition for resources such as food or territory. However, fitness might also mean the ability to occupy a previously uninhabitable biological niche. In any case, as populations experience the selective pressures of the environment, those entities, which have traits that increase their reproductive chances, will be more likely to be represented in succeeding generations.

The end of the nineteenth century was an age dominated by Newtonian physics. In this scientific milieu it is interesting to consider that Darwin called natural selection a "force." But a force must act on some-*thing*. On what did Darwin's force of natural selection act? Significantly, Darwin had no answer for this. And so, in this respect, his theory was scientifically lacking.

Two other nineteenth-century events, taking place within a decade of the publication of Darwin's book, would ultimately provide the answer he needed. In 1868, Augustinian monk Gregor Mendel published the results of his experiments with pea plants, resulting in his model for the quantitative nature of inheritance. This quantitative unit he referred to as *the gene*, from the Greek *genos* meaning offspring. In 1869 Frederick Miescher reported the isolation of a substance from white blood cells which he called nuclein and which has come to be known as DNA. Research synthesizing Mendel's gene and Meishner's DNA would eventually provide the "object" on which Darwin's force of natural selection acts.

The Neo-Darwinian Synthesis of the Twentieth Century

By the early part of the twentieth century the work of Gregor Mendel, ignored for almost fifty years, had been rediscovered. The proliferation of the field of genetics at centers such as Columbia University in New York City led to a rapid advance in the understanding of what is called the chromosomal basis of inheritance. What was a theoretical concept of quantitation for Mendel had become a physical entity: the genes located along the length of the fibrous structures called chromosomes within the nucleus of the cell. By the middle of the twentieth century it had been shown that the chemical nature of the gene was embodied in the molecule called DNA, the very stuff that Frederich Meischer had observed nearly a century before. The merging of genetics with the new discipline of molecular biology resulted in what has been called the Neo-Darwinian synthesis.

The new model developed from this merger added the following features to Darwin's hypothesis:

1. Genes represent information in the form of the linear array of the nitrogenous bases that make up the DNA molecules of chromosomes.
2. The traits of an organism, the so-called phenotype, are the expression of the information found in the genes, the genotype.
3. Variations that are seen in individual organisms are the result of subtle differences in this information. These differences are changes in the array of nucleotide base pairs that make up specific genes.
4. Changes in the genes arise by mutational events. These events occur in a random way. "Random" here means that the events are unpredictable in the quantum mechanical sense. Random does not mean that the changes are simply chaotic.

5. A population of entities (to use John Maynard Smith's language) will have variations in traits that are the result of mutational events.
6. Thus, the force of natural selection operates on this pool of genetic variants, allowing those with greater reproductive fitness to be represented in succeeding generations.

With the Neo-Darwinian paradigm in place, modern biology has been able to gather an impressive and convincing array of data to support the Darwinian model of natural history. In addition to the phenotypes that can be observed at the level of the entire organism (the beaks of finches, for instance), Darwinian evolution is seen to explain data obtained at the level of DNA structure itself. The field of genomics and bioinformatics provides great storehouses of data that support the notion of descent from a common ancestor. The Neo-Darwinian model is applied in biological thinking at all levels of organization, from the molecular to the ecosystem.

This re-visioning of nature, however, did not just affect the natural sciences. Let us turn to how this paradigm has influenced the philosophical positions of scientists and theologians.

The Role of Scientific Materialism and Reductionism

The scientific worldview of which biology forms an integral component has certain philosophical presuppositions. The Enlightenment turn to reason as the most reliable foundation for knowledge of nature, combined with the assumption that nature is intelligible, encouraged the development of that method which is now the hallmark of the scientific enterprise. The refinement of this approach between the sixteenth and twentieth centuries resulted in the tacit understanding that scientific investigation – science itself – would be limited to the following range of concerns:

1. Science would only consider the material aspects of the natural world.
2. Science would restrict itself to secondary causes and would forgo consideration of a primary cause (such as a divine primary cause) as part of its explanatory structure.
3. Science would seek to reduce the systems observed to their component parts as a way of simplifying observation and explaining the behavior of the higher levels of organization.

When applied to evolutionary biology, these limiting principles exorcized from explanation of natural life everything spiritual. Only the material remained. And this material lacked teleology. No purpose could be found in nature. Through the lens of evolution, nature seems to wander with no ultimate goal.

In this way, the Darwinian model revises our interpretation of nature. Even though living organisms are observably complex and higher forms of life exhibit purposeful behavior, finally everything can be reduced to chemical components and physical laws. What appears spiritual seems to be reducible to what is physical. What appears purposeful seems to be reducible to what is random. What appears designed seems to be reducible to the blind interaction of law and chance. The presuppositions of reductionism and materialism have grown like philosophical ivy around the empirical trunk of scientific research.

For instance, the interpretations of Richard Dawkins, James Watson, and Edward Wilson all rely heavily upon these particular presuppositions. When Dawkins, in his various writings including *The Blind Watchmaker* and *The Selfish Gene*, argues that the essential explanation for any biological feature can be found in the DNA sequences of the genes that give rise to that entity, he is making a statement that derives its power from the positions of reductionism and materialism. When Watson writes in *Of Molecules and Men* that all of biology will ultimately be explained at the level of chemistry and physics, he is engaging in a philosophical reductionism. And when Wilson holds in *Consilience* that behavioral aspects of humans can be best explained by genes whose traits gave survival value to the descendants carrying them, his explanation assumes that the material aspect is all that exists.

The use of the evolutionary and molecular biological models to explain all aspects of human biology, including the behavioral and social, has led to the development of two derivative areas of study: sociobiology and evolutionary psychology. The later field attempts to discern common features of human behavior that have identifiable roots in our evolutionary past. The hypothesis is that such features were fixed in our genetic make-up during a period called the environment of evolutionary adaptedness, a time in our species history when certain selective pressures resulted in survival of individuals with these behaviors. Thus, the Darwinian model of natural history is utilized as an explanatory device for virtually all that it means to be human.

In each of these cases the scientist is assuming, sometimes uncritically, a particular philosophical stance. This assumption can result in the problematic blurring of the distinction between science and the interpretation of science. It is important to realize this when reading these texts. Such arguments are consistent within the assumptions of the science they are interpreting. Here are some questions with respect to their position:

- Does the scientific method exhaustively explain all of reality?
- Are conclusions that are drawn about philosophical issues valid within the constraints of the scientific method?
- Is reductionism justified as a philosophical view of the world?
- Is the Neo-Darwinian model an adequate explanatory device for human behavioral and societal features?

Theological Responses to Darwinian Evolution

Almost immediately upon the publication of Darwin's book there was a reaction from the theological community. A common view up to that point had been that God had created the world, in its entirety, in the form in which we see it at present. As a result many argued that Darwin's model was at odds with the Judeo-Christian understanding of creation. More than a hundred years later, some are still drawing this conclusion. We must ask, however, is this conclusion justified? Need we interpret evolution as inherently at odds with theology of divine creation? Does the Judeo-Christian tradition include understandings of nature which might be more consonant with the Darwinian model of natural history?

In fifth-century North Africa, St Augustine of Hippo wrote a treatise on the biblical view of creation entitled *On the Literal Meaning of Genesis*. In that work he said:

> In the seed, then, there was invisibly present all that would develop in time into a tree. And in this same way we must picture the world, when God made all things together, as having had all things which were made in it and with it when day was made. This includes not only heaven with sun, moon, and stars . . . but also the beings which water and earth produced in potency and in their causes before they came forth in the course of time.

The idea of evolution, that is change over time, seems to be implied in this passage, although certainly one should not argue that this statement corresponds to Darwin's model. Nonetheless, we can modestly suggest that at least in the patristic tradition the concept of creation

yet-to-be-complete is not inherently incommensurable with Darwinian evolution.

About one thousand years after Augustine, in the thirteenth century, St Thomas Aquinas also commented on the interpretation of the
scriptural text dealing with the question of how nature was created.
Citing Augustine, Thomas wrote in the *Summa Theologica*:

> In these first days God created all things in their origin or causes,
> and from this work He subsequently rested. Yet afterwards, by
> governing His creatures, in the work of propagation, "He worketh
> until now."

The notion of continuing creation (*creatio continua*) implies a role
for God within an evolutionary theory. In other words, reading
evolutionary history in light of Thomas's work, one might conclude
that it is through the laws governing descent with modification that
God's creative work is seen. Note the implication here. It is not that
Thomas's work confirms or is confirmed by the Darwinian model, but
that it provides a theological understanding of nature that does not
contradict the Darwinian model. In fact, it is, in limited respects, consonant with some of the basic assumptions of the Darwinian model.

Thomas, later in the *Summa*, further develops his understanding of
nature when he characterizes God's creative work as threefold: creation from nothing (*creatio ex nihilo*), distinction, and embellishment
(together seen as *creatio continua*). It would seem that evolution would
be best described again as consonant with distinction and embellishment, those creative activities that lead to the kaleidoscopic diversity
of the biological world. This, of course, is the essence of evolutionary
theory.

That a Darwinian view of nature need not be intrinsically at odds
with theological models of nature can be seen in the work of contemporary theologians as well. Pope John Paul II has acknowledged
the power and importance of evolutionary theory in reshaping our
theological assessment of nature. Referencing the work of one of his
predecessors, he wrote:

> Today, almost half a century after the publication of [*Humani
> Generis*], new knowledge has led to the recognition of the theory of
> evolution as more than a hypothesis. It is indeed remarkable that
> this theory has been progressively accepted by researchers, follow-
> ing a series of discoveries in various fields of knowledge. The con-
> vergence, neither sought nor fabricated, of the results of work that

was conducted independently is in itself a significant argument in favor of this theory.

Using the thought of Augustine, Thomas, and Pope John Paul II as examples, we should conclude that Christian understandings of creation are not inherently incommensurable with the Darwinian model. In fact, we might venture the tentative suggestion that certain Christian theologians provide descriptions of creation that are in fundamental ways consonant with the assumptions of the Darwinian model. Given that these theological statements are separated by nearly the entire history of Christianity, how is it that the popular view of Darwinian evolution is that it is in direct and incontrovertible opposition to Christian belief?

Christian Fundamentalism and Creationism

Within the spectrum of religious reflection, some worldviews rely upon a literalist view of the scriptural texts of those particular traditions. This is especially true in the Abrahamic religions where the inspired writings, be they the Torah, the Qur'an, or the Bible, are interpreted by some in these traditions as providing literal descriptions of all aspects of reality. This treatment of scripture comes into conflict with Darwinian evolution at those places where the scripture describes the work of creation.

An historically significant example of this conflict can be found within the Christian tradition. Within Christianity those who subscribe to a literal interpretation of scripture hold an understanding of the history of nature that relies upon a literal reading of the creation events described in the book of Genesis. This reading assumes that the events as described in scripture represent not simply a theological account of God's creative relationship to the world, but a reliable "scientific" portrayal of what happened in real historical time.

Based upon this assumption the idea of *creation science* was born. This conflation of scripture and science attempts to represent physical reality such that it is consistent with the Genesis description. For instance, the age of the earth is given in Old Testament terms, and the conclusions of geological dating studies are discounted. The fossil record is interpreted in light of the flood story rather than in terms of the paleontological record. For the creation scientist, everything must square with the literal truth of Genesis.

We must pose questions for theologians here, just as we did for the scientific materialist position:

- Is the creation science view a reasonable position, in the light of both scientific inquiry and biblical scholarship?
- Is it appropriate to treat scripture as a scientific document?
- Is Darwinian evolution inconsistent with Christian thought?

Intelligent Design as a Possible Scientific Approach

A philosophical challenge results from the methodological self-limitation of the scientific enterprise. Because science investigates only secondary causes, the idea of purpose, integral to the question of primary cause, is excluded from the explanatory process. This limitation, in turn, results in the exclusion of any idea of design from the *scientific* model that is being considered. This becomes particularly critical in the case of biological systems, where design or purpose seems much more evident.

The idea of design as part of the philosophical consideration is deeply entrenched in the Western tradition. Aristotle considered the purpose for which something exists as an important part of the description of that thing. St Thomas Aquinas, in the *Summa Theologica*, used the idea of design as one way that one could consider the existence of God:

> The fifth way is taken from the governance of the world. We see that things which lack intelligence, such as natural bodies, act for an end, and this is evident from their acting always, or nearly always, in the same way, so as to obtain the best result. Hence it is plain that not fortuitously, but designedly, do they achieve their end. Now whatever lacks intelligence cannot move towards an end, unless it be directed by some being endowed with knowledge and intelligence; as the arrow is shot to its mark by the archer. Therefore some intelligent being exists by whom all natural things are directed to their end; and this being we call God.

While Thomas did not offer this as a "proof" of God's existence, later natural theologians such as Bishop William Paley used the existence of design in biological systems as direct evidence of God's creative action. Indeed, the "blind watchmaker" that Richard Dawkins raises in his book of the same name is a reference to this design argument found in Paley's early nineteenth-century work.

Recently, the idea of design in biological systems due to the intervention of some intelligence has again been raised. Michael Behe (*Darwin's Black Box*) and William Dembski (*The Design Inference*) have

both made a case for reintroducing design as a necessary consideration in the scientific explanatory process. Behe attempts this by using
the concept of "irreducible complexity" to argue that the cell, as a
biochemical structure, could not have arisen by the process of gradual
change and selection, as predicted by the strict Neo-Darwinian
model. He uses a mousetrap analogy to speak about structures and
systems in cells that he argues are too complex to have arisen by
gradual changes (single base changes in DNA) and selection. The
argument is that such irreducibly complex systems cannot be selected
for by standard Darwinian mechanisms. The alternative hypothesis is
that the cell had to be designed. The identity of the designer may be
said to be God, although this is not explicitly stated. Dembski holds
a similar position, though his approach draws on mathematics and
philosophy.

The intelligent design movement has been proposed by its academic supporters as a testable hypothesis, as distinct from creation
science, which relies upon an acceptance of a literal reading of the
Judeo-Christian scriptures. It does include, however, the ideas of
design and purpose (teleological arguments) that are outside of the
accepted scientific paradigm.

Again, we must ask questions about the arguments for design as a
description of the natural world:

- Is it possible to experimentally detect design using the standard
  scientific method? If not, should design be considered scientific or
  philosophical?
- Is the idea of a designer, who is responsible for irreducible complexity, really a "God of the gaps" argument? That is, will scientific
  investigation eventually show how these systems might arise by
  methods consistent with natural laws?
- Does this argument apply only if gradualism is the sole source for
  variations during Darwinian evolution? Could other mechanisms
  of variation be used that would not require the intervention of an
  intelligent designer?

Summary and Conclusion

The great insight of Charles Darwin has for nearly a century and a half
dominated the intellectual landscape of both the sciences and the
humanities. In order to fully appreciate, and competently navigate,
this changed and changing intellectual landscape we distinguish
three components of the Darwinian influence: the science of the

Darwinian model itself; philosophical interpretations of the Darwinian model as applied to human behavior; and the relationship between the Darwinian model and theological views of nature which are and are not hostile to it. These distinctions have been clarified as we've addressed them through the lens of our threefold inquiry articulated in the introduction. First, we have seen that this theory rested initially upon observations made in the best tradition of the scientific method. Second, with the modern understanding of genetics combined with molecular biology, we have noted how the Neo-Darwinian synthesis has expanded the reach of Darwin's original investigations. Moreover, we now see evidence for descent with modification through the filter of natural selection in every aspect of our biosphere, from the micro- to the macro-level. And third, we have outlined aspects of the intellectual challenge of incorporating this view of the natural world into philosophical and theological reflection.

The Darwinian model will not be the last word spoken on the nature of nature; nor will it stand alone as a complete description of reality. Its strength lies in its impact on both science and philosophy, along with the concomitant reaction of theology. If our general, or common-sense, picture of the nature of reality is to approximate what actually exists, we must be willing to consider multiple points of view. In this sense, Darwinian evolution provides several, but perhaps not all, of the colors with which we will paint our picture. It would be a mistake for theology and philosophy to ignore the fact that this is a very powerful way of envisioning creation. Yet it would also be a mistake to assume that the Darwinian model provides an exhaustive resource for understanding reality.

5

Genetics, Theology, and Ethics

TED PETERS

Genetics is the field of scientific research that studies gene activity in plants, animals, and humans. Genes are segments of DNA (deoxyribonucleic acid) found in each living cell, and each of these DNA segments codes for a protein, thereby yielding a bodily effect. All of life on planet Earth shares the chemical make-up of DNA, even though each species differs in the number and function of genes. Human DNA contains approximately 30,000 genes arrayed over two pairs of 23 chromosomes. The 46 human chromosomes are strands of DNA, with each of the 23-strand pairs arranged as a double helix. The DNA strands are composed of four base chemicals: adenine (A), guanine (G), cytosine (C), and thymine (T). These four bases are typically identified by their single-letter abbreviations (A, G, C, T) and constitute an alphabet, so to speak, that carries genetic information from DNA to tissue formation and bodily activity.

Modern genetics began in the nineteenth century with the research of an obscure Austrian monk, Gregor Mendel, who discovered patterns of inheritance in pea plants. Mendelian laws of inheritance still stand as the foundation for contemporary genetics. What the twentieth century added is the chemical work of molecular biology, such as the post-World War II discovery of the double helix structure of DNA by James Watson and Francis Crick. At the turn of the twenty-first century, the Human Genome Project had sequenced the 3 billion base pairs and identified nearly all the genes in the human genome. The complete genomes of a handful of plants and animals have also been identified.

In addition to molecular biology, which directly studies the chemical processes of genes, two other branches of genetics have become significant for religious reflection, behavioral genetics, and sociobiology. Behavioral genetics employs statistical studies of phenotypical characteristics and social preferences to discern heritability probabilities. Central to such studies are monozygotic and heterozygotic twins who have been raised apart. The assumption in such studies is that twins who are raised apart are excellent subjects because they provide opportunity to distinguish between genetic and environmental influences on development.

Sociobiology appeared on the scene in 1975 with publications by Harvard entomologist Edward O. Wilson. Wilson, having studied how ant societies are socially held together by chemical signals, purported by analogy that human breeding patterns, gender dominance, and caste systems are similarly explainable. Richard Dawkins shortly thereafter coined the term "selfish gene," which reinforced the central thesis of sociobiology: in Darwinian fashion the human organism does not live for itself; rather, its function in nature is to reproduce the genes for which it is the temporary carrier. In short, genetic forces drive evolution, including human evolution; and human social history including religious history can be explained by reference to genetic drives.

Theological Issues Raised by Genetics

The apparent growth in knowledge regarding human nature cultivated by genetic research leads some religious thinkers to review their inherited anthropologies. Most theologians see the field of genetics as a challenge – requiring response; a few see new genetic knowledge as a complement to long-standing religious insight. Distinctively theological issues are few, and are frequently embedded within the more plentiful and visible issues of ethics and public policy. Theological issues will be taken up immediately; ethical issues surrounding cloning and stem cell research will follow.

The first theological concern is *genetic reductionism*. Reductionism poses a theological threat everywhere in modern science, to be sure. The form it takes here is the vague cultural belief that "it's all in the genes." In the laboratory, methodological reductionism is necessary to foster research into gene function; but a threat comes with onto-logical reductionism and surmises that all of what constitutes human nature is reducible to the genes. During the early years of the Human Genome Project DNA was described by some scientists as the "code of codes" or the "blueprint of humanity." Such biological reductionism seems to leave no room for independent influence on the part of spirit or culture, the dimensions wherein most religious traditions work.

A second and related concern is *genetic determinism*. If "it's all in the genes," and the DNA is the blueprint of who human beings are, then genes move into the position of determiners of human nature and human value. In the historical struggle between nature and nurture in the minds of intellectuals trying to explain human complexity, the new breed of genetic determinists stake their claim on nature. Relatively few molecular biologists advocate strong genetic determinism, while behavioral geneticists and sociobiologists reinforce it. Molecular biologists and philosophers who oppose an exclusive genetic determinism frequently appeal to two-part determinism: genes plus environment. Some theologians locate human freedom in three-part determinism: genes, environment, and the human self or person. In the latter case, the human self is emergent; the self is not reducible to merely biological or environmental influences.

A third and related concern is *Neo-Darwinian evolution*. Nineteenth-century Darwinism employed natural selection as the mechanism for explaining evolutionary change over time. Twentieth-century Neo-Darwinists add genetic mutation to the theory, adding detail to the manner in which natural selection works. Sociobiology extrapolates on Neo-Darwinism by attempting to explain all of human culture including religious belief in terms of biological determinism. Sociobiologists (sometimes called evolutionary psychologists) contend that human culture is on a leash, a short leash, held by a genetic agenda. That agenda is the self-replication of genes using the human species as its vehicle. Human culture is structured so as to encourage reproduction and, hence, the perpetuation of genes. Human religion and human morality, whether theologians know it or not, is reducible to the agenda of selfish genes.

Those theologians who are attempting to incorporate sociobiology into their religious vision feel they must justify human transcendence of biology and the emergence of soul or spirit. Philip Hefner's theological anthropology, for example, argues that through evolutionary processes the genes have determined that we humans would be free. Some Christologies, for another example, contend that Jesus marks a significant advance in evolutionary history, because with the Nazarene a precedent-setting life is led that transcends the selfish genetic agenda and the possibility is opened for self-sacrificial loving. In contrast, some Muslim scholars find they must simply reject Neo-Darwinian evolutionary theory because it makes no room for human spirit and because it fails to cohere with the anthropology of the Qur'an.

In summary, the theological community is accepting of methodological reductionism within molecular biology that functions to yield advance in scientific research. However, theologians resist philosophical extrapolations that tend toward ontological reductionism or genetic determinism. Reductionism and determinism are insufficient, say theologians, to explain spiritual reality or ethical transcendence. Theologians will defend human freedom and moral transcendence whether it complements the science or requires abandoning the science.

Genetic Engineering

Genetic engineering consists of selecting, inserting, or removing individual genes in order to manipulate the genome of an organism. In agriculture and animal husbandry selective breeding to obtain preferred strains has been practiced for millennia. What modern genetic engineering adds is chemical and mechanical methods for more sophisticated results.

In agriculture, the genomes of plants are altered by genetic engineering to confer resistance to blight; or to herbicides, in order to preserve the crops while eliminating weeds. Tomato genomes, for example, can be modified so as to stall final ripening during transport to market, the fruit ripening just prior to going on sale. Such techniques dramatically increase the percentage of produce that becomes saleable. In Europe and other parts of the world popular movements against *Genetically Modified Foods* (GMFs) have arisen. Fearing unknown possible health effects, opponents of GMFs lobby for accurate labeling so that the market can freely choose whether to consume them or not.

The engineering of farm animal genomes has two purposes. One is to obtain preferred strains of livestock, especially beef cattle. The other is to produce foods or pharmaceuticals for human consumption. An example of the latter case is the insertion of a human gene into a sheep genome to produce in the animal's milk a certain protein, a protein usable for treatment of a human disease. This use of animals for human betterment is itself controversial, with opponents arguing that turning animals into a means for human ends violates animal dignity.

To date, the genetic engineering of human genomes in the reproduction process has been limited to gene selection; it has not included gene insertion or removal. When *in vitro* multiple fertilized ova can be examined, only those with the preferred genome will be implanted in the mother's uterus. This process is typically employed to eliminate known deleterious genes such as that for cystic fibrosis. In somatic therapy on living persons, however, more than selection is being tried. Genes that produce healthy blood have been inserted into bone marrow cells. Attempts are being made to send knock-out genes into cancer tumors to turn off telomerese activity, that is, to turn off tumor growth.

An implicit theological issue that arises more often in the wider cultural debate than within specific religious communities is *naturalism*. Naturalism is the belief that nature apart from intervention by human technology is the source of value. Genetic engineering is a form of technology that alters the natural world we have inherited from evolutionary history. The Promethean question arises implicitly: is the natural world we have inherited the source of human value; or, on the basis of humanly superimposed purposes, do we have the right to manipulate nature to meet these purposes? Much of the energy driving opposition to GMFs derives from naturalism. A similar naturalism is implicit in theological arguments that presume that God's will is manifest in the genetic lottery resulting from sexual intercourse rather than through deliberate selection *in vitro* of the genetic code of future children.

This Promethean question also arises with genetic futurism. As the present generation manipulates plant, animal, and human genomes, will this place us in the position of guiding our evolutionary future? Does the human race possess the wisdom to choose a wholesome future, or, like the Prometheus of ancient Greek tragedy, will we overstep our finite bounds and create an irreparable tragedy? Select conservative as well as liberal theologians along with naturalist advocacy groups wish to put the brakes on genetic engineering and let nature take its course; whereas other religious leaders foresee immense benefits for health and well-being to be gained through genetic technology and contend that the human race must steward scientific advance.

The Human Genome Project

The worldwide effort, originally named the "Human Genome Initiative" but later known as the "Human Genome Project" or HGP, began in 1987 and was celebrated as complete in 2001. When begun, HGP was dubbed "big science," comparable to placing human beings on the moon. It was international in scope, involving numerous laboratories and associations of scientists around the world, receiving public funding in the US at $200 million per year, with a scheduled fifteen-year time line. The US Department of Energy (DOE) began funding in 1987, followed by the National Institutes of Health (NIH) in 1990.

The scientific goal was to map the genes and sequence the human DNA. Mapping would eventually tell us the position and spacing of the then predicted 100,000 genes in each of our bodies' cells; and sequencing would determine the order of the four base pairs – the A (adenine), T (thymine), G (guanine), and C (cytosine) nucleotides – that compose the DNA molecule. The primary motive was that which drives all basic science, namely, the need to know. The secondary motive was perhaps even more important, namely, to identify the 4,000 or so genes that were suspected to be responsible for inherited diseases and prepare the way for treatment through genetic therapy. This would benefit society, HGP architects thought, because a library of DNA knowledge would jump-start medical research on many fronts. Many early prophecies found their fulfillment. Some did not.

What was not anticipated was the competition between the private sector and the public sector. J. Craig Venter led the private sector effort. While on a grant from NIH, Venter applied for nearly 3,000 patents on Expressed Sequence Tags (ESTs). The ESTs located genes but stopped short of identifying gene function. A furor developed over applying for a patent on government money that merely reports knowledge of what already exists in nature – knowledge of existing DNA sequences – and this led to the 1992 resignation of James Watson from the directorship of NIH's National Center for Human Genome Research (NCHGR). Venter then established The Institute for Genomic Research (TIGR) and began employing Applied Biosystems' automatic sequencers twenty-four hours per day to speed up nucleotide sequencing and locating ESTs. By 1998 Venter had established Celera Genomics, with sequencing capacity fifty times greater than TIGR, and by 17 June 2000 he concluded his 90 percent complete account of the human genome. It was published in the 16 February 2001 issue of *Science*.

Francis Collins took over NCHGR leadership from Watson and found himself driving the public sector effort, racing with Venter toward the mapping finish line. Collins drew twenty laboratories worldwide with hundreds of researchers into the International Human Genome Sequencing Consortium, which he directed from his Washington office. Collins repudiated patenting of raw genomic data, and sought to place DNA data into the public domain as rapidly as possible so as to prevent private patenting. His philosophy was that the human genome is the common property of the whole human race. The public project finished almost simultaneously with the private, and the Collins map, also 90 percent complete, appeared one day prior to Venter's, 15 February 2001, in *Nature*.

Human DNA, as it turns out, is largely "junk" – that is, 98.6 percent does not code for proteins. Half of the junk DNA consists of repeated sequences of various types, most of which are parasitic elements inherited from our distant evolutionary past. Only 1.1 percent to 1.4 percent constitute sequences that code for proteins, which function as genes.

Of dramatic interest is the number of genes in the human genome. Francis Collins estimates there are 31,000 protein-encoding genes; and at the time of the announcement he could actually list 22,000. Venter could provide a list of 26,000, to which he added an estimate of 10,000 additional possibilities. For round numbers, the estimate in 2001 stood at 30,000 human genes.

This is philosophically significant, because in 1987 the anticipated number was 100,000. It was further assumed that human complexity lodged in the number of genes: the greater the number of genes, the greater the complexity. So, when, near completion, HGP scientists could find only a third of the anticipated number, confusion appeared. Confusion was enhanced when the human genome was compared to a yeast cell with 6,000 genes, a fly with 13,000 genes, and a worm with 26,000 genes, and a rice cell with 50,000 genes. On the basis of the previous assumption, a grain of rice should be more complex than Albert Einstein.

With the near completion of HGP, no longer could human unique-ness or complexity or even distinctiveness be lodged in the number of genes. Francis Collins began to speculate that perhaps what is distinctively human could be found not in the genes themselves but in the multiple proteins and the complexity of protein production. Culturally, DNA began to lose some of its magic, some of its associa-tion with human essence.

Ethical and Public Policy Issues Arising out of HGP

It is significant to note that HGP scientists at the outset anticipated ethical and public policy concerns; they were acutely aware that their research would have an impact on surrounding society and were willing to share responsibility for it. When in 1987 James D. Watson counseled the US Department of Health and Human Services to appropriate the funds for what would become HGP, he recom-mended that 3 percent of the budget be allotted to study the ethical, legal, and social implications of genome research. Watson insisted that society learn to use genetic information only in beneficial ways; and, if necessary, the government should pass laws at both the federal and state levels to prevent invasions of privacy or discrimination on genetic grounds. As mentioned, Watson, who along with Francis Crick is famed for his discovery of the double helix structure of DNA, was the first to head the Office of Human Genome Research at the National Institutes of Health (NIH). He later resigned amidst a dispute with former NIH director Bernadine Healey over the morality of patenting of DNA sequences. Moral controversy broke out repeatedly during the near decade and a half of research.

Religious responses to the advancing frontier of genetic knowledge emerge mainly from faith's concern to relieve human suffering and employ science to improve human health and well-being. A statement prepared by the National Council of Churches under the leadership of Union Seminary ethicist Roger L. Shinn affirms that churches in the United States must be involved with genetic research and therapy. "The Christian churches understand themselves as communities dedicated to obeying the will of God through service to others. The churches have a particular concern for those who are hurt or whose faith has been shaken, as demonstrated by the long history of the churches in providing medical care . . . Moreover, the churches have a mission to prevent suffering as well as to alleviate it."[1]

In 1990 the Center for Theology and the Natural Sciences (CTNS) at the Graduate Theological Union (GTU) in Berkeley, California, obtained one of the first grants offered by the Ethical, Legal, and Social Issues (ELSI) division of NCHGR at NIH. A team of molecular biologists, behavioral geneticists, theologians, and bioethicists monitored the first years of HGP research to articulate theological and ethical implications of the new knowledge. Many religious and ethical issues eventually became public policy concerns. These are adumbrated in what follows.

Genetic Discrimination

When James Watson recommended the establishment of ELSI, the first public policy concern was what he called *privacy*, what is here called *genetic discrimination*. An anticipated and feared scenario took the following steps. As researchers identify and locate most if not all genes in the human genome that either condition or in some cases cause disease, the foreknowledge of an individual's genetic predisposition to expensive diseases could lead to loss of medical insurance and perhaps loss of employment opportunities. As HGP progressed, the gene for cystic fibrosis was found on chromosome 7 and Huntington's chorea on chromosome 4. Alzheimer's disease was sought on chromosome 21 and colon cancer on chromosome 2. Disposition to muscular dystrophy, sickle-cell anemia, Tay Sachs disease, certain cancers, and numerous other diseases turned out to have locatable genetic origins. More knowledge is yet to come. When it comes, it may be accompanied by an inexpensive method for testing the genome of each individual to see if he or she has any genes for any diseases. Screening for all genetic diseases may become routine for newborns just as testing for phenylketonuria (PKU) has been since the 1960s. A person's individual genome might become part of a data bank to which each of us, as well as our health care providers, would have future access. The advantage is clear: alert medical care from birth to grave could be carefully planned to delay onset, and to appropriately treat, and perhaps even cure, genetically based diseases.

Despite the promise for advances in preventative health care, fear arises due to practices of commercial insurance. Commercial insurance around which much of the US health care system is structured works by sharing risk. When risk is uncertain to all, then all can be asked to contribute equally to the insurance pool. Premiums can be equalized. Once the genetic disorders of individuals become known, however, this could justify higher premiums for those demonstrating greater risk: the greater the risk, the higher the premium. Insurance even may be denied those whose genes predict extended or expensive medical treatment.

Some ethicists operating out of rights theory are seeking protection from discrimination by invoking the principles of confidentiality and privacy. They argue that genetic testing should be voluntary, and the information contained in one's genome should be controlled by the patient. This argument presumes that if information can be controlled, then the rights of the individual for employment, insurance, and medical care can be protected. There are some grounds for thinking this approach will succeed. United States Title VII of the 1964 Civil Rights Act restricts pre-employment questioning to work-related health conditions, and its paragraph 102.b.4 potentially protects coverage for the employee's spouse and children. Current legislative proposals seem to favor privacy.

Other ethicists argue that privacy is a misguided cure for this problem. Privacy will fail, say its critics, because insurance carriers will press for legislation more advantageous to them; and eventually, protection by privacy may slip. In addition, the existing state of computer linkage makes it difficult to prevent the movement of data from hospital to insurance carrier and to anyone else bent on finding it. Most importantly, the privacy argument overlooks the principle that genome information should not, finally, be restricted. The more society knows, the better the health care planning can be. In the long run, what society needs is *information without discrimination*. The only way to obtain this is to restructure the employment–insurance–health care relationship. The current structure makes it profitable for employers and insurance carriers to discriminate against individuals with certain genetic configurations – that is, it is in their best financial interest to limit or even deny health care. A restructuring is called for so that it becomes profitable to deliver, not withhold, health care. To accomplish this the whole nation will have to become more egalitarian – that is, to think of the nation itself as a single community willing to care for its own constituents.

The Abortion Controversy Intensifies

Given the divisiveness of the abortion controversy in the United States and certain other countries, fears arise over possible genetic discrimination in the womb or prior to the womb in the petri dish. Techniques have been developed to examine *in-vitro* fertilized (IVF) eggs as early as the fourth cell-division in order to identify so called "defective" genes, such as the chromosomal structure of Down's syndrome. Prospective parents may soon routinely fertilize a dozen or so eggs in the laboratory, screen for the preferred genetic make-up, implant the desired zygote(s), and discard the rest. What will be the status of the discarded embryos? Might they be considered abortions? By what criteria do we define "defective" when considering the future of a human being? Should prospective parents limit themselves to eliminating defective children, or should they go on to screen for enhancing genetic traits such as blue eyes or higher intelligence? If so, might this lead to a new form of eugenics, to selective breeding based upon personal preference and prevailing social values? What will become of human dignity in all this?

Relevant here is that the legal precedent set by *Roe* v. *Wade* (1973) would not serve to legitimate discarding pre-implanted embryos. This US Supreme Court case has served to legalize the use of abortion to eliminate a fetus from a woman's body as an extension of a woman's right to determine what happens to her body. This would not apply to pre-implanted embryos, however, because they are life forms outside the woman's body.

The Roman Catholic tradition has set strong precedents regarding the practice of abortion. The Second Vatican Council document *Gaudium et spes* (1965) states the position still held today: "from the moment of its conception life must be guarded with the greatest care, while abortion and infanticide are unspeakable crimes." The challenge to ethicists in the Roman Catholic tradition in the near future will be to examine what transpires at the pre-implantation stage of the embryo to determine if the word "abortion" applies. If it does, this may lead to recommending that genetic screening be pushed back one step further, to the gamete stage prior to fertilization. The genetic make-up of sperm and ovum separately could be screened, using acceptable gametes and discarding the unacceptable. The Catholic Health Association of the United States pushes back a step still further by recommending the development of techniques of gonadal cell therapy to make genetic corrections in the reproductive tissues of prospective parents long before conception takes place – that is, gametocyte therapy.

Genetic Determinism, Human Freedom, and the Gene Myth

With rising public attention given to the Human Genome Project in the early 1990s, there grew up with it an increased belief in genetic determinism. The cultural construction was: "it's all in the genes." Scholars referred to this widespread belief as "geneticism," the "strong genetic principle," "genetic essentialism," "genetic fatalism," and the "gene myth." The gene myth was fed minimally by molecular biology but maximally by behavioral genetics and sociobiology. In the classic war between nature and nurture, the genetic determinists sided with nature.

The gene myth can be dissected into three subtenets: puppet determinism, Promethean determinism, and the commandment against playing God. The first is seemingly fatalistic: *puppet determinism*. According to puppet determinism the DNA defines who we are and the genes, like a puppeteer, pull the strings that make us dance. To speak of "genetic essentialism" or to see genetics as the ultimate explanation of human being is to place DNA in the position of defining who we are and who we can be. To speak of "genetic fatalism" or to say "it's all in the genes" is to assume that genetic influences are unchangeable, that we are immutably destined to express our DNA programming. The psychological corollary to genetic determinism is that what we assume to be personal freedom is only a delusion. The ethical corollary to genetic determinism is that we are not responsible for what we do; our genes are. We have natural innocence in a new form: blame my genes, not me.

The second subtenet is *Promethean determinism*. Promethean determinism assigns our scientists the task of understanding just how the genes work, plus that of making the decision to develop appropriate technologies based upon this understanding; and this will then give the human race control over what nature has bequeathed to us. Because the history of genes constitutes the history of human evolution, once scientists have gained control we will be able to guide the future evolution of the human race. We will have wrested from nature her secrets, and this will transform us from the determined into the determiners.

One significant difference between the two types of determinism is notable. In the case of puppet determinism, there is no human self that transcends our DNA. Genetic essentialism is reductionistic; it means that who we are is exhaustively reducible to genetic determinism. There is no "I" or "we" that stands independently. The self is a puppet. What we know as human freedom simply does not exist, except as a delusion.

Promethean determinism is more humanistic in that it entails the unspoken trust that some sort of decision-making entity, perhaps the human self, has gained a degree of critical distance over against its own genetic make-up. This self is presumed without question to exist, and it cannot be exhaustively reduced to its genetic determinants. The self cannot be reducible if we can advocate pressing the determining power of genes into the service of higher human purposes. This must be the case if the scientific members of the human race are going to be able to determine how the determining genes will determine the future of humankind. The gene myth is not itself a highly developed philosophy or ideology that requires internal consistency. Rather, it is a barely articulated thought-form present in culture that provides a framework for interpreting the human reality in light of genetic research.

In addition to these two forms of determinism, the gene myth also voices an ethical maxim: thou shalt not play God. This derives from the Frankenstein fear of the mad scientist who, in trying to take control of the mysterious forces of life, oversteps the invisible boundary intended by nature to contain human pride and lets loose uncontrollable destructive forces. Blockbuster movies such as *Jurassic Park* and *Gattaca* warn us to not play God with genetic nature. On the one hand, the gene myth lures us toward Promethean prowess, toward taking control of human destiny. On the other hand, it causes us to shrink back in horror over the possibility that we might precipitate nature's backlash.

As mentioned above, many are tempted to embrace a two-part

determinism of genes plus environment to avoid genetic determinism. Yet, even here, our everyday human experience of freedom cannot be accounted for by either one-part or two-part determinism. The self or person determines things through deliberation, decision, and action. Although constrained and enabled by genes and environment, the self constitutes the third determinant.

Genes, Sin, Crime, and Racial Discrimination

The belief in determinism promulgated by the gene myth raises the question of moral and legal culpability. Does a genetic disposition to antisocial behavior make a person guilty or innocent before the law? Over the next decade, our legal system will have to face a rethinking of the philosophical planks on which we have constructed concepts such as free will, guilt, innocence, and mitigating factors. There is no question that research into the connection between genetic determinism and human behavior will continue and new discoveries will become immediately relevant to the prosecution and defense of those accused of crimes. The focus will be on the concept of free will, because the assumption of the Western philosophy coming down to us from Augustine that underlies our understanding of law is that guilt can only be assigned to a human agent acting freely.

The specter on the genetic horizon is that genetic dispositions confirmable to certain forms of behavior will constitute compulsion, and this will place us at a fork in the legal road: either we declare the person with a genetic disposition to crime innocent and set him or her free, or we declare him or her so constitutionally impaired as to justify incarceration and isolation from the rest of society. The first fork would jeopardize the welfare of society; the second fork would violate individual rights.

That society needs to be protected from criminal behavior, and that such protection could be had by isolating individuals with certain genetic dispositions, leads to further questions regarding insanity and race. The issue of insanity arises because we can predict that the genetic defense may rely upon precedents set by the insanity defense. The courts treat insanity with a focus on the insane person's inability to distinguish right from wrong when committing a crime. When a defendant is judged innocent on these grounds, he or she is incarcerated in a mental hospital until the medical evaluators judge that the individual is cured. Once cured, the individual is then released. In principle, such a person might never be judged "cured" and spend more time in isolation than the prison penalty prescribed for the crime, maybe even the rest of his or her life. Should the genetic defense tie itself to the insanity defense, and if one's DNA is thought to last a lifetime, then the trip to the hospital may become the equivalent of a life sentence. In this way the genetic defense may backfire.

With this prospect, we have returned to the specter of genetic discrimination once again. The current discussion of possible genetic influence on antisocial behavior is riddled with fears of discrimination, especially its racial overtones. Within the United States, the percentage is growing of black men among the population of incarcerated prisoners. Because of this, society could invoke the gene myth to associate genes with criminal predispositions and these two with race. A stigma against black people could arise, a presumption that they are genetically predisposed to crime. University of California sociologist Troy Duster fears that if we identify crime with genes and then genes with race, we may inadvertently provide a biological support for prejudice and discrimination.

The Gay Gene

Theological and ethical debate has arisen over the 1993 discovery of a possible genetic disposition to male homosexuality. Dean H. Hamer and his research team at the US National Cancer Institute announced that they discovered evidence that male homosexuality – at least some male homosexuality – is genetic. Constructing family trees in instances where two or more brothers are gay combined with actual laboratory testing of homosexual DNA, Hamer located a region near the end of the long arm of the X chromosome that likely contains a gene influencing sexual orientation. Because men receive an X chromosome from their mother and a Y from their father (women receive two Xs, one from each parent), this means that the possible gay gene is inherited maternally. Mothers can pass on the gay gene without themselves nor their daughters being homosexual. A parallel study of lesbian genetics is as yet incomplete; and the present study of gay men will certainly require replication and confirmation. Scientists do not yet have undisputable proof.

The ethical implications, should a biological basis for homosexuality be confirmed, could go more than one direction. The scientific fact does not itself determine the direction of the ethical interpretation of that fact. The central ethical question is this: does the genetic disposition toward homosexuality make the bearer of that gene innocent or guilty? Two answers are logically possible.

On the one hand, a homosexual man could claim that because he inherited the gay gene and did not choose a gay orientation by his own free will, he is innocent. The biological innocence position could be buttressed by an additional argument that homosexual activity is not itself sinful; it is simply one natural form of sexual expression among others. One could go still further to say that because it is biologically inherited it is God's will; that a person's homosexual pre-disposition is God's gift.

On the other hand, one could follow the opposite road and identify the gay gene with a carnal disposition to sin. Society could claim that the body inherited by each of us belongs to who we are – who I am as a self is determined at least in part by what my parents bequeathed me – and that an inherited disposition to homosexual behavior is just like other innate dispositions such as lust or greed or similar forms of concupiscence which are shared with the human race generally; and all this constitutes the state of original sin into which we are born. Signposts point in both ethical directions.

Beyond the question of guilt or innocence ethicists anticipate another issue, namely, the risk of stigma. Might the presence of the gay gene in an unborn fetus be considered a genetic defect and become grounds for abortion? Would routine genetic testing lead to a wholesale reduction of gay men in a manner parallel to that of children with Down's syndrome? Would this count as class discrimi-nation?

Somatic Therapy vs. Germline Enhancement

The debate over two distinctions – somatic vs. germline intervention and therapy vs. enhancement intervention – involves both secular and religious discussions. The term "somatic therapy" refers to the treatment of a disease in the body cells of a living individual by trying to repair an existing defect. The term "germline therapy" refers to intervention into the gametes perhaps for the purpose of eliminating a gene such as that for cystic fibrosis so that it would not be passed along to future generations. Both somatic and germline therapies are conservative when compared to genetic enhancement. Enhancement goes beyond merely therapy for existing genes that may be a threat to health by selecting or adding genes to make an individual superior in some fashion. Enhancement might involve genetic engineering to increase bodily strength or intelligence or other socially desirable characteristics.

Ethical commentators almost universally agree that somatic therapy is morally desirable, and they look forward to the advances

HGP will bring for expanding this important work. Yet they to stop short of endorsing genetic selection and manipulation for the purposes of enhancing the quality of biological life for otherwise normal individuals or for the human race as a whole. New knowledge gained from HGP might locate genes that affect the brain's organization and structure so that careful engineering might lead to enhanced ability for abstract thinking or to other forms of physiological and mental improvement.

Religious ethicists argue that somatic therapy should be pursued, but enhancement through germline engineering raises cautions about protecting human dignity. In a 1982 study, the World Council of Churches stated: "Somatic cell therapy may provide a good; however, other issues are raised if it also brings about a change in germline cells. The introduction of genes into the germline is a permanent alteration . . . Nonetheless, changes in genes that avoid the occurrence of disease are not necessarily made illicit merely because those changes also alter the genetic inheritance of future generations . . . There is no absolute distinction between eliminating defects and improving heredity."[2] The primary caution raised by the WCC here has to do with our lack of knowledge regarding the possible consequences of altering the human germline. The problem is that the present generation lacks sufficient information regarding the long-term consequences of a decision today that might turn out to be irreversible tomorrow. Thus, the WCC does not forbid forever germline therapy or even enhancement; rather, it cautions us to wait and see.

The Catholic Health Association is more positive: "Germline intervention is potentially the only means of treating genetic diseases that do their damage early in embryonic development, for which somatic cell therapy would be ineffective. Although still a long way off, developments in molecular genetics suggest that this is a goal toward which biomedicine could reasonably devote its efforts."[3]

Another reason for caution regarding germline enhancement, especially among the Protestants, is the specter of eugenics. The word "eugenics" connotes the ghastly racial policies of Nazism, and this accounts for much of today's mistrust of genetic science in Germany and elsewhere. No-one expects a resurrection of the Nazi nightmare; yet some critics fear a subtle form of eugenics slipping in the cultural back door. The growing power to control the design of living tissue will foster the emergence of the image of the "perfect child," and a new social value of perfection will begin to oppress all those who fall short.

Are We Asking Our Scientists to Play God?

The debate over germline intervention brings us directly to the question popularized by newspaper headlines: should we ask our scientists to play God? Should we ask them to refrain from playing God? The way the question is posed in the press is usually so superficial as to be misleading. Yet beneath the superficiality we find a theological issue of some consequence, namely, do we as human beings share with our creator God some responsibility for the ongoing creativity of our world? The concept of creation includes anthropology and the notion that the human race is created in the divine image. If the *imago dei* means, as some contemporary theologians say, that the human race is God's "created co-creator," then ethics begins with envisioning a better future. This suggests we should, at minimum, keep the door open to improving the human genetic lot. The derisive use of the phrase "play God" attempts to deter us from such intervention into what nature has bequeathed us in our genome.

The acerbic rhetoric that usually employs the phrase "play God" is aimed at inhibiting if not shutting down certain forms of scientific research and medical therapy. This applies particularly to the field of human genetics and, still more particularly, to the prospect of germline intervention for purposes of human enhancement – that is, the insertion of new gene segments of DNA into sperm or eggs before fertilization, or into undifferentiated cells of an early embryo that will be passed on to future generations and may become part of the permanent gene pool. Some scientists and religious spokespersons are putting a chain across the gate to germline enhancement, with a posted sign reading, "Thou shalt not play God."

The issue of "playing God" raises the question of naturalism. Does our genetic make-up represent a divine creation in such a way that it is complete and final as it is? Is our DNA sacred? Are we desecrating a sacred realm when we try to discern the mysteries of DNA, and are we exhibiting excessive human pride when we try to engineer our genetic future?

Those who work with a "created co-creator" anthropology argue that we cannot *not* be creative. The ethical mandate, then, has to do with the purposes toward which our creativity is directed and the degree of zeal with which we approach our creative tasks.

Cloning

The first successful experiment in reproductive animal cloning was accomplished at the Roslin Institute in Edinburgh, Scotland, where embryologist Ian Wilmut cloned the world-famous sheep Dolly. The details were published in the 27 February 1997 issue of *Nature*. Wilmut's Roslin team removed cells from the udder of a pregnant Finn Dorset ewe, placed them in a culture, and starved them of serum nutrients for a week until the cells became quiescent – that is, they arrested the normal cycle of cell-division, inviting a state akin to hibernation. Second, they took an unfertilized egg, or oocyte, from a Scottish Blackface ewe and removed the nucleus. When removing the nucleus with the DNA, they left the remaining cytoplasm intact. Third, the scientists placed the quiescent cell next to the oocyte; and then they introduced pulses of electric current. The gentle electric shock caused the cells to fuse, and the oocyte cytoplasm accepted the quiescent DNA. A second electric pulse initiated normal cell-division. Fourth, after six days of cell-division, the merged embryo was implanted into the uterus of another Blackface ewe and brought through pregnancy to birth on 5 July 1996. The newborn babe was named Dolly. The procedure was called *somatic cell nuclear transfer* (NT).

An important scientific question was answered with this experiment: is cell differentiation reversible? The answer seems to be yes. Embryonic cells are pre-differentiated. Adult cells are normally differentiated in order to perform the particular tasks of particular parts of the body. For example, genes for hair are turned on in the hair while genes for toenails are turned off in hair but on where the toenails belong. In theory, cloning could be accomplished by employing embryonic cells in their pre-differentiated state. The accomplishment here was to make an adult differentiated cell function as an undifferentiated embryonic cell.

The procedure was not clean and easy. The successful cloning of Dolly was accompanied by numerous misfires. Out of 277 tries, the Roslin scientists were able to make only 29 embryos survive beyond six days. At fourteen days 62 percent of the fetuses in ewe wombs were lost, a significantly greater proportion than the estimate of 6 percent after natural mating. Eight ewes gave birth to five lambs, with all but one dying shortly thereafter. Dolly is the only one to survive. Triumph is accompanied by loss. Noting this, many scientists including Wilmut himself have opposed the prospect of human cloning because of the safety argument – that is, until the process is perfected too many human embryos would be destroyed as misfires.

Ethical issues arising from cloning technology can be divided into two areas, human reproductive cloning and human therapeutic cloning. Therapeutic cloning will be taken up later in the discussion of stem cells. The public discussion over reproductive cloning seems to focus on human reproduction, not animals. Cloned cattle and sheep do not elicit the religious opposition connected to human births.

The overriding ethical issue is this: should we clone human beings? Back in 1971 James Watson predicted this debate. Watson, along with Francis Crick, won the Nobel Prize for the discovery of the double helix structure of DNA. Writing on cloning for the *Atlantic* of May 1971, he predicted that the first reaction of most people to the arrival of these asexually produced children would be one of despair. He then went on to suggest that people with strong religious backgrounds would want to de-emphasize all those forms of research that would circumvent the normal sexual reproductive process. The Watson prophecy seems to have found its fulfillment.

In a press release of 22 February 1997, Donald Bruce, Director of the Society, Religion and Technology Project of the Church of Scotland, said that cloning human beings would be ethically unacceptable as a matter of principle. According to Christian belief, he said, cloning would be a violation of the uniqueness of human life, which God has given to each of us and to no-one else. This argument that each individual person has a unique identity that would be violated by cloning has been repeated in religious and secular circles with a high degree of frequency.

The structure of this argument applies three assumptions to the issue of cloning. The first assumption is that in order for a human person to have an individual identity he or she must have a unique genome. The second assumption is that God has ordained that each person have a genome that differs from every other person. The third assumption is that through this genetic technology we human beings could accidentally produce two persons with the same identity and, thereby, violate the divine creator's intention. On the basis of these scientific and theological assumptions, the ethical conclusion drawn here is this: no cloning.

Those holding the alternative position reject these assumptions. Scientifically speaking, even though two individuals might end up with identical genotypes, they would not end up with identical phenotypes. DNA does not always express itself in lock-step fashion. There are variations in expression and spontaneous mutations. In addition, environmental factors such as food and exercise and health care influence gene activity. If the DNA donor and clone are reared a generation apart in time, let alone in separate locations, similarities will be noticeable, to be sure, but differences will abound.

The existence of monozygotic twins is instructive. Like clones, identical twins are born with identical genomes. Despite what they share in common, they grow up as separate and distinct individuals. Each has his or her own interior consciousness, sense of self, thought processes, and ethical responsibility. Even if studies in behavioral genetics eventually show strong DNA influence on predispositions to certain forms of behavior, they remain two separate individuals with separate lives to lead. A clone would in effect be a delayed twin; and, due to the delay, would probably experience even more independence than two born at the same time.

During the debate, the question arose: Would two clones share a single soul? No theological position to date has held that two twins share a single soul. Each has his or her own soul, his or her own connection to God. This by analogy would seem to apply to clones as well. The human soul, theologically speaking, is not formed from DNA as the phenotype is formed from the genotype. The soul is not a metaphysical appendage to the physical. In sum, the theological argument against cloning based on an alleged violation of a God-given identity appeared early in the debate but eventually dissipated under critical review.

On 10 July 2002 the US President's Council on Bioethics released a report, *Human Cloning and Human Dignity: An Ethical Inquiry*, recommending a total ban on cloning-to-reproduce-children. This followed a precedent. The United States National Bioethics Advisory Commission (NBAC) studied cloning – a study which included interviews with leaders in Judaism, Islam, Hinduism, Buddhism, Evangelical Protestantism, Liberal Protestantism, and Roman Catholicism – and issued a report on 6 June 1997 with the following conclusion: At this time it is morally unacceptable for anyone in the public or private sector, whether in a research or clinical setting, to attempt to create a child using somatic cell nuclear transfer cloning. The principle argument against cloning was the safety argument, as enunciated above by Ian Wilmut. The NBAC further recommended that religious groups carry on an ongoing discussion of the ethics of cloning. Even though legislation did not follow, religious groups have carried on the recommended discussion.

In addition to the safety argument and the identity argument, a third has been raised against human reproductive cloning: the commodification argument. Cloning – as a form of designer baby-making – might lead to the commodification or commercialization of children;

and this would constitute an assault on a child's dignity. Dignity in this case is not based upon genetic individuality but upon treatment as an end rather than a means. Designer babies serve the ends of the designers, the parents, not the ends of the child. Critics fear that cloning, along with other genetic technologies, may play into the hands of economic forces that will tend to commodify newborn children. Commodification, not genetic uniqueness, would deny the sacred character of human individual life.

Stem Cells

The cloning controversy deals primarily with human reproduction. With the stem cell controversy we move into therapeutic cloning and related matters. The therapeutic promise is dramatic. Specifically, rejuvenation through transplantation of tissue grown in a laboratory from stem cells would be of enormous value for *cardiomyocytes* to renew heart muscle to prevent congestive heart failure; replacement of *hematopoietic stem cells* for producing healthy blood in bone marrow to resist infection by the HIV virus and to treat AIDS and possibly sickle cell anemia; cultivating *endothelial cells* to reline blood vessels as treatment for atherosclerosis, angina, and stroke due to arterial insufficiency; rejuvenating *islet cells* in the pancreas to produce natural insulin to fight diabetes; renewal of *neurons* in the brain to treat Parkinson's disease and victims of stroke; *fibroblast and keratinocyte cells* to heal skin in the treatment of burns; and *chondrocytes* or cartilage cells to treat osteoarthritis or rheumatoid arthritis. All this promise arises from human embryonic stem cells (hES cells), which are self-renewing – virtually immortal – and have the capacity to develop into any or all tissue types in the human body.

Two momentous laboratory discoveries are relevant. First is the isolation of human embryonic stem cells (hES cells) by James Thomson, an associate veterinarian in the University of Wisconsin's Regional Primate Research Center. Thomson began with fertilized ova – spare embryos from *in-vitro* fertilization (IVF) not placed in a uterus – and culturing them to the blastocyst stage, about four to six days. At this point he removed the outer shell of the blastocyst, separated out the individual cells, and placed them on a feeder tray. The cells divided. They reproduced themselves. Because these cells are as yet undifferentiated – that is, they are pluripotent and able to make any part of a human body – they are the cells from which other cells stem. Because they replicate themselves indefinitely, Thomson in effect created an immortal line of embryonic stem cells.

Second, John Gearhart, a professor of gynecology and obstetrics at Johns Hopkins University School of Medicine, drew human embryonic germ cells (hEG cells) from fetal gonadal tissue. These cells, when taken from an aborted fetus, resemble in nearly all respects the pluripotent stem cells described above.

It is not yet clear whether or not hES cells are identical to hEG cells. Both are pluripotent and equivalent in function, to be sure. Yet, it may be discovered that different alleles appear in different hES, because hES cells could be imprinted by either the male or female source. The blastocyst stage of embryogenesis is a stage that avoids the gender imprint. What is not yet known is whether original gender imprint will matter. For the foreseeable future the two types of stem cells will be treated the same; yet the controversy rages over Thomson's destruction of the blastocyst to obtain hES cells.

One goal of the research agenda is to learn just what turns genes on and off. Once scientists have gained the knowledge of triggering gene expression, they can apply it to pluripotent stem cells and direct the growth of selected bodily tissue. Particular organ tissue could be grown in culture. Heart tissue or other organs such as the pancreas or liver could be grown in the laboratory. These would be healthy rejuvenating organs ready for transplantation.

In order to transplant the laboratory grown organs, however, medical scientists need to override our immune system in order to avoid organ rejection. Several scenarios lie before us; two deserve attention here. One would be to create a *universal donor* cell that would be compatible with any organ recipient. The task here would be to disrupt or alter the genes within the cell responsible for the proteins on the cell's outer surface that label them as foreign to the recipient's immune system. This approach would be difficult. It would involve disrupting genes within the same DNA in which we are trying to express certain other genes. Exposing such cells to harsh conditions with rounds of different drugs may damage more than just the targeted surface proteins.

A preferable second scenario would be to make cells that are genetically compatible (histocompatible) with the organ recipient – that is, to make cells with an identical genotype. If the organ genotype matches that of the recipient, no immune system rejection will take place.

This is the connection to cloning, or somatic cell nuclear transfer. One hypothetical scenario is to begin with an enucleated human oocyte, with an egg with the DNA nucleus removed. Via somatic nuclear transplantation – cloning – one could insert the DNA nucleus of the future transplant recipient. By turning on selected genes, selected tissue could be grown *ex vivo*, outside the body, and then through surgery placed within the recipient. Because the implanted heart or liver tissue has the same genetic code as the recipient, no rejection would occur. This is in part the Dolly scenario. It differs in part because it grows only organ tissue and not an entire fetus.

Another variant or second scenario distinguishes itself sharply from Dolly, namely, one that eliminates the use of a fresh oocyte. Instead of an oocyte, the recipient's DNA nucleus would be placed in a non-egg cell, in the stem cell itself. The goal here would be to accomplish laboratory organ growth in a stem cell that is not an egg. To accomplish this, further research on cytoplasm's role in gene expression is required, as well as development of the nuclear transfer technology for insertion into the tiny stem cell.

On 9 August 2001 US President George Bush announced to his nation that his government would support research on existing lines of stem cells; but it would refrain from supporting the destruction of embryos to create new cell lines. The US president thought he was settling an ethical dispute. Public policy, science, and ethics are inextricable.

Formulating the central ethical question raised by stem cell research is difficult, because each of the two sides is oriented toward a different question. The *embryo protection* position begins with the question: How can we protect the dignity of the embryo? The *beneficence* or healing opportunity position begins with the question: How can scientific research lead to advances in human health and well-being? Each position is internally coherent, perhaps even compossible; yet they are locked in controversy.

Those holding the embryo protection position lift their voices in defense of the apparently helpless embryo threatened with death at the hands of the laboratory executioner. The use of blastocysts and aborted fetuses leads opponents to criticize the scientific community for devaluing human life. They argue: The devaluation of humans at the very commencement of life encourages a policy of sacrificing the vulnerable; and this could ultimately put other humans at risk, such as those with disabilities and the aged, through a new eugenics of euthanasia. Pope John Paul II, in an elocution at Castel Gandolpho in August 2001, likened the destruction of blastocysts to obtain hES cells with infanticide. In effect, the embryo protection position sees the stem cell debate in terms of the abortion debate.

The major premise of this position is that each human embryo is the tiniest of human beings. The unspoken second premise is that, because an embryonic stem cell is a tiny human being, it has dignity. And, having dignity, the embryo providing the stem cell deserves protection from scientists who would use the name of medical research to destroy it. The non-malificence, or "do no harm," medical maxim applies here; and this maxim is violated in embryonic stem cell research.

In contrast, the healing opportunity position notes that the principle of beneficence goes beyond that of non-malificence. Beyond avoiding harm, appeal to beneficence requires the active pursuit of human health and well-being. The central focus here is the good promised by stem cell research. Beneficence is a form of *agape*, selfless love. Decisive in the thinking of Christian supporters of medical research is Jesus' own ministry of healing, which set an example for his disciples. In many cities Christian groups have named their hospitals "Good Samaritan" after the key figure in one of Jesus' parables who administered healing to an abandoned victim of violence. From this perspective, secular medical research contributes to God's healing work on earth.

Embryo protectors accuse beneficence supporters of crass utilitarianism, of sacrificing innocent human beings *in vitro* for future hospital patients. Stem cell supporters repudiate the charge of utilitarianism, some even conceding the possibility of dignity applied to the early embryo. Relevant here is the observation that hES cells are derived from surplus embryos, from fertilized ova discarded in clinics. Such surplus embryos are slated for destruction regardless, either due to freezer burn or overt disposal. The beneficence position does not necessarily endorse the actual creation of new embryos for sacrifice to laboratory research; rather, it is satisfied with drawing some life-giving potential from an entity otherwise marked for disposal. Rather than deny dignity to the early embryo, beneficence advocates believe they can affirm embryo dignity yet still sustain justification for proceeding with health-yielding research on stem cells.

The deliberate creation of fresh embryos for destruction in the laboratory would require an additional premise to attain ethical justification. The additional premise could be supplied by the developmentalists. Ethicists holding the developmentalist position frequently apply the fourteen-day rule. This is based on the observation that until an embryo attaches itself to the uterine wall and gastrulation occurs, a single individual fetus is not yet formed. Twinning can still occur up until the appearance of the primitive streak, which will become the backbone, thereby defining a single individual over against multiple fetuses. By denying individuality to the embryo prior to the fourteenth day, some ethicists justify research at prior stages of development. Stem cells are harvested between the fourth and sixth days.

The Vatican has steadfastly rejected the fourteen-day rule. *Donum Vitae* in 1987 and subsequent papal elocutions have reiterated the classic doctrine of creationism and applied it to the so-called moment of conception: when the sperm fertilizes the egg during sexual intercourse, says Pope John Paul II, a third factor is present. God imparts a freshly created soul to the zygote. The presence of this eternal soul establishes personhood and dignity to the embryo. This makes it morally inviolable and, hence, protectable.

The Vatican and others, who hold the embryo protection position, claim not only that the use of embryonic stem cells is unethical, but that it is also unnecessary. Those who make this claim argue that stem cells derived from non-embryonic sources, that is, from adult tissues or "adult stem cells," offer therapeutic value equal to that of embryonic stem cells. The use of adult stem cells, according to this argument, makes the use of embryonic stem cells superfluous, thus bypassing several ethical problems altogether.

However, the scientific jury is still out on the relative therapeutic value of adult stem cells. While it has been long established that adult stem cells are valuable for some therapies, such as bone marrow transplant, the scientific question remains: are they valuable in the same way as embryonic stem cells are held to be valuable? Recall that the potential therapeutic value of embryonic stem cells is due to two unusual characteristics of these cells: (1) they are pluripotent, that is, they can produce all tissues in the body; and (2) the cell lines are immortal, that is, they can self-replicate indefinitely. Do adult stem cells share these same characteristics? The answer, it seems, is no. Several recent studies suggest that adult stem cells may be able to produce more cell types than once thought. However, adult stem cells are not as plastic as embryonic stem cells, and they appear to not be immortal. For many, these limitations make the adult stem cells less therapeutically promising than embryonic stem cells.

Science changes. Studies that suggest that adult stem cells are pluripotent may indeed be on target. Tomorrow's researchers may demonstrate that the therapeutic value of adult stem cells is identical to that of embryonic stem cells. For this reason, proponents of adult stem cell research are correct in reminding us of the therapeutic value that these adult tissues offer. They are incorrect, however, when they cite the value of adult stem cells as warrant for shutting down embryonic stem cell research. Adult stem cell research is valuable, but that value does not preclude the value of embryonic stem cell research.

Those who hold the embryo protection position may reject embryonic stem cell research for ethical reasons, but they should not do so for scientific reasons. Scientifically speaking, adult stem cell research and embryonic stem cell research are not competing for the same intellectual turf.

Genetics, Culture, and Religion

With the field of genetics the unavoidable interpenetration of science, culture, and religion becomes visible. Laboratory researchers cannot separate their daily work from wider cultural interpretations, and the wider culture in this case has elected to interpret genes deterministically. Theologians, who represent the intellectual segment of religious traditions, find themselves simultaneously listening to the bench scientists and the wider cultural cacophony, trying to respond to both. The pressure is increased by the demand from the political sector to establish public policy regarding what is permissible in basic research and resulting medical technology. Society cannot do without either the scientists or the theologians.

Virtually all Roman Catholics and Protestants who take up the challenge of the new genetic knowledge seem to agree on a handful of theological axioms. First, they affirm that God is the creator of the world and, further, that God's creative work is ongoing. God continues to create in and through natural genetic selection and even through human intervention in the natural processes. Second, the human race is created in God's image. In this context, the divine image in humanity is tied to creativity. God creates. So do we. With increasing frequency, we humans are described by theologians as "co-creators" with God, making our contribution to the evolutionary process. In order to avoid the arrogance of thinking that we humans are equal to the God who created us in the first place, we must add the term "created" to make the phrase "created co-creators." This emphasizes our dependency upon God while pointing to our human opportunity and responsibility. Third, these religious axioms place a high value on human dignity.

By "dignity" they mean what philosopher Immanuel Kant meant, namely, that we treat each human being as an end, not merely as a means to some further end. As church leaders respond responsibly to new developments in HGP, we can confidently forecast one thing: this affirmation of dignity will become decisive for thinking through the ethical implications of genetic engineering. Promoting dignity is a way of drawing an ethical implication from what the theologian can safely say, namely, God loves each human being regardless of our genetic make-up and, therefore, we should love one another according to this model.

6

Neuroscience, the Human Person, and God

PHILIP CLAYTON

Two extreme positions would, if true, block any significant dialogue between the neurosciences and the accounts of the self in many of the world's religions. On the one hand, strong forms of *dualism* – those that make "mind" into a substance separate from the body – remove our mental experience forever from the realm of scientific study. On the other hand, *eliminative* forms of materialism try to explain mental phenomena by reducing them to nothing but the underlying physical processes of which they are the product. The first of these two extreme positions, strong forms of dualism, has been successfully critiqued in recent scholarship. The second extreme position has been less often and less successfully critiqued. This relative absence is significant. Eliminative approaches to interpreting the neurosciences remove belief in God, and sometimes even belief in mind, from the realm of the plausible altogether. One form of eliminative materialism is referred to as the *Sufficiency Thesis*, according to which neuroscientific explanations will finally be sufficient to fully explain human behavior. In this chapter I challenge the sufficiency thesis.

Once the block created by these two views – dualism and eliminative materialism – has been removed, a wide range of interesting possibilities for understanding the relationship between the neurosciences and religious accounts of the self remain. In these few pages I would like to explore some of the ways in which recent neuroscience might be supplemented by insights from the world's religions in order to produce a more adequate theory of the person. The neurosciences show us how deeply our subjective mental experience is controlled by physical inputs and processing. Nonetheless, the acts of referring and constructing a meaningful world, as well as the individual experiences of *qualia* (the subjective components of conscious experience) remain irreducible to those inputs and processes.

In this chapter I advocate a form of *supervenience theory*, which holds that mental events are dependent on their physical substrata but not reducible to them. Challenging the determinism of "strong" supervenience, I defend a version of "weak" supervenience that allows for genuine mental causation; not all causes of human behavior are purely neuronal causes. This view gives rise in turn to an *emergentist* theory of the person: mental phenomena result from an incredibly complex physical system, the brain; at the same time, they represent a genuinely new causal and explanatory level within the world. In the end, though, this position is *monistic* rather than *dualistic*: we encounter many types of properties in the world, but it is only the one nature that bears all these properties. The resulting position, *emergentist monism*, thus allows for wide diversity of properties within the one world. This view is open at the top for religious applications and interpretations, while retaining the close link to neuroscientific study and its results. In other words, it allows for a scientifically informed view of the human person, without that scientific view precluding religious and philosophical claims. Many religious traditions offer an interpretation of the whole world based on a yet higher order of emergence, although the notion of an ultimate reality would clearly move beyond the natural order as a whole.[1]

The contemporary debate about neuroscience, psychology, and mind presents one with a confusing clutter of possibilities with regard to how one ought to understand the human person. And yet these possibilities return again and again to one fundamental choice: are the neurosciences sufficient to explain all there is to know about the human person? Many neuroscientists, but not all, maintain the *Sufficiency Thesis*. These choose the view that in the future neuroscience will indeed be sufficient to explain all that we know about the human person. This view contrasts with the *Insufficiency Thesis*, which predicts that neuroscience will *not* be sufficient to explain all we come to know about the human person. I defend the Insufficiency Thesis in what follows not because of blindness to the explanatory power of the neurosciences (far from it!), but because there are parts of what it is to be a person that lie *in principle* beyond their reach. This "something more," which is rooted in, but extends beyond, the explanatory scope of neuroscience, has been called variously *consciousness* (Chalmers, Nagel, Jackson, McGinn), *original intentionality* (Searle), or perhaps *caring* (Haugeland). In order to comprehend this debate concerning sufficiency versus insufficiency, one must understand what *intentionality* is and why it plays the decisive role in the present debate about neuroscience, the human person, and even God.

Emergentist Non-Reductionism and Mind

The study of the human person involves not only all the knowledge we can glean about the brain and its workings, but also study of the emergent level of thought, *described and explained not only in terms of its physical inputs and nature, but also in terms intrinsic to itself.* This presents a challenge: How is one to integrate these two vastly differ- ent levels, and what framework should one use for doing so? I suggest beginning with the notion of the human person as *psychosomatic unity.* Humans have physical, biological, and mental properties, and we have them in a deeply interconnected manner. How does this inter- connectedness work?

It is not difficult to describe what is normally connoted by the word "person." A person is one who is able to enter into human social inter- actions: praising your work colleague, planning your dinner party, carrying out your intention to graduate from university by next year – and being aware of (at least some) other humans as moral agents who have value and rights equal to your own. These are concepts of personhood that are basic to research in the social sciences (psy- chology, sociology, and cultural anthropology); they are reflected in the literature of all the world's cultures; and they play a central role in most of the world's religious traditions. Of course, there are many questions that still leave us unsure: when does personhood start? Does personhood demand a metaphysical basis, such as the intro- duction of the soul or person-substance? Does it develop and end gradually? Can it be effaced within a human being? Is it a legal or social fiction, or a theological reality? Such broad philosophical ques- tions are crucial to the complete definition of personhood and hence part of the discussion that neuroscientists and religious persons must have if they are to find common ground.

Personhood, seen from the vantage of these broad questions, thus requires a level of analysis that has no complete translation into a state of the body or brain – no matter how complete our neuroscientific descriptions might be. Of course, personhood presupposes such states; yet it represents an explanatory level that is distinct from explanations at the level of our "hardware." As Brian Cantwell Smith writes:

> First, you and I do not exist in [physical explanations] – *qua people.* We may be material, divine, social, embodied, whatever – but we don't figure *as people* in any physicist's equation. What we are – or rather what our lives are, in this picture – is a group of roughly

aligned not-terribly-well delineated very slightly wiggling four-dimensional worms or noodles: massively longer temporally than spatially. We care tremendously about these noodles. But physics does not: it does nothing to identify them, either as personal, or as unitary, or as distinct from the boundless number of other worms that could be inscribed on the physical plenum . . . [2]

The languages of physics and of personhood only partly overlap; one cannot do justice to the one using only the tools of the other. To give a purely physics-based account of the person is like saying that, because a university cannot survive without being financially viable (i.e., receiving income from some source), it *just is* the economic unit that economists describe in terms of income and expenditures. The confusion, one might say, is a confusion of necessary and sufficient conditions. A living body and a functioning brain are *necessary* conditions for personhood, yet the wide discrepancy in the "logic" of the vocabularies suggests that they are not *sufficient* conditions. Personhood is not fully translatable into "lower-level" terms; persons experience causal and phenomenological properties (*qualia*) that are uniquely personal.

Emergentist Supervenience

The philosophical notion of supervenience is especially attractive as a bridge framework when discussing neuroscience and the human person. Simply put, the notion of supervenience grants that mental phenomena depend on physical phenomena while at the same time denying that the mental is reducible to the physical. Note that supervenience is about properties or groups of phenomena, and not about relations between two "things" or substances called *mind* and *body*.

The early uses of the concept of supervenience described the way in which ethical judgments are dependent upon certain physical states and yet not reducible to them. The notion made its major entrance into the mind/body debate in the early article "Mental Causation" by Donald Davidson. Davidson wrote,

Although the position I describe denies there are psychophysical laws, it is consistent with the view that mental characteristics are in some sense dependent, or supervenient, on physical characteristics. Such supervenience might be taken to mean that there cannot be two events alike in all physical respects but differing in some mental respects, or that an object cannot alter in some mental respects without altering in some physical respects. Dependence or supervenience of this kind does not entail reducibility [*sic*] through law or definition: if it did, we could reduce moral properties to descriptive [ones], and this there is good reason to *believe* cannot be done.[3]

What about the relationship of dependence between the mental and the physical? We might call those views *strongly supervenient* in which the physical determines the mental in its emergence and in all its subsequent behavior. Godehard Bruntrup writes of the strong supervenience relation, "Micro-properties determine completely the macro-properties (micro-determinism) . . . If mental properties are macro-properties in this sense, they are causally inefficacious qua mental properties."[4] On this view of the physical/mental relationship, for example, one might hold that there are general physical laws such that, if they were known, the occurrence of any given mental event could be predicted from a complete enough knowledge of the brain, its structure, and its past and present inputs.

There is a certain inherent tension in strong supervenience, however. As Jaegwon Kim, one of its best known (former) advocates, admits, "nonreductive materialism is not a stable position. There are pressures of various sorts that push it either in the direction of an outright eliminativism or in the direction of an explicit form of dualism."[5] One of the reasons that "nonreductive materialism" is such an unstable position is that it appears to leave no room for genuine mental causes; in the end, the determination of outcomes seems to flow from the bottom (the physical substratum), leaving no "room for play" for the mental actually to do anything. At worst, mental phenomena become mere epiphenomena: their reality is bought at the cost of causal impotence.

So the question becomes: Can any framework that is consistent with what we know today about the brain, and with what we may reasonably be expected to *come* to know, also be consistent with a real causal influence of mental phenomena? Not only folk psychology – the common-sense way of speaking of human persons – depends on a successful theory of mental causation, but the viability of key beliefs in many of the world's religious traditions does as well. Strong supervenience theories might suggest how religious beliefs and experiences could arise as a product of human physiology. But however much such accounts might explain the psychological or evolutionary *functions* of religious beliefs, they could not explain the *truth* of religious beliefs. On physicalist accounts, there is no way to conceive how religious insights might be *true or false* (unless physicalists just assume that they are all false); and there is definitely no place for any influence of a disembodied divine force on the world. At first the supervenience concept seemed to offer the sort of framework required for drawing the links between the brain sciences and the mental life that we experience. But strong supervenience conflicts both with folk psychology and with many religious truth claims.

Is it possible, then, to formulate a "weaker" version of the dependence relationship between mind and body? Suppose we define *weak supervenience* as the view that, although physical structures and causes may determine the initial emergence of the mental, they do not fully or solely determine the outcome of the mental life subsequent to its emergence. This view amounts to a dependence of genesis, since it grants that the origins of mentality can be traced back to the physical conditions without which there would be no mental phenomena. But it does not grant a full, bottom-up determination of the mental by the physical – hence my defense of the "Insufficiency Thesis" above – even though the degree of bottom-up influence will certainly far exceed our present knowledge. Weak supervenience thus retains the central tenet of supervenience theory: the mental is dependent on, yet not reducible to, the physical. One reason for choosing "weak" over "strong" supervenience is the belief in mental causation: there are genuine mental causes that are not themselves the product of physical causes. The causal history of the mental cannot be told in simply physical terms, and the outcome of mental events is not determined by phenomena at the physical level alone.

Weak supervenience is the stepping-off point for an emergentist theory of supervenience, and thus for an emergentist theory of human personhood. The background for emergentist supervenience comes from the British Emergentists in the 1920s and 1930s. As Jaegwon Kim notes, the early emergentists held "that the supervenient, or emergent, qualities necessarily manifest themselves when, and only when, appropriate conditions obtain at the more basic level; and some emergentists took great pains to emphasize that the phenomenon of emergence is consistent with determinism. But in spite of that, the emergents are not reducible, *or reductively explainable*, in terms of their 'basal' conditions."[6]

A property is thus emergent only if laws *cannot* be formulated in lower-level terms that fully predict its occurrence and behaviors, for example by reducing it to a boundary condition of other well-established laws at that level. In cases where we can relate higher-level and lower-level phenomena with the same bottom-up precision with which we can formulate the physical conditions that produce conductivity or the development of a thermodynamic system in phase space, then we do not have emergentist supervenience. A set of phenomena is emergent only when an exhaustive description of the underlying physical state of affairs, although necessary, is not sufficient for explaining the emergent properties. Thus an emergent condition seems to be implied in the neuroscientist Leslie Brothers' explanation of human social behavior in terms of "the representation of the generalized other" and the irreducible nature of first-person language – assuming that she means these terms to refer to a genuinely psychological reality that is something more than, and not just a different manifestation of, the underlying physical realities.[7] One would also need to use the language of emergence if qualia (human subjective experiences, such as seeing red or being in love) are, at least in part, self-explanatory.

To reiterate my argument, emergentist supervenience offers a viable framework for conceptualizing mental properties in human persons in light of contemporary neuroscience. Does it also offer a view of the person that is compatible with what many of the world's religious traditions teach about the nature of the person? I believe the answer is yes. As we know, the religious traditions have many *more* things to say about these emergent properties, their sources, and their ultimate purpose. Not bound by the scientific demand to be "value neutral," religions advocate right actions, just relations between persons, and (in theistic cases) a right relationship to God. To explain this normative picture of human personhood, theologians often offer explanations, drawn from their tradition, of why the biological world could or would give rise to such emergent properties as we find in humanity. The difference in perspective should be underscored, however, lest it appear as a contradiction between religion and science. When speaking normatively, religious thinkers and theologians do not limit themselves to what can be concluded on the basis of empirical evidence; thus their claims are often not open to empirical verification in the way that neuroscientific research is. Conversely, there is nothing in emergentist supervenience that *requires* a religious interpretation; it is not a form of natural theology. Emergentism is, in my view, a necessary condition for an adequate interpretation of the human person, but it is emphatically not a sufficient condition for a religious anthropology.

Coming from the viewpoint of science, one might worry that the position I have defended closes off research and hence progress in neuroscience. Does it introduce a constraint on the actual work of empirical scientists? I would argue that it does not. Emergentists should have no less interest than physicalists in knowing more about actual brain functions and in seeing neural explanations extended as far as possible. It is just that they wager that the "as far as possible" does not extend as far as an exhaustive explanation of the mental – unless part of that explanation is given in irreducibly mental terms! Talk about the subjective experience of being in love or the sense of self-awareness is irreducibly mental; such mental phenomena exercise a type of causal influence of their own.

Three Ways to Depend on Your Brain

By avoiding both dualism and strong reductionism, and by turning instead to the resources of contemporary emergence theory, I have sought to describe a philosophical framework which does justice to recent studies of the brain's role in producing mental phenomena, as well as to the human experience of personhood. Following contemporary usage, I have characterized the resulting positions as belonging to the family of supervenience theories of mind. We discovered, however, that some of the same tensions arise within this family as were present in the old *dualism versus reductionism* debate. Specifically, scholars in the debate either do or do not accept the Sufficiency Thesis, the view that the causal explanations of human behavior will ultimately and exhaustively be given in neuroscientific terms.

Since both sides of this *new* debate accept the dependence of mental phenomena on the brain, one begins to suppose that the ambiguity lies in how this dependence is understood. And indeed this turns out to be the case: one finds in the literature at least three different ways of characterizing the dependence relation of mental states on physical states. All three presuppose that mental phenomena represent levels of complexification that depend on physiological states and processes, yet without being fully reducible to those lower levels. How might the complexity of mental experience be related to its neurological basis?

(1) The more complex level could be related to the lower level by a clear set of laws (call it *nomological supervenience*). On this view, mental phenomena can be understood scientifically in terms of the laws that govern the behavior of neurons and synaptic connections, even if the supervenient properties can only be fully expressed at the level of the brain as a whole. Nomological supervenience is presupposed in the groundbreaking work of R. M. Hare, who says explicitly,

"supervenience brings with it the claim that there is some 'law' which binds what supervenes to what it supervenes upon." For Hare such laws are necessary conditions for supervenience: "what supervenience requires is that what supervenes is seen as an instance of some universal proposition linking it with what it supervenes upon."[8]

(2) By contrast, the higher level could have all of the attributes listed in (1), yet without the condition just expressed by Hare, which we might call the "nomological condition." This second position is best known in the guise of what Donald Davidson calls "anomalous monism." Davidson holds that "mental entities (particular time-space and space-bound objects and events) are physical entities, but . . . mental concepts are not reducible by definition or natural law to physical concepts."[9] Davidson disputes the law-likeness of mental events: such events are of a different *type* than physical events, although there may be a token identity of every mental event with a physical event. Still, in other respects his view stands fairly close to (1). Certainly he does not speak of mental phenomena as strongly emergent. He insists only that at least one portion of the physical world does not admit of the kinds of causal explanation by means of natural laws that science has been successful in formulating in so many other areas. Still, no emergentist conclusions would need to be drawn from this particular failure of law-like explanation; mental phenomena simply obey different constraints than physical laws, such as the unique constraint of rationality.

(3) The final type of supervenience is the one that I have been defending; we might call it *strong emergence*. It finds in mental phenomena and their dependence on brain events a supervenient relationship not unlike that accepted by the first two positions. Yet it also finds grounds in the nature of this relationship to support the belief that mentality represents an emergent level. That is, without questioning the dependence of mental properties on the brain, it understands them to be different in kind from the properties that one observes at lower levels, exercising a type of causal influence unique to this new emergent level.

Emergentist Monism

We have appealed to emergence to explain how one can grant the distinctive features of mental properties without denying their dependence on the brain that produces them. In these final sections, we step back from the explicit concern with the neurosciences to ask about the philosophical and theological implications of the argument.

What kind of ontological position do these emergent properties entail? Is it monism or property dualism or panpsychism?

The ontological view that is implied might be called *emergentist monism*.[10] Monism asserts that only one thing exists. There are not two substances in the world with essentially different natures, such as the *res cogitans* and *res extensa* (thinking and extended substance) propounded by Descartes and the Cartesians. But unlike dual-aspect monism, which argues that the mental and the physical are two different ways to characterize the one "stuff," emergentist monism conceives the relationship between them as temporal and hierarchical.

In one sense, monism is a necessary assumption for those who wish to do science. For instance, we can (and must) assume that the total physical energy of the universe as a whole is conserved. No action that you perform, no thought that you think, can add to the total energy of the system without invalidating calculations based on physical laws. Herein lies one of the chief problems with dualism, and with the idea of direct interventions into the world by a God who breaks natural laws. If a so-called spiritual cause gives rise to an unmediated physical effect, it has brought about a physical change in the world without there being any physical cause or the expenditure of any physical energy. But this fractures the natural order in a way that would make science impossible. For example, there could be no scientific study of a world in which cups spontaneously fly across the room and objects released from your hand could go either up or down according to spiritual forces. Science does not need a world that is fully deterministic (see the next paragraph). But it does need the world to reflect at least patterns of probability over time.

Note that monism is not only in the interests of science; one can *also* give theological arguments in defense of monism. Monism makes the assertion that the world is one, that it constitutes a distinct order. Religious persons who are theists, for example, speak of the universe as a whole as *finite*, in order to specify its single ontological status and to contrast it with a creator whose nature is essentially infinite. Herein lies the importance of the phrase, "the unity of nature": in comparison to the creator, all things in the universe share a common nature. Theologians have also argued that creatures can only exercise freedom within an ordered world that has an integrity and law-like structure of its own.

It doesn't matter if you want to think of this monism as a *sort* of materialism, but only if you mean by this interpretation that the "things" in the world – rocks and computers and persons – are all made out of *some material or other*. What's crucial is that we develop theories that do justice to the specific qualities that we actually find associated with the various "things" in the world. For example, after Newton, Western philosophers thought that physics presupposed at least the possibility of a fully determinate, and determined, account of the world. But when we found out that microphysical or quantum events simply don't work this way, we had to develop an essentially stochastic or probability-based science to deal with them. Likewise, when scientists began to research chaotic "systems," or systems far from thermodynamic equilibrium, they discovered that such systems are *essentially* unpredictable (for finite agents). But science did not simply end; instead, a fascinating new science of chaotic systems has been developed. An equally complex story can be told about the convertibility of matter and energy.

Now we come to a *very* complex object in the world: humans. With 10^{14} neural connections, the brain is the most complex interconnected system we are aware of in the universe. This object has some *very* strange properties that we call "mental" properties – properties such as being afraid of the environmental crisis, or wishing for universal peace, or believing in divine revelation. On the one hand, to suppose that mental properties of this sort will be fully understood in terms of physics as we now know it, is only that: a supposition, an assumption, a wager on a future outcome. A deep commitment to the study and understanding of the natural world (which I share with my scientific colleagues) does not necessitate taking a physicalist approach to the human person – if by "physicalist approach" one means that the actions and beliefs of persons must be fully explained through a series of explanatory sciences reaching down (finally) to physics, or, more simply, that all causes are ultimately physical causes.[11] On the other hand, *for both scientific and religious reasons*, I do not advocate introducing an occult entity instead, such as Descartes's soul substance, in order to explain the human person. To say that each person is a *psychosomatic unity* is to resist both positions. It is to assert that the person is a complexly patterned entity within the world, one with diverse sets of naturally occurring properties, each of which needs to be understood *by a science appropriate to its own level of complexity*. We need multiple layers of explanatory accounts *because* human persons represent a physical, biological, psychological, and (I believe also) spiritual reality, and because these aspects of its reality, though interdependent, are not mutually reducible. Call the existence of these multiple layers *ontological pluralism*, and call the need for multiple layers of explanation *explanatory pluralism*, and my thesis becomes clear: ontological pluralism begets explanatory pluralism. (Or, to put it differently: the best explanation for explanatory pluralism is onto-logical pluralism.)

In a helpful essay, Nancey Murphy draws on the work of Ian Barbour and Arthur Peacocke in chronicling the multiple meanings of "reductionism."[12] Using her distinctions, we could say that an emergentist position rejects causal reductionism, since it accepts mental causes. It therefore rejects explanatory (i.e., theoretical or epis-temological) reductionism, insofar as mental properties need to be explained using a theoretical structure appropriate to their place on the ladder of increasing complexity. At first blush, emergentist monism may *seem* like a version of ontological or metaphysical reduc-tionism, since it breaks with dualism and refuses to postulate non-physical entities such as souls. But emergentists must finally declare themselves opposed to reductionism even with respect to ontological (metaphysical) questions. For our central assertion is that the history of the universe is one of development and process. The one cosmos exists at each stage in its history, but what the entities are that popu-late it at any given time is not always identical. Genuinely new properties emerge that are not reducible to what came before, although they are continuous with it.

What *emerges* in the human case is a particular psychosomatic unity, an organism that can do things both mentally and physically. Although human mental functioning depends upon its physiological basis, the mental and physical attributes of persons are intercon-nected and exhibit causal influences *in both directions*. We therefore need a "science of personhood" that begins (as a science should) with a theoretical structure adequate to this level of complexity. To defend an emergentist account of the self is not to turn science into meta-physics. Instead, it is to acknowledge that the one natural world is vastly more complicated and more subtle than physical explanations can ever express. "Person properties," such as *thinking about general relativity* or *wishing for a just society* or *being devoted to God* cannot be omitted in the final explanation of personhood. You can *wager* that the only *real* things that exist in the world are physical processes within organisms, and that everything else – intentions, free will, ideas like love or ultimate reality – are "constructs," complicated manifesta-tions of neural processes. But I'm wagering on the other side. I wager that no level of explanation short of irreducibly psychological explanations will finally do an adequate job of accounting for the human person. This position holds to the real existence and causal efficacy of the conscious or mental dimension of human personhood.

Neuroscience, the Person, and God

In the introduction I suggested that if the extreme positions of strong dualism and eliminative materialism can be avoided, significant dialogue between the neurosciences and accounts of the self in religion could be pursued. I will close this chapter by considering the question of neuroscience and personhood in a religious context – and, more specifically, in the context of belief in God.

The difference between world and God has to come out somewhere. God does not simply arise out of the world (this would mean that there was no creation by God, and many billions of years where God didn't exist or existed only in preliminary form). And the world is not simply identical with the eternal God: it had a beginning in time; its present structure is not eternal but will run down eventually; and the marks of its finitude and imperfection are too ubiquitous to need listing.

It is against the backdrop of this difference that one must formulate the differences, but also the similarities, between persons and God. Where and when in the world does one first find signs of the mental or spiritual? Process thinkers, for example, believe they find full units of mental experience even at the earliest stages of natural history. By contrast, theologians who are physicalists (cf. the "non-reductive physicalism" defended in some recent publications[13]) retain the emphasis on the physical construal of the human person even at the end of natural history.

Between these two views stands the emergentist view of the human person. The foundation of personhood lies in physical mass and energy; at this level we are a physical system, developing according to the patterns of natural law. But we are *also* organisms, inheritors of a long process of biological evolution that has been adding to and modifying our basic DNA code through natural selection since the most primitive organisms. Every organ in the human body, and most especially the brain, is the product of a history of genetic developments, each of which was (directly or indirectly) selected for at some point in natural history. If every sinew and tissue of our bodies bears the mark of this evolutionary history of selection, surely we should be "non-reductive evolutionary biologists" even more than "non-reductive physicalists" when it comes to specifying the nature of the brain and its properties!

But biology is not the end of the story. Just as those biochemical systems that we call organisms require evolutionary biology to make sense of their properties and behaviors, so also the more complex organisms among them – higher primates such as *Homo sapiens* – begin to evidence properties that require a discipline of their own. These "inner" or "first person" properties that we call *psychological* have a Darwinian root (hence the power of the new discipline of evolutionary psychology, which uses Darwinian evolution to account for psychological properties). But our mental lives are also non- or meta-Darwinian: we pass on acquired characteristics to our offspring (personality features, attitudes, behaviors); one charismatic individual can spread his or her ideas rapidly to an entire population (for good or for evil); and the mind can preoccupy itself with issues that have little or no impact on the survival of the organism (such as your reflection on whether the argument of this chapter is sound!). Psychological qualities are genuinely emergent properties in higher primates like ourselves. From a religious perspective, we say that humans reflect something of the nature of God in our *trans*-biological abilities to reason, to introspect, to make moral assessments, and to turn our minds toward the transcendent, the metaphysical, the eternal.

Indeed, could it be that we witness yet another emergent level in the "intimations of transcendence" that humans have? Human persons are not divine; we remain an all-too-finite component of the one cosmos, tracing our lineage back through elements of earth to exploded stars. And yet in us matter has become conscious of itself, of its history, and perhaps even of its ultimate origins. Moved by considerations of right and wrong, hungry for immortality, feeling awe and reverence toward the world around us, and – sometimes – longing to be transformed into the image of God, we *are* the stage at which evolution has begun to reflect consciously on the source and goal of all things finite. If the religious traditions are right, personhood is bounded by its physiological basis, its body and brain, on the one side, and by its divine source on the other. We are, as Pascal noted in another context, positioned between two infinities. A full account of human personhood can no more afford to omit the theological goal of our existence than it can omit the physiological conditions that allow us to pursue this goal.

Part Three
Constructing Religious Spans

7

God's Two Books: Special Revelation and Natural Science in the Christian West

PETER M. J. HESS

For the invisible things by him from the creation of the world are clearly seen, being understood by the things that are made.

Romans 1.20

Hence there are two books given to us by God, the one being the book of the whole collection of creatures or the book of nature, and the other being the book of sacred scripture.

Raimundus Sabundus

Human language, as a medium of communicating our experience in every sphere, is seldom intended to be understood merely literally. Indeed, the use of metaphor is central to the language we use in realms as widely diverse as religion and science. In interpreting our human history we consciously employ metaphors and models, discovering a past that is colored by our experience precisely as we would expect it to be. That is to say, we interpret our history through a lens conditioned by factors such as popular tradition, established historiography, and the cultural assumptions of our own society. In the case of the Judeo-Christian West, this interpretive lens increasingly has reflected the assumptions of a technologically and scientifically oriented society. Modern Western science has, since 1850, come to be regarded more and more as normative, even enjoying an epistemologically privileged position.

When examining the historical relationship between religion and science in the West, we must bear in mind that for more than a century the model dominating its interpretation has been the "warfare model." This model was first crafted in the nineteenth century by

John William Draper in his work *History of the Conflict Between Religion and Science*, and Andrew Dickson White in his work *History of the Warfare of Science with Theology in Christendom*. The popular misconception that science and religion are natural enemies resulted from these works and is regularly reinforced. Historical portrayals of these disciplines as having been at each other's throats since time immemorial are sometimes rehearsed.[1] Fortunately, considerable work has been done in the last two decades to redress the balance and construct a more sophisticated understanding of the complex relationship between religion and science.[2] The "bridge" model, according to which science and religion are connected by similar methodologies or by a shared concern for particular subject matter, is attracting increased attention. In the past, however, neither the warfare nor the bridge model dominated the Christian West. Rather, the relationship between science and religion, or nature and faith more broadly, was understood through the metaphor of "God's two books" of revelation – the books of scripture and nature.

The Knowledge of God in Western Traditions

That science and religion have enjoyed a more complex association than one merely of conflict is made clear by the history of the metaphor most central to the natural theological tradition, that of "God's two books." "Natural theology" is a branch of theology in the Western tradition that historically has been regarded by many as complementary to revealed doctrine. What we know about God can be derived from two coordinated sources: the created world and the revealed scriptures, or "the book of nature and the book of scripture."[3] The idea was used by many early modern English natural theologians as shorthand for the assumed validity of the design argument for the existence of God. Thomas Browne notes in *Religio Medici*:

> Thus are there two books from whence I collect my divinity: besides that written one of God, another of his servant, nature, that universal and public manuscript that lies expansed unto the eyes of all. Those that never saw him in the one have discovered him in the other. This was the scripture and theology of the heathens: the natural motion of the sun made them more admire him than its supernatural station did the children of Israel.[4]

Although Browne emphasizes his care not to lose sight of the distinction between nature and God, he notes that Christians have tended to "cast a more careless eye on these common hieroglyphics, and disdain to suck divinity from the flowers of nature."[5]

A number of intriguing questions are raised by these references to the two books. First is the question of the origins of the metaphor, which seventeenth-century English authors ascribe variously to Chrysostom, Ambrose, Augustine, or Lactantius. In addition to this intriguing problem of identifying the origins of the metaphor of God's two books of nature and scripture, a number of questions concerning its precise use also lack clear answers. What was the history of its use and development in ancient, medieval, and early modern theology and natural science? When did the idea finally fall into neglect, and in response to what circumstances? This chapter will endeavor to answer these questions by reconstructing the sources and development of the theme of "God's two books of nature and scripture" in Western Christian intellectual history, offering insights on its significance throughout that history and its relevance for a contemporary challenge of constructing models and metaphors for bridging science and religion.

Birth of the Two Books Metaphor

Historically, human spiritual and religious life has been predicated upon the premise that the divine can be known through revelation. In primal religious traditions, stories about sacred times and sacral space, about the ancestors, and about manifestations of the divine through weather, the seasons, and personal intervention, have been transmitted orally across countless generations. Revelation of the divine, as told by these oral traditions, permeates the natural world, an all-encompassing reality in which people are seamlessly embedded as part of a unified, living, spiritual ecology. To know nature, and the human place in it, is to know something of the divine.

The development of written communication brought important modifications to this notion of a pervasive natural revelation. In many cultures, oral tradition as the primary mode of cultural transmission became replaced by the mode of fixing truth in written texts. Religious wisdom could now be recorded in a more permanent form, and the immediacy of myth passed down by word of mouth was replaced by the mediating text, just as the verbal transmission of moral norms became replaced by their codification into law. With the advent of the Abrahamic faiths – Judaism, Christianity, and Islam – the idea of revelation took on a significantly new character. Although the Hebrew scriptures, the New Testament, and the Qur'an represent, in important respects, substantially different literary genres, they are all nevertheless understood by their followers to be transmitting the very word of God. The "book" became of paramount importance in these religions, and it is here in the Judeo-Christian tradition that we can trace the origins and development of the two books metaphor.

Scriptural Foundations

Within the Judeo-Christian tradition there are clear scriptural prece-dents for the idea that God may be known through both divine word and divine works. There are hints of the metaphor in the Hebrew scriptures, both in the Psalms and in the later books. Psalm 19.1 majestically articulates a theme that would remain common currency throughout the history of natural theology: "The heavens declare the glory of God, and the firmament proclaims his handi-work." The Book of Wisdom, composed in the middle of the first century BCE, articulates the idea that God is known through the divine works, even by non-Jews who have not enjoyed the benefit of special revelation (Wisdom 11.6–9). The argument is essentially designed to remove from non-believers any excuse for not knowing God, who may, by analogy with a human author, contemplate the author of creation through the grandeur and beauty of creatures. This argu-ment initiated a key strain of thought within the Christian theological tradition, persisting at least until the time of Calvin, in whose theolo-gy humanity is regarded as standing without excuse before the awe-some justice of God. The analogy of the two books hence serves to justify God's judgment of all humanity, humans standing both within and outside of traditions of special revelation.

The classical New Testament source for the natural knowledge of God, the Pauline declaration in Romans, builds upon this Hebrew idea of God's authorship of nature:

> For what can be known about God is plain to them, because God has shown it to them. Ever since the creation of the world his invisible nature, namely, his eternal power and deity, has been clearly perceived in the things that have been made. (Romans 1.19–20)

But if the roots of this theme are Hebrew, the particular intensity of its Pauline expression seems to reflect the confrontation of first-century Jewish religious thought with the cultural life of the Roman empire, and particularly with Hellenistic philosophical categories. Non-Christians can be held accountable for knowledge of God.

Patristic Thought on the Two Books

There are clear precedents for important elements of the "two books" metaphor scattered throughout patristic literature. Justin Martyr's second-century apologetic in his *Second Apology* builds on the seeds-of-knowledge (*logos spermatikos*) notion of Stoicism, the idea that the world is permeated by seeds of the divine Word.[6] And Irenaeus of Lyons (*c*.130–202) in *Adversus haereses* (AD 180/199) provides two essential ingredients of the theme: the works and the word of God: "One God formed all things in the world, by means of the Word and the Holy Spirit; and although he is to us in this life invisible and incomprehensible, nevertheless he is not unknown; inasmuch as his works do declare him, and his Word has shown that in many modes he may be seen and known".[7]

The first significant thinker of the Latin church, Tertullian (*c*.160–*c*.225), prefigures the two books metaphor by suggesting that "God has from the beginning of all things given as primary witnesses for the knowledge of Himself, nature in her [manifold] works, kindly providences, plagues, and indications of his divinity." Tertullian regards these evidences as counterparts to scripture, and claims that because his heretical opponent Marcion has rejected most of scripture, he cannot provide a counterpart in revelation to the knowledge of God we derive from nature.[8] Origen (*c*.185–254), suggests in the *Philocalia* that anyone who believes the scripture to have proceeded from him who is the author of nature may well expect to find the same sort of difficulties in it as are found in the constitution of nature.

But the clearest instance we have of a formal patristic statement of the metaphor of the two books may be found in St John Chrysostom's (*c*.347–407) *Homilies to the People of Antioch*. An eloquent Antiochene preacher known as "John the Golden Tongued," Chrysostom implies in Homily IX that "nature" serves the function of a book of revelation:

> If God had given instruction by means of books, and of letters, he who knew letters would have learnt what was written, but the illiterate man would have gone away without receiving any benefit ... This however cannot be said with respect to the heavens, but the Scythian, and Barbarian, and Indian, and Egyptian, and every man that walks upon the earth, shall hear this voice; for not by means of the ears, but through the sight, it reaches our understanding ... Upon this volume the unlearned, as well as the wise man, shall be able to look, and wherever any one may chance to come, there

looking upwards towards the heavens, he will receive a sufficient lesson from the view of them . . . [9]

This passage by Chrysostom aptly summarizes what we might term the patristic attitude toward the complementarity of natural and revealed theology. There is ample evidence that the ingredients of the two books metaphor were available in the patristic period. However, it would not be until the High Middle Ages that the metaphor would reach full articulation with the progressive rediscovery of Aristotelian natural philosophy. The two books would become the primary model for expressing a mature binary epistemology of revelation.

The Two Books in the Middle Ages

The metaphor of God's two books became firmly established in the High Middle Ages. Alain of Lille's judgment was influential: *Omnis mundi creatura / Quasi liber et pictura / Nobis est et speculum* (Every creature is to us like a book and a picture and a mirror). Hugh of St Victor regarded both the creation and the incarnation as "books" of God, and compared Christ as primary revelation to a book.[10] Bonaventure (1217–74) noted in his *Collations on the Hexaemeron* that sensible creatures are "a book with writing front and back," spiritual creatures are "a scroll written from within," and scripture is "a scroll written within and without."[11] We should note that Bonaventure's writing illustrates the plasticity of metaphors: here we have three books, and while the two books would become the norm in our particular model, a multiplicity of books would crop up repeatedly in the next six hundred years.

The fullest articulation of the metaphor in medieval philosophy and literature may be found in Raimundus Sabunde's *Natural Theology, or Book of the Creatures* (*Theologia Naturalis sive Liber Creaturarum*) (1436). Sabundus was a Barcelona native, a graduate in arts and medicine, who died prematurely at Toulouse while on his way to take up a post at Paris. His statement of the two books metaphor, which would become the classic source for early modern appropriators of the theme, is as follows:

Hence there are two books given to us by God, the one being the book of the whole collection of creatures or the book of nature, and the other being the book of sacred scripture. The first book was given to human beings in the beginning, when the universe of creatures was created, since no creature exists that is not a certain letter, written by the finger of God, and from many creatures as from many letters is composed one book, which is called the book of the creatures. Within this book is included humanity itself, and human beings are the first letters of this book. But the second book, Scripture, was given to human beings secondarily to correct the deficiencies of the first book, which humanity could not read because it is blind. The first book is common to everyone, but the second book is not common to all, because only clerics are able to read what is written in it.[12]

A number of interesting points are suggested by this passage. For one thing, the idea that we ourselves are letters in the book of nature carries the intriguing implication that the book of nature can never in its entirety be deciphered, since it will never cease being written, at least not until the eschaton. For another, the idea that the book of scripture is limited to the interpretation of clerics would ultimately be antithetical to the Protestant confidence that the book of scripture is open to reading and interpretation by all.

An additional, and perhaps more serious consequence – and what led to the condemnation of Sabunde's work as heretical – was his incautious insistence that the book of scripture is a less accurate revelation. *Theologia Naturalis* was placed on the Roman Index of Prohibited Books in 1595, a victim both of the frigid ideological climate of the Counter-Reformation, and of Sabunde's own incautious exaltation of the "Book of Nature." As Clement Webb noted in his *Studies in the History of Natural Theology*, the problem with Raymond of Sabunde's articulation of the two books metaphor was not its glorification of the Bible at the expense of Tradition, but rather an assertion of the pre-eminent importance of natural knowledge, in the spirit of Roger Bacon.[13] Sabunde's confidence in the "book of nature" was supreme:

> this science is accessible alike to laymen and to clerks and to every condition of men and can be had in less than a month and without trouble, nor to possess it need one have learned anything by heart or keep any written book . . . and so in the order of our procedure it comes before Holy Scripture.[14]

Humanism, Printing, and the Reformation

There were influences at work in both the Renaissance and Reformation movements that would exercise profound impact on the idea of the complementary books of nature and scripture. Renaissance scholars initiated the subjection of literary texts ecclesiastical as well as secular to intense critical scrutiny, and it would not be many centuries before the application of their methods would extend even to biblical texts. Such textual criticism would inevitably undermine both scripture and the received texts of classic natural philosophy as authoritative books. In addition, the technological innovations leading to the Western invention of mechanical printing in 1453 created a sea change in the literary world. Paradoxically, printing would serve to weaken the hold that "science" texts had held on the medieval mind. The effect of the work of Theophrastus Phillippus Aureolus Bombastus von Hohenheim (1493–1541) – Paracelsus for short – is a good example. Peter Harrison suggests that

> He [Paracelsus] took a lead in refashioning the medieval metaphor, contrasting the book of nature with both the scriptures and the writings of ancient authorities. In place of Galen, Avicenna, and Aristotle, Paracelsus set Nature – that library of books which God himself wrote, made, and bound. Every country, he insisted, is a page of nature's book, and he who would explore her must tread her books with his feet. Scripture is explored through its letters, but nature from land to land.[15]

The implications of this empirical approach to nature – however much it may have been a literary conceit – would be far-reaching for science, and also for the idea of nature as a book.

The emphasis placed by the Protestant Reformers on scripture as the primary source of God's revelation would likewise have a significant impact on the development of the two books theme. For Luther, a sober appreciation of the primary meaning of language as literal rather than allegorical, and as the medium by which God's word is accessible to all, would cut through the wild profusion of "meanings" and "signatures" that medieval people had found in the book of nature. John Calvin shared this emphasis on the literal sense of scripture with Luther, emphasizing its revelatory clarity over against the revelation of God in nature, a revelation that might be obscured given the fallenness of human nature. Appealing to the Pauline notion that we are without excuse for the knowledge of God, he writes in the *Institutes of the Christian Religion*:

> Therefore, though the effulgence which is presented to every eye, both in the heavens and on the earth, leaves the ingratitude of man without excuse, since God, in order to bring the whole human

race under the same condemnation, holds forth to all, without exception, a mirror of his Deity in his works, another and better help must be given to guide us properly to God as Creator.[16]

The two books are not equal partners, in Calvin's theology; rather, the revealed word of God in scripture is a necessary corrective to the deficiencies of nature.[17] The Reformed tradition retained this Calvinist interpretation of the two books, and in the *Belgic Confession* adopted by the Dutch Reformed Church, we read in article 2, "The Means by Which We Know God":

> We know him by two means: First, by the creation, preservation, and government of the universe, since that universe is before our eyes like a beautiful book in which all creatures, great and small, are as letters to make us ponder the invisible things of God: his eternal power and his divinity, as the apostle Paul says in Romans 1.20. All these things are enough to convict men and to leave them without excuse. Second, he makes himself known to us more openly by his holy and divine Word, as much as we need in this life, for his glory and for the salvation of his own.[18]

The Scientific Revolution

The centuries that saw the development of the anti-Aristotelian "new philosophy" are among the most complicated in terms of tracing the ramifications undergone by the two books metaphor. Descartes (1596–1650) appears to have rejected the book of nature, since it necessitated an empiricism that was inimical to his rationalist epistemological project. Pierre Gassendi (1592–1655), on the other hand, saw purpose in all of nature, and suggested to Descartes that if he wanted to prove the existence of God, he ought to abandon reason and look around him, that the two books were not to be kept on separate shelves.[19] Johannes Kepler considered astronomers to be priests of God in the book of nature, not surprising if Kepler "elevated nature as a revelation of God to a status equal to that of the Bible."[20]

Although for Francis Bacon (1561–1626) the two books seem in practice ultimately to have been kept on separate shelves, in *The Advancement of Learning* he articulates their essential connection:

> Our Saviour lays before us two volumes to study, if we will be secured from error: first, the scriptures, revealing the Will of God; and then the creatures expressing his power; whereof the latter is

a key unto the former: not only opening our understanding to conceive the true sense of the scriptures, by the general notions of reason and rules of speech; but chiefly opening our belief, in drawing us into a due meditation of the omnipotency of God, which is chiefly signed and engraven upon his works. This much therefore for divine testimony and evidence concerning the true dignity and value of learning.[21]

James Bono suggests that Bacon, in a sense, distinguishes between two aspects of the "Word of God": "The first is revelatory of God's intentions for man, for his salvation and redemption . . . The second aspect of the 'Word of God' is his creative word, that 'word' that is productive of the created order itself – of 'God's Works.' " Through knowledge of God's works, humanity can "read" the book of nature, uncovering the signatures in nature, and beginning to reconstruct this second aspect of the "Word of God" – the language of nature known to Adam in his earthly paradise.[22]

The theme of two books plays an important role in the thought of Galileo, particularly in his *Letter to the Grand Duchess Christina*. As is well known, Galileo argued that the book of nature is written in the language of mathematics, not only implying that mathematics is the most sublime expression of the world because divine, but de facto restricting its full comprehension to those who are appropriately educated. It is worth quoting at length:

And to prohibit the whole science [of astronomy] would be but to censure a hundred passages of holy Scripture which teach us that the glory and greatness of Almighty God are marvelously discerned in all his works and divinely read in the open book of heaven. For let no-one believe that reading the lofty concepts written in that book leads to nothing further than the mere seeing of the splendor of the sun and the stars and their rising and setting, which is as far as the eyes of brutes and of the vulgar can penetrate. Within its pages are couched mysteries so profound and concepts so sublime that the vigils, labors, and studies of hundreds upon hundreds of the most acute minds have still not pierced them, even after continual investigations for thousands of years.[23]

The two books metaphor flourished in the natural theological climate of seventeenth-century England, but its two terms were not always held in comfortable balance. The dissenting theologian Richard Baxter, for example, felt that "nature was a 'Hard Book,' which few could understand. It was therefore safer to rely more heavily on Scripture."[24] Newton's thought on the relationship between science and religion is notoriously complex, and interpreters differ considerably about it. Richard Westfall suggests that for Newton, nature was perhaps more truly the source of divine revelation than was the Bible, noting that Newton adds "revelation" almost as an afterthought.[25] On the other hand, Frank Manuel argues that Newton, in virtually abolishing the distinction between the two books, which he revered as separate expressions of the same divine meaning, was attempting to keep science sacred and to reveal scientific rationality in what was once a purely sacral realm, namely, biblical prophecy. Manuel suggests that even Newton was uneasy about the amalgam, and that he was aware that science and its uses were becoming independent of theology "despite the proliferation of books of *physica sacra* and the depth and pervasiveness of his own religious feelings."[26]

Waning and Survival of the Two Books Metaphor

The theme of the two books persisted vigorously right through the nineteenth century, and there are a number of intriguing (if repetitive) book-length treatments of it. However, we can also begin at this time (around 1800) to see cracks in the edifice of the metaphor. The deist movement challenged the uniqueness of the Christian revelation. One telling example is Thomas Paine, who writes defiantly in his *Age of Reason*:

> But some, perhaps, will say: are we to have no word of God – no revelation? I answer, Yes; there is a word of God; there is a revelation. The Word of God is the creation we behold, and it is in this word, which no human invention can counterfeit or alter, that God speaketh universally to man . . . In sum [fine], do we want to know what God is? Search not the book called the Scripture, which any human hand might make, but the Scripture, called the creation.[27]

Paine admits the possibility of revelation, but rejects the idea that God has ever communicated with humankind otherwise than through the universal display of Godself in the works of the creation, and through the moral sense of repugnance to bad actions and attraction to good ones. Creation is the Bible of the deist:

> Instead then, of studying theology, as is now done, out of the Bible and the Testament, the meanings of which books are always con-

troverted and the authenticity of which is disproved, it is necessary that we refer to the bible of the creation. The principles we discover there are eternal and of divine origin; they are the foundation of all the science that exists in the world, and must be the foundation of theology. We can know God only through his works.[28]

The deist challenge would have a profound impact in philosophical circles, attacking one of the pillars of the two books theme. But there were other trends in the nineteenth century that would exercise an even more widespread effect, including the revolutions in geology and biology which challenged long-standing traditions of a young Earth and an immutable creation, and therefore of a coherent book of nature temporally coextensive with the book of scripture. Charles Babbage (1791–1871) advanced a view in his *Ninth Bridgewater Treatise* (1838) that seems to have verged almost on asserting the superfluity of scriptural revelation:

> In the early stages of the world, before man had acquired knowledge to read the book of nature ever open to his view, direct revelation might be as necessary for his belief in a deity, as for his moral government; and this might from time to time be repeated. When civilization and science had fixed their abode amongst mankind, and when observations and reason had enabled man to penetrate some little way into the mysteries of nature, his conviction of the existence of a first great cause would gradually acquire additional strength from the use of his own faculties, and when accumulating proofs had firmly established this great step, the recurrence of revelation might be less necessary for his welfare.[29]

Babbage continues by arguing that even if "the ancient revelation" lost its ability to convince through its transmission through the centuries, modern science can give it a degree of force that can compel "our understandings to assent to it even with a conviction great as that which had compelled the belief of those to whom it was originally delivered."[30]

In addition to the "historicization" of geology and biology, the nineteenth century saw the development of an historical-critical approach to study of the Bible. This would affect the two books theme no less importantly, challenging the entire received tradition about the nature of scripture as a unitary record of the Word of God. Simultaneously, these innovations in both hermeneutics and science would push some in the more conservative wings of society to vigorously defend both the verbal inerrancy of scripture and the ancient understanding of Earth history, a twofold attempt to insulate scripture from historical criticism. The metaphor of God's two books of revelation served as one of the cornerstones of their defense.

Survival of the Two Books Metaphor

The theme of "two books" would continue to thrive under both conservative and liberal interpretations. Commenting on Genesis 2.15, "conservative" Seventh Day Adventist leader Ellen G. White (1827–1915) expanded upon the theme that Adam and Eve were committed to the care of the garden, "to dress it and to keep it." White argued that "the book of nature, which spread its living lessons before them, afforded an exhaustless source of instruction and delight. On every leaf of the forest and stone of the mountains, in every shining star, in earth and sea and sky, God's name was written . . . all of these were objects of study by the pupils of earth's first school." The laws and operations of nature, and the great principles of truth that govern the spiritual universe these were opened to Adam's and Eve's minds by the infinite Author of all.[31]

The theme survived as well among numerous nineteenth-century "liberal" thinkers, who had, by and large, adopted the principles and findings of contemporary science. Herbert W. Morris, in *Science and the Bible* (published a decade after Charles Darwin's *Origin of Species*), argues that scripture and nature represent respectively the verbal and the pictorial representation of divine wisdom. Morris intended to illustrate the "Inspired Record of Creation" with references to the marvelous developments of modern science, taking great pains to obtain the latest and most accurate results of science.[32] Paul A. Chadbourne used the metaphor extensively in his 1867 Lowell Lectures delivered in Boston, *Lectures on Natural Theology, or Nature and the Bible from the Same Author*, and starkly articulated the challenge posed to contemporary science by the book of God's word:

> Above all the sources of knowledge, we have a Book, claiming divine origin, claiming to be the written word of the Being we are searching for, revealing His character and answering every question we need to propound respecting Him and our relations to him . . . but we freely acknowledge that the Bible must stand the tests which science can fairly put it to. If, by fair interpretation, it is shown to conflict with the revelations of nature, it can no longer claim authority as the word of God.[33]

But Chadbourne was curiously out of date. A decade after the appearance of the *Origin of Species*, he had set up for meticulous "scientific" examination a safe, immutable, pre-Darwinian concept of the world. He championed the idea that nature is an unchangeable record, a "temple inscribed," contending that geology, chemistry, and biology constitute the language in which nature is written, with geology being the most clearly comprehended volume. It is no wonder, given his idiosyncratic reading of science, that he could confidently conclude that "the two revelations are one in their teaching."[34]

In stark contrast is the very progressive writer Joseph Le Conte, professor of geology at the University of California, Berkeley. Writing in an apologetic pro-evolutionary context, Le Conte declared, "the whole object of science is to construct the theology or the divine revelation in nature," and contended that "while Metaphysics has been disputing as to whether watches are made or whether they are eternal, Geology comes forward and tells us the date of manufacture."[35]

He mounted a vigorous defense of the theory of evolution, but was quite clear on the limits of science as a commentary on the book of nature, which passes from sensible phenomena to immediate causes, and from these to other higher causes, and by a continuous chain reaches the Great First Cause, where "she doffs her robes, lays down her scepter, and veils her face."[36] For Le Conte, "Of these two books, Nature is the elder born, and, in some sense, at least, may be considered the more comprehensive and perfect." But he hastens to qualify this: "Nature cultivates primarily the intellect, while Scripture cultivates primarily the moral nature of man."[37] The originality of Le Conte's careful and detailed exposition of the two books theme is his thorough integration of contemporary science, and his attention to emerging issues in the philosophy of science.

Breakdown of the Two Books Metaphor

Despite the healthy survival of the theme of "God's two books" in some theological circles, and the works of some scientists late in the nineteenth century, during the following hundred years it would fail to command the same attention. Some prominent examples are instructive in this regard.

Princeton Theologian Charles Hodge investigated the issue of the human knowledge of God in a thoroughly systematic way in his *Systematic Theology* (1873), arguing that the mind proceeds to form its idea of God by way of analogy: if we are like God, then God is like us, and the works of God manifest a nature like our own.[38] However, he nowhere employed the metaphor, and one wonders whether in the era of a critical approach to scripture it was considered unsophisticated to appeal to God's two books. Hodges' later Princeton colleague, the influential J. Gresham Machen, argued in *The Christian Faith in the Modern World* (1936) without appealing to the theme that "the revelation of God through nature has the stamp of approval put on it by the Bible."[39]

We find evidence for part of the reason for the breakdown of the metaphor in Frederick Temple's *Nature, Man and God*, the Gifford Lectures for 1932–4:

> The supposed clearness of the distinction between Natural and Revealed Religion, as it existed in the minds of our grandfathers, was partly illusory. For us it has, in that form, been completely destroyed by recent study of what has been taken to be the main source of revealed religion – the Bible. In the eighteenth century, and for much of the nineteenth, the theologian believed himself to draw his principles from the lively oracles of God contained in Holy Scripture, and developed his theology as a deductive science. But we are now vividly conscious that whatever the books of the Bible may contain of divine self-disclosure, they are also the record of a very rich and significant human experience.[40]

Temple does not refer in any way to the metaphor of God's two books, suggesting that through the revolutions in scientific method and understanding, and in biblical history and exegesis, the theme of two coordinated revelations of nature and scripture was well on its way to retirement.

Conclusion

The metaphor of God's two books has enjoyed an extraordinarily complex history, from its roots deep in antiquity right up to the present time. Our survey of its intriguing life-cycle leads us to some important conclusions about why the metaphor was significant in the Christian West, and why it began to erode and eventually died out in most circles.

We have seen that the metaphor was born at the confluence of a number of streams: the common human experience of the transcendent, the conviction of the possibility of divine communication, and the Western fascination for books as repositories of knowledge.

Though the two books metaphor varied in use throughout the development of thought in the West, it functioned throughout its history to mark a theological understanding both of nature and of God's relationship to humanity through nature. The metaphor emphasized the capacity of nature to reveal the divine, to mirror characteristics of its creator. The metaphor also served to justify God's judgment of all humanity. If God is revealed in the book of nature as well as the book of scripture, then all humanity can be held fairly and equally under God's judgment.

The theme underwent a complex process of development, as the natural world was paralleled first by the book of the scriptures in Hebrew history, then by the increasing number of written records in late antiquity, and later by the printed book in 1543. This process of development saw both the flourishing and decline of the metaphor. Though its use persisted throughout the nineteenth century, as early as the sixteenth century, with the advent of printing and the production of books on a mass scale, the force of the metaphor began to wane, brought about by a radical change in both the nature of book learning and the character of the book itself. Books became more commonplace and clearly reflected new mechanical techniques of production. Combined with the shift in scholarship with the rise of humanism, this no doubt contributed to the loss of the quasi-sacred character of the "book."

Though early scientists such as Galileo advanced the metaphor in defense of the exploration of nature, by the time of Newton, science and the study of nature began to shift away from theology. Though nature was certainly held to reveal God's handiwork, this "one book" began to gain independence, if not prominence, over against scriptural revelation. This shift can be thought of as the second factor underlying the decline of the metaphor in some circles, and might be termed a "deistic drift." We have seen that for Thomas Paine the scriptures testifying to a particular people's experience of God are no longer as trustworthy as the universal book of nature; indeed, perhaps they are not trustworthy at all. Could scripture defend its place as the Book of all books in a deistic worldview?

The decline of the metaphor continued with the advent of a third circumstance, the gradual development of an historical-critical approach to biblical interpretation, paralleled by the historical treatment of geology. As the Bible came to be recognized as a compendium of many different genres of writing, assembled over centuries and through numerous and diverse redactions, it became more difficult to read it as a unitary and timeless presentation of the divine word.

Scripture came to be understood as a contextualized document proceeding from varied and (often contradictory) human experience. Likewise, we can trace a gradual historicization of nature through the eighteenth-century development of the deep history of time. The geological record showed a progressive revelation, and while this was accommodated reasonably well by some, such as Le Conte, it would not be accommodated well by others. Though this period of biblical criticism and the scientific historicization of nature was accompanied by an appeal to the two books metaphor by conservatives and liberals alike, the metaphor began to fall into disuse.

Parallel to this historicization was a growing loss of confidence in the idea that we can easily interpret scientific evidence teleologically. Beginning with the eighteenth-century discovery of extinction in the fossil record, the evidence mounted that species are not immutable, and that the physical world is not always, or even usually, a harmonious God-reflecting environment. All this rendered it increasingly difficult to look upon the book of nature as self-evidently revealing the divine plan, or at least as a plan worthy of admiration.

A fifth factor behind the decline of the metaphor is the gradual professionalization of the sciences in the nineteenth century. As natural philosophy split into physics, chemistry, and astronomy, and as natural history was divided into biology, ecology, and paleontology, each with its own discreet subject matter and unique methodology, the "nature" underlying the book of nature lost its metaphorical cogency. Moreover, the virtually complete replacement of commentary on ancient texts by the empirical exploration of the physical world, essentially took the book out of the book of nature. Thus, the metamorphosis of "natural philosophy" or "natural history" into the professional disciplines as we know them today undercut both terms in the metaphor of God's two books.

A final factor particularly relevant in the late twentieth century might be the changing flow of information consequent upon the computer revolution and the rise of global communications. We are so inundated with information at all times and from every conceivable source, that the medieval idea of two "books" as primary sources of revelation seems hopelessly anachronistic. It has even become common, since the 1960s, to speak of the eventual abandonment of the book as a human artifact of knowledge, replaced by the explosion of the almost infinite and instantaneous transmission of information now available over the Internet. To be sure, information is hardly the same as revelation or wisdom, but information appears to outcompete the latter for attention in many spheres.

The complex theme of God's two books has enjoyed a long and convoluted history. Although during the last century it has gradually fallen into disuse, the metaphor has for nearly two millennia variously framed, constituted, negated, or otherwise reflected the relationship between the two human enterprises that would in time become science and religion. In a postmodern era it appears to be a less convincing rhetorical device. Understanding the life-cycle of the metaphor is, however, pedagogically very useful, since the history of its employment provides clues to how science and religion were viewed. More importantly perhaps, understanding the development and use of the two books theme provides insights into the way in which metaphors frame and serve to mediate or bridge the relationship between such complex spheres of human existence as science and religion.

Can the theme of God's two books be useful in a world of historical-critical interpretation of scripture, and in a world in which evolutionary or developmental paradigms hold sway in scientific disciplines ranging from cosmology and geology to biology and neuroscience? Whether or not it can be rehabilitated, the changing fashions of metaphor cannot mask the need to revisit the question of the relationship between nature and faith, between science and religion. If God does speak to God's creatures, is it through pluriform ways? Is it only through religious traditions, through immediate intuition, through personal relationships? Or is it also through the twofold revelations of scripture and nature?

8

Traditional Islam and Modern Science

MUZAFFAR IQBAL

That modern science has transformed our lives is self-evident. In the most mundane things of life, from the way we procure our food to the way we communicate with one another, we rely on science and its various technological by-products. The power of modern science to transform our lives has attained universal proportions.

This universal character of modern science is unprecedented in human history; science is able to penetrate cultural and religious traditions as different as Islamic, Hindu, Chinese and those of the North American aboriginal people. Wondrous is the fact that on a small part of this tiny planet that orbits around a star in the suburbs of a galaxy of a billion stars, which, in turn, is only a galaxy among millions of galaxies, there arose a science which was able to penetrate diverse cultures within the short span of three centuries and change the way humans live, die, communicate, marry, give birth to children, and produce their food, clothing, and housing.

The transformative impact of modern science has perhaps been felt most forcefully as advances in cosmology, quantum physics, neuroscience, and evolutionary biology have provided purely "scientific" answers to some of the oldest and most fundamental questions humans have ever asked: What is the nature of Nature? Is Nature merely a huge coagulate of purposeless matter that has somehow emerged on the cosmic plane? Or is there any teleology observable in natural phenomena? Does God act in the physical world, or are natural causes sufficient to explain everything – from the thunderstorm to the formation of galaxies? In the past, these kinds of questions have been given religious answers. And this encroachment of science into a territory held by religions for centuries has inspired a revision of religion's relationship to knowledge of the universe and the human place in it.

These developments have, in turn, produced a new discourse between science and religion, sparking novel insights in theological reflection. During the last forty years, a surging interest in this discourse has produced a large body of scholarly responses and inter-actions that seek to build bridges between science and theology. These bridges have most often been built between science and Christianity. Other religious traditions, though equally affected by the proliferation of science and technology, have been slower in spanning the distance between the worlds of their traditions and that of modern science.

Building an Islamic Bridge

This need for a bridge of new interaction takes particular form in the case of Islam. The relationship of Islam to contemporary science is historically unique. Islam mothered the birth of a vibrant science from the ninth to the twelfth centuries. In its adolescent stage science went off to Europe and was adopted by the Christian West. During the Enlightenment, science matured. Now science is returning to its Islamic home as an independent adult, and the Muslim mother must adapt to its child become stranger.

If Islamic scholars are to build a bridge parallel to those being built in other traditions, what materials will they use? Given the unique historical relationship Islam shares with modern science, the materi-als will need to include at least three things: first, an historical retrieval of Islamic science; second, a reassessment of transitions and transformations of Islamic science to European thought; and third, a retrieval of the Qur'anic picture of, and approach to, the cosmos. These three things will provide the materials needed to construct methods and models appropriate to an Islamic dialogue with modern Western science.

The Muslim world received modern Western science at a time when most of the traditional Muslim lands were under direct colonial rule. Seen from the perspective of the colonized, it was the sheer force of Western science and technology that had made it possible for nations such as England and France to colonize such a large part of the world. In retrospect it seems only a partial truth, but for the early twentieth-century Muslim reformers, science and technology was *the* reason for their subjugation. They saw Western science and tech-nology as providing political and military power. It was thus seen as the most desirable aspect of Western civilization and many Muslim reformers implored their people to acquire it at all costs. This attitude has persisted. The desire for increased access to science and technology continues to be the reigning paradigm in various develop-ment-related debates in the Muslim world.

In spite of this desire for Western science, few Muslim scholars or institutions have been interested in studying the relationship between the philosophical and metaphysical foundations of Islam in relation to those of modern science. On the one hand, most Muslim scientists appear to be neither qualified nor interested in this study. Religious scholars, on the other hand, generally know too little about modern science to contribute on their own to this discourse. Thus, one finds little in the Muslim world that compares with the relatively sophisti-cated and mature discourse on science and religion in the Christian tradition. At best one finds literature attempting to show that particu-lar modern scientific discoveries were prefigured in the Qur'an. This apologetic literature often, in fact, attempts to prove that the Qur'an is the word of God *precisely because* (they claim) it contains theories and facts which modern science has only recently discovered. The result of this work, however, is that neither science nor Islam is granted the intellectual integrity each deserves; no genuine dialogue takes place.

The Islam and science discourse is not completely uncharted terri-tory. There exists a small body of literature – most of which is written by scholars who reside outside the traditional Islamic lands – which has explored the relationship between Islam and modern science. Mainstream scholarship within the Muslim world, however, has shown few signs of interest in this disciplined engagement. For all practical purposes, despite a persistent desire for Western science and technology, Islam and science remain in two separate, non-overlapping zones of discourse for most Muslims, even Muslim scientists.

Given the widespread impact and colonial history it has had, larger numbers of Muslim scientists and scholars should engage in the task of examining modern science from Islamic perspectives. This essential if daunting task must be undertaken by Muslim scientists and scholars with an understanding of the history of Islamic science, those with an appreciation for the way in which that science has been fundamentally transformed in the West, and knowledge of the Qur'anic view of the cosmos. Work developed in Christian theology cannot serve as a substitute counterweight to science in the science–religion discourse for Islam. Islamic theology functions differently within the Islamic tradition from the way Christian theology does in the Christian tradition. Because of this, it must build its own bridges to modern science. These bridges should reflect the tasks and com-mitments native to Islam.

It has been noted that the Islam and science discourse cannot attain any degree of authenticity without a careful retrieval of the Islamic scientific tradition. This retrieval consists, at its most rudimentary level, of asking the question: What was Islamic about so-called Islamic science, and how was the Islamic scientific tradition rooted in the Qur'anic worldview? Inseparable from this task is the need to reassess the transition and transformation of that tradition as it was inherited by European thought during the centuries prior to the emergence of modern science. This reassessment will provide insights into the making of the foundational structure of modern science and the relationship of its underlying philosophical structure to the Islamic worldview. Equally important are considerations concerning the status of the Qur'an in relation to modern science. This involves Qur'anic epistemology, concepts of cosmos, concepts of nature and divine action, and, finally, God's relationship to created beings as defined by the Qur'an. Note that in the West, attempts to include a scriptural worldview within the science–religion dialogue, because of association with biblical literalism, have resulted in a slamming shut of intellectual doors. Perhaps this is because in the West, "legitimate" dialogue has been framed only as "theology and science," and rarely, if ever, as "the Bible and science." However, despite this difficulty, one cannot engage in genuine Islam and science discourse that does not take account of the Islamic commitment to the Qur'an. On the basis of these explorations one can begin building models and methodologies for discourse with modern science appropriate to Islam.

The Islamic Scientific Tradition and Modern Science

We have ample historical resources to reconstruct, at least in general terms, the process that brought the Islamic scientific tradition to Europe. It is reasonable to believe that it was the transmission of the Islamic scientific tradition to Europe that made it possible for the re-awakened interest in sciences to rapidly mature and develop during the centuries prior to the Renaissance. However, it is of vital importance to note that modern science is not simply an outgrowth or continuation of the Islamic scientific tradition; rather, modern science arose on the basis of a concept of nature essentially different from the one that was at the heart of Islamic scientific tradition. The process of *transmission* of the Islamic scientific tradition to European thought was followed by a process of fundamental *transformation* of this tradition. Put another way, historical evidence suggests that the Islamic scientific tradition had a contribution in the process that led to the emergence of the *medieval* European scientific tradition, a tradition that viewed nature from a perspective not wholly alien to the Islamic perspective. This shared perspective, however, was short-lived, and as the Middle Ages gave way to the Renaissance and medieval science to the seventeenth-century scientific revolution, the common conception of nature that had been shared between the Islamic scientific tradition and European science began to disappear with the emergence of the new, what was to become modern, scientific tradition. Finally, this emerging tradition replaced medieval science entirely, leaving little or nothing of that former commonality.

The dissimilarity thus produced was only to increase with time. The inner dynamics of the post-Renaissance European civilization, the abandonment of the essential status of qualities – which were considered to be an integral part of matter in the Islamic as well as in the Greek scientific traditions – the emphasis on the geometric properties of corpuscles (shape, size, motion), and lastly the mathematization of nature at an unprecedented scale, was to produce a final philosophical separation from the inheritance received from the Islamic scientific tradition.

Transition and Transformation

The Islamic scientific tradition arrived in Europe through translation of essential texts from Arabic into Latin. One of the first to be translated was none other than the Grand Shaykh (*al-Shaykh al-Ra'is*) of Islamic science, Ibn Sina (980–1037), whose name was Latinized as Avicenna. The physical and philosophical portions of his *Kitab al-Shifa'* (*The Book of Healing*) were translated in the twelfth century; the chemical and the geographical parts translated in Spain at the beginning of the thirteenth century; and his magnum opus *al-Qanun fi'l-Tibb* (*The Canon of Medicine*), the ordered Summa of all the medical knowledge up to his time, was translated between 1150 and 1187. Divided into five books, this major work of Islamic medical tradition was used as the basic textbook for teaching medicine for seven centuries both in the East as well as in the West. The *Canon* formed the basis of teaching at all European universities. It appears in the oldest known syllabus of teaching given to the School of Medicine at Montpellier, a bull of Clement V, dating from 1309, and in all subsequent ones until 1557.

Among others who were translated between the eleventh and the thirteenth centuries are Ibn Rushd (1126–98), known to Latin

Christendom as Averroes, who was translated in the early thirteenth century; Ibn al-Haytham (965–1039), called Alhazen by his Latin translators, was translated by more than one translator toward the end of the twelfth century; Al-Farabi (d. 950) was translated in Toledo during the twelfth century; Abu Bakr al-Razi (c.854–925), known to his translators as Rhazes, was translated in Toledo and Sicily in the twelfth and thirteenth centuries; Al-Kindi (c.801–66) was translated in Toledo, in the twelfth century; al-Khwarazmi (c.800–c.847) was translated in the twelfth century; and Jabir ibn Hayyan (d. 815) was translated by various translators in the twelfth and thirteenth centuries.

The large-scale translation activity of the twelfth and thirteenth centuries that opened the floodgates of knowledge from an Islamic civilization which was considered to be hostile, pagan, and dangerous, posed a serious threat to the status quo of intellectual life in Europe. The new material was simply irresistible in its utility, power, and quality. Much of this new material was considered religiously and philosophically "harmless." Thus treatises on mathematics, optics, meteorology, and medicine were welcomed. Euclid's *Elements*, al-Khawarazmi's *Algebra*, Ibn al-Haytham's *Optics*, Ibn Sina's *Canon of Medicine*, and even Ptolemy's *Almagest* were thought to pose no serious threat to belief. However, when it came to works that had profound metaphysical implications, welcome was less forthcoming. Once translated and circulated, these works could not, of course, be untranslated and removed from the intellectual horizon of Western Europe, and their presence posed a challenge to reigning philosophical paradigms.

Aristotle and his Muslim commentators met with some legal resistance from the Christian Church. In 1210, a council of bishops issued a decree forbidding instruction on Aristotle's natural philosophy within the faculty of arts; this decree was renewed in 1215 by the papal legate Robert de Courçon. Though the decree was only applicable to Paris, it marks the beginning of a long process that would eventually cast shadows over the later history of science and religion discourse in the West. Bans on Aristotle, however, had a short life, and by 1240 Aristotle's works on natural philosophy were being taught in Paris as they had been in taught in Oxford and Bologna. By 1255, Aristotle had won a respectable place in the academia; in that year the faculty of arts at Paris passed new statutes making mandatory study of all known works of Aristotle.

The works of Aristotle did not enter the intellectual tradition of the West unaided: they were received in the company of Ibn Sina, whose Platonized versions of the Aristotelian corpus provided support for pantheism. However, around 1230, the commentaries of Ibn Sina started to be replaced by those of Ibn Rushd, in whose works Europe discovered a more authentic and less Platonized Aristotle. It was for this reason that Ibn Rushd, who became famous as *the* Commentator, was to enjoy immense respect and popularity in the West. Though Dante, in the *Inferno*, placed him in Limbo, in the first circle of Hell, he placed him there in the company of the greatest of all non-Christian thinkers – Euclid, Ptolemy, Hippocrates, Avicenna and Galen – and called him *che'l gran comento*.

In spite of the positive influence of his new companion, Aristotle often was held to be as unacceptable to much of Christendom as he had been to the Muslim worlds when he first arrived in his Arab home. Both the Islamic and the Christian traditions struggled to incorporate an Aristotelian cosmos that was made up of eternal elements and destined to last forever because the elements had not come into being at any moment and would never cease to be. This contradicted both the Christian and Muslim belief in a God who brought the finite world into being out of nothing. Likewise, both traditions were threatened by the Aristotelian notion of the Prime Mover as the deity who was eternally unchanging and hence incapable of intervening in the operation of the cosmos that ran on its own – established for eternity on the basis of cause and effect relationships. In this cosmos there was no room for miracles, for a God who acted on behalf of creation at specific times and places – a major element in both the Islamic as well as the Christian traditions. Other troubling elements in the Aristotelian system that had sparked intense debates in the Muslim world a few centuries earlier had reappeared in Europe with the translations. For example, the astrological theories that accompanied Aristotle's philosophy taught that human acts and will were influenced by celestial objects and hence impinged upon Christian notions of sin and salvation. Likewise, the nature of the soul in Aristotle's philosophy troubled many Christian scholars: Aristotelian philosophy conceived of the soul as form and organizing principle of the body that had no independent existence, and that needed a body to exist. Hence at death, both the individual's body and soul ceased to exist. This notion was incompatible with various Christian teachings that espoused the Platonic idea of an immortal soul, just as it had been unacceptable to Muslims.

But these specific concepts that seemed incompatible with much of the philosophy underlying Christian teachings posed a far less serious threat than the more fundamental threat of Aristotle's view of knowledge. Latin Christendom faced the same challenge Muslims had faced only centuries earlier: Aristotle's system of thought was a purely rational alternative to the revealed knowledge of religious tradition. This view of knowledge allowed Aristotelian philosophy to stand on equal philosophical footing with theology, and appeared to be a rival to scriptural studies. A dilemma arose within European intellectual life: assuming the validity of Aristotle's approach to knowledge, one could follow theological methods and arrive at one conclusion, or follow philosophical methods to arrive at a different conclusion, both claiming to be true. This was a re-emergence of a challenge early Christianity had faced in Neoplatonism, the classical fight for authority, the rivalry between Athens and Jerusalem.

With the beginning of the scientific revolution of the seventeenth century, Europe was to reappraise its Islamic inheritance. In the fourteenth century, Chaucer (*c.*1340–1400) had given places of honor to seven Muslim scientists and sages in his *Canterbury Tales*, reflecting the generally accepted status these men held in the European eye, a favorable appraisal of their contributions to the Middle Ages. In the new appraisal, however, Islam and Muslims were cast out of the European memory as major players in the advancement of science, their role denigrated to second-class citizenship – a position that was to remain firmly entrenched in Western scholarship for almost five hundred years, yielding only to a revised twentieth-century appraisal. The Renaissance brought a violent reaction against Ibn Sina. Leonardo da Vinci rejected Ibn Sina's anatomy; Paracelsus burned the *Canon* in Basle. It was left to Harvey to dislodge Ibn Sina from his throne by publishing a new theory of the circulation of blood in 1628.

The scientific revolution was soon followed by the invasion and colonization of most of the Muslim world. This process brought almost the entire Muslim world under European colonial rule. During the era of colonization, the Islamic scientific tradition was pulled out of the intellectual soil and Western science was planted in its place. In time, this gave rise to our contemporary milieu in which Islam and Muslims have to negotiate a relationship with an entity (modern science) that did not take form within the Islamic intellectual tradition. It is this odd historical situation that is chiefly responsible for the schizophrenic currents in contemporary scholarship on Islam and science. On the one end of the spectrum there are Muslim scholars who insist that modern science arose directly out of Europe's inherited Islamic scientific tradition. On the other end of the spectrum are scholars who reject modern science in its entirety as an un-Islamic entity. This complete rejection is ultimately a naive enterprise, however, for even those who reject the trappings of modern Western science and technology cannot live without them. Between these poles, there is an emerging group of scholars engaged in an intense effort to define and explore a healthy relationship between Islam and modern science.

The Qur'an and Modern Science

A sophisticated assessment of the relationship between Islam and science involves an exploration of the relationship between the Qur'an and science. In response to Big Bang cosmology, for example, scholars should reflect on the nature of the relationship between the fundamental assumptions of modern cosmology and the Qur'anic cosmos, its metaphysical roots, and its ontological structure. Likewise, rather than simply debating the consonance or dissonance between Islam and the theory of evolution, first one ought to explore the Qur'anic data on creation, life, death, and resurrection in its totality and then examine the underlying principles of the theory of evolution.

This assessment of the Qur'an and science involves epistemological and hermeneutical questions. Ultimately, discourse on Islam and science will have to be framed within theories of knowledge to which Islam is amenable. Certain recent attempts at writing scientific commentaries on the Qur'an (*al-Tafsir al-'ilmi*), for example, have failed to accomplish this, ignoring fourteen centuries of tradition on the grounds that new scientific facts dictate a totally new approach to the Qur'anic hermeneutics. This has met with general disapproval by the majority of contemporary scholars. Their position is that the fourteen hundred years of tradition of Qur'anic hermeneutics provides ample guidelines and foundational principles for any new interpretation, and any attempt to reinterpret the verses of the Qur'an has to be rooted in this tradition. This does not foreclose the possibility of new interpretation; rather it seeks to build the new interpretations on a solid foundation. Likewise, the language of the Qur'an has been the focus of continuous scholarship, and any new interpretation requires the support of this long tradition. Thus, by relying on these two solid traditions, one can explore the relationship between the Qur'anic cosmos and the one envisioned by modern science with reasonable assurance of arriving at a correct understanding.

The Islamic cosmos has the same essential features as those of the two other Abrahamic religions – Judaism and Christianity. In these three monotheistic faiths, God is the originator of everything that exists. In Islam, this creative act of God, through a simple command, *Kun* ("Be"), became the subject matter of Islamic cosmogony that elucidates the modalities of creation. The Qur'anic creation theme, let us note, includes the physical as well as non-physical worlds – all ontologically linked and existentially dependent upon God.

This intrinsic nexus between various levels of existence transforms the multiplicity of appearances into a unity. The ultimate foundation of their interrelatedness at the level of cosmic existence is their onto-logical dependence on God. Hence the world of nature is related to all other levels of creation. This common ontological foundation made it possible for the Islamic scientific tradition to forge links and share a language of discourse with other disciplines of knowledge, all of which were arranged in a single hierarchy.

The unity of existence is a recurrent theme of the Qur'an that relates it to its central concept of *Tawhid*, the Unicity of God. Thus linked ontologically with the realm of the divine, the realm of nature becomes more than the physical entity that it is; it becomes a sign (*aya*, pl. *ayat*), pointing to a transcendent reality beyond itself. This transcendence is semantically linked to the verses of the Qur'an which are also called *ayat*. But this elegant nexus between the world of nature and the word of God is much more than mere semantics; it is an essential feature of the Qur'anic metaphysics of nature which establishes an inalienable link between various levels of created things by relating them to an All-Encompassing (*al-Muheet*) and All-Knowing (*al-'Aleem*) God who is above and beyond all human conceptions.

Since all things exist through and because of God, their ontological dependence on the creator simultaneously ennobles them by raising their status from being mere things (*ashya'*) to signs (*ayat*) of a tran-scendent Real (*al-Haqq*), who, nevertheless, remains beyond them. Thus rather than being mere dialectical utterances, the "sign verses" of the Qur'an have an irresistible urgency which draws our attention to that which lies beyond the phenomena being mentioned. It is this ennoblement that makes the common elements of the natural world – the rhythmic alteration of the day and the night and the emergence of a grand oak from a small acorn – much more than the natural phe-nomena that occur according to certain laws of nature.

Seen from within the Islamic tradition, sciences that explore various aspects of the natural world actually explore aspects of the one Qur'anic cosmos. This cosmos is made up of both the physical as well as non-physical beings according to a grand scheme, conceived and executed by the creator. While the ultimate destination of this created cosmos remains part of God's mystery, the Qur'an insists that humans discover the modalities through which nature works. It draws attention to the regularities, beneficence and design of various observable natural processes through concrete examples drawn from the world of nature. These processes fall in the domain of various scientific disciplines such as astronomy, physics, mathematics, geology, and botany. When studied in their proper metaphysical context, these processes become means to gain knowledge of that which lies beyond the laws that govern them. This Qur'anic invitation to reflect on these natural processes is repeated with such urgency that the spatio-temporal plane that contains the world of nature seems to form the very background of the Qur'anic universe.

These intrinsic links make the drama of creation, existence, and the moral response to revelation out of human volition an integrated whole uniquely anchored in the metaphysical realm though operating in a historical setting. These linkages become apparent when the sign verses are seen in the context of the creation theme of the Qur'an – a context that provides us with a fundamental framework of inquiry for what has been called the religious order of nature.

The Qur'an does not contain any explicit physical cosmological theory. What it does reiterate, however, is that the cosmos is ontologically dependent upon divine sustenance and will, and that it exists only for a specific duration. This is not to suggest that certain verses of the Qur'an that mention specific physical processes are not relevant to the discourse. A prime example is the verse, "Are they, who are bent on denying the truth, not aware that the heavens and the earth were one single entity, which We then parted asunder? – and [that] We made out of water every living thing" (Q. 21.30), which is often cited in support of the Big Bang theory. Rather than simply attempting to correlate theories in science with specific Qur'anic texts, scholars working in the discourse on Islam and science must situate that discourse within the broad context of Qur'anic themes. This Qur'anic contextualization must be stressed.

Life, like the cosmos, arises out of divine command through a process that is explained in many verses that neither negate nor affirm specific modern theories. The enigmas of life – birth (described as an embryogeny in several stages, Q. 23.12–14; 40.69), death, resurrection, and life after death – are mentioned in detail as fundamental facts. With regard to divine action and human free will, the Qur'an gives humans (and *jinns*) the moral choice of accepting or rejecting the divine trust, prescribes the legal limits of human activity, and gives humanity the freedom to choose between the two paths (Q. 90.10).

Summary

These, then, are the broad parameters for creating models and methods of discourse appropriate to the relationship between Islam and science. Muslim scientists and religious scholars need to engage in a historical retrieval of Islamic science, including a reassessment of the transitions and transformations of Islamic science to European thought. Perhaps most importantly, scholars who wish to bridge Islam and science must do so within a context of inquiry sensitive to the Qur'anic worldview, and consonant with the Islamic intellectual tradition. The task of constructing this bridge involves drawing on the various resources of Islamic scholarship: Qur'anic hermeneutics, scholastics (*kalam*), philosophical and mystical traditions – all of which have served to elucidate the Islamic view of God's relationship to creation, and, in consonance with that view, Islam's relationship to science.

9

Buddhism and the Sciences: Historical Background, Contemporary Developments

RICHARD K. PAYNE

While discourse on the relation between Christianity and science has a long history, it has only been in the last century that Buddhists and Buddhist scholars have begun to consider the relation between their own religious tradition and the promises and challenges of modern science. This does not mean that there has not been a long history of a relation between Buddhism and the sciences. However, rarely has that relation been conceived of in terms of "discourse on religion and science" as such. As a result, much of the recent work done in the area of science and religion, though significant in its own right, inadequately considers many core Buddhist concerns.

That much of the discourse on science and religion is structured according to assumptions and concerns particular to the theistic traditions generally, and Christian theology specifically, is understandable. However, the fundamental concerns of Buddhist thought differ substantially from those of Christianity and other theistic traditions. While Buddhist scholars can learn from the models of discourse developed in the relationship between Christianity and modern science, in order for them to enter fully into constructive dialogue with science basic presuppositions about the nature of science–religion interaction will need to be revisited.

What might this revisitation look like? In this chapter I propose three steps. First, in order to bring fundamental Buddhist concerns into conversation with science, it is necessary to clear the intellectual ground upon which dialogue between science and Buddhism will be established. The first portion of this chapter concerns itself with this task. This ground-clearing will involve the clarification of several key issues, assumptions, and terminology involved in discussing the relation between Buddhism and science.

Having cleared some of the intellectual ground, the second step in the process of building constructive dialogue between Buddhism and science involves asking the question: What is it about the Buddhist tradition that appears to be amenable or open to dialogue with the sciences? The second section of this chapter takes up this question, which can be answered by considering various instances of constructive interaction throughout the history of Buddhism. This examination is organized so as to develop a typology of relations. This typology, outlining ways in which Buddhism seems open to discourse with the sciences, should provide a reliable foundation upon which dialogue can be established.

The third step in establishing constructive dialogue involves assessing how contemporary scholars have begun to re-envision discourse between science and religion so as to more adequately consider fundamental Buddhist concerns. The final section of this chapter takes that step. A significant area of work for contemporary scholars is the dialogue between Buddhism and the cognitive sciences, philosophy of mind, and psychology.

Much popular literature has concerned itself with similarities between varieties of Asian religious thought and certain theories from physics. These claims of similarity, however, appear to be grounded on little more than an inadequately nuanced analogy, that is, Buddhist doctrine is portrayed so as to appear fully consonant with theories from contemporary physics. These analogies depend heavily upon particular ways of expressing Buddhist doctrines, entailing selective interpretations, which heighten the appearance of similarity. Moreover, these articulations frequently extract doctrine from its own intellectual context. The result is that genuine dialogue between Buddhism as it is practiced and science is compromised. In contrast, recent developments in Buddhism and cognitive science, for example, are more sensitively conceived, and, significantly, remain in keeping with the priorities of Buddhist thought itself.

A final introductory note should be made concerning the difficulty of representing the Buddhist tradition. There is no "orthodox" interpretation of Buddhist thought. Hence, there can be no single authoritative Buddhism. The Buddhism that anyone describes cannot be anything other than Buddhism as that person understands it. Given this, the reader needs to take into consideration that throughout this chapter, when I speak of "Buddhism," it is a shorthand way of referring to "Buddhism as I understand it." My reading of Buddhism is not intended to be either normative or essentialist. In other words it should not be taken as a claim regarding what Buddhism should be, or as a claim regarding what the essence of Buddhism is. Moreover, I do not intend the description of Buddhism that follows to arbitrate what is or is not Buddhism, nor do I presume that everyone who identifies him/herself as a Buddhist would necessarily agree with the entirety of what I have to say. The object "Buddhism" differs greatly depending upon one's mode of engagement with the tradition. Having made these qualifications, it will be enough that many of those who identify themselves as Buddhists would at least be able to recognize a significant similarity between what follows and their own religious commitments.

Clearing the Ground

Because dialogue between religion and science has involved Buddhism less frequently than some other traditions, it is important to clear the intellectual ground – gaining a better sense of the terrain – before beginning constructive work. This process of ground-clearing involves (1) reviewing ways in which the landscape has been misunderstood and consequently misrepresented – mistakes which inhibit solid construction; (2) removing this rubble of misunderstanding by defining terms, allowing us to survey the ground more effectively; and (3) noting several key landmarks on the Buddhist terrain that will need to be incorporated into our construction plans.

Reviewing the Landscape: Neither Apologetics nor Polemics

Any claim that an entire religious tradition either supports or impedes science is generally nothing more than a simple rhetorical strategy designed for apologetics or polemics. This chapter is neither. Such unambiguous claims tend to be ahistorical, assuming some unchanging essence as characterizing both religion and science, and then selectively drawing upon historical evidence to support the position taken. Beginning from an essentialized view of the tradition, rather than examining what the relations actually have been, the apologetic or polemical position builds an argument about what the consequences of that essential nature must be. Such arguments are referred to as *a priori* or as *retrodictive*.

An example in which this essentializing is evident is Joseph Needham's famous series of studies on *Science and Civilization in China*. His is a polemical argument that the failure of China to achieve a "scientific revolution" was due to the "inhibitory influence" of the supposedly other-worldly tendencies of Buddhism. He asserts that the teaching that the world is illusory (the doctrine of *maya*) precludes Buddhists from actively engaging in empirical research, and that the other-worldliness of the goal of *nirvana* (the cessation of suffering) precludes Buddists from engaging in technological projects which seek to improve the human condition in this world.

In the background of this argument are the British colonialist representations of Indian religions as contributing to a culture of passivity, a representation that was used to justify both evangelism and imperialism. More specifically, Needham represents Buddhism as reducible to a single, unchanging essence: the doctrines of maya and nirvana. Thus, Buddhism is represented as teaching that all of existence is an illusion from which one must escape, without any reference to the vastly different forms Buddhism has taken over its history. This latter failure makes his representation of Buddhism ahistoric, and thus untenable. Not only is it problematic to represent Buddhism as essentially a teaching of illusion and escape, but Needham fails to ask whether the interpretations of the concepts of maya and nirvana which he employs are accurate. At the same time he does not establish that these concepts were of central importance in the history of Chinese Buddhism, or that they actually played any role at key moments in the history of the Chinese sciences. Rather, he presents Buddhism as *essentially* this negative worldview, and then deduces from that dubious premise the conclusion that Buddhism must have impeded scientific development in China.

Finally, the argument seems to assume that the intellectual cultures of all societies ought to develop in such a fashion as to culminate in experimental science, and that if a society did not develop that way, then something must have deleteriously impeded that development. From that conclusion, he looks backwards for the cause, retrodictively examining various aspects of Buddhism in his attempt to identify the culprit. This is a conception of cultural progress as a unilinear development, another historically untenable view.

Although Needham's polemical evaluation of Buddhism portrays a negative relation to science, much the same kinds of problems would also be found with apologetic attempts to assert that Buddhism has an unambiguously positive relation with science. Such arguments might assert that:

- Buddhism is conducive to science;
- Buddhism is in agreement with science;

- Buddhism has already discovered what science only now has learned, sometimes called "the ancient wisdom argument."

These arguments tend to select particular doctrinal views to represent the entirety of the tradition, simplifying them, and treating them as true of the entire tradition throughout its history. Arguments of this kind, based on essentialized, decontextualized and ahistorical portrayals of the religious tradition, can only serve rhetorical ends. They cannot provide the basis for a historical study of the actual relations between a religious tradition and the sciences.

Removing the Rubble: Definitions, Distinctions, and Clarifications

For our discussion of science and Buddhism, it is important to clear the ground of misconceptions by defining key terms and making key distinctions. First we need to distinguish between *Science* and *the sciences*. The idea of Science as a single, unitary entity would seem to be the product of late nineteenth and early twentieth-century positivism, which envisioned a single, unified scientific realm in which all explanations could, at least in principle, be reduced to physics. When religious authors reject scientific explanations as reductionist, it is quite often this positivist conception of science – this idea that physical explanations are the only legitimate explanations – which they have in mind.

In contrast to Science, there is what one might refer to as the sciences. These are specific fields of study with (1) organized bodies of knowledge, (2) recognized procedures for adding to that knowledge, (3) shared criteria for evaluating such knowledge, and (4) usually having a distinct terminology. Note that when conceived of as a single, unified entity, Science is something other than the cumulative total of the sciences.

In addition to the distinction between the sciences and Science, the sciences can be divided into observational sciences and experimental sciences. While much of the discussion regarding science and religion has tended to focus on experimental sciences (also sometimes referred to as modern or hard sciences), in order to engage core Buddhist concerns, one should also consider the observational sciences (traditional or soft sciences), systematic forms of knowledge developed through observation rather than experimentation. This distinction expands the scope of discussion to allow for consideration of the traditional sciences, such as those developed in India and China, which were rarely experimental in character, but did accrue extensive bodies of systematic knowledge. The assumption that science necessarily means experimental science is not universal. The equivalents of "science" in various European languages, e.g., *Wissenschaft* (German), *science* (French), *scienza* (Italian), *ciencia* (Spanish), and *nauk* (Russian), do not refer to experimental science as such, but include a broader range of systematic forms of knowledge.

The so-called experimental sciences are subject to two kinds of limitations: cultural and practical. The cultural limitation is due to social mores concerning experimentation on human beings. Increasingly these mores are strictly codified into what are sometimes called "human subjects protocols." Such constraints limit certain forms of experimentation in fields such as medicine, psychology, sociology, and anthropology. There are also several sciences in which the constraint on experimentation is practical. Meteorology, economics and astronomy are examples of such observational sciences. Being an observational science does not preclude making predictions and waiting to see if these are confirmed. However, in such a situation one is not actively controlling an experimental situation, attempting to hold all variables except one steady. Thus, observational sciences can also be ones that engage in theory-formation and hypothesis-testing, but the method for testing hypotheses is not experimental in nature. However, both experimental and observational sciences are equally committed to systematic and reliable explanation.

We should note here that the characterization of science as theory-formation and hypothesis-testing is itself not uncontested. On the one hand studies have sought to discern the social and cultural dimensions of scientific practice. On the other there are instances in which competing theories are equally confirmed by experimental results.

These different uses are reflected in different uses of the term science itself. Many fruitless disagreements about the relation between Buddhism and science can be avoided by a further set of distinctions with regard to the definition of the term science. Science can be understood to mean several things:

- science as a body of authoritative knowledge;
- science as method producing authoritative knowledge;
- science as a social institution; and
- science as a set of practices.

Each of these is sometimes meant when reference is made to science. Without our clarifying which definition or combination of definitions is intended, only confusion can result. These four categories overlap, making clarity all the more important.

"Scientific knowledge" is one of the most common usages for the term science, and is often used – quite mistakenly – to mean that which is unquestionably true, irrefutable knowledge. This colloquial reference to science as "that which is assuredly the case" pervades contemporary American culture. Ironically, this rhetorical use misrepresents the strength of scientific knowledge. At its best, science remains open to doubt, question, reconsideration, and reexamination. Such knowledge is distinct from but closely tied to the question of the methods used to create it, i.e., the scientific method. Although commonly equated with experimentation, scientific knowledge is more appropriately identified with this method – theory-formation and hypothesis-testing, employing empirical information, with results that are publicly verifiable.

The definition of science and scientific knowledge also needs to be distinguished from its social institutions. As a social entity, the institutional organization and societal support for science affects its pursuit of knowledge. In contemporary American society, institutional location of science has increasingly shifted from governmentally supported research institutions in universities to privately supported, business-based research. It is this social institution that is meant when people blame science for such ills of contemporary society as air pollution or atomic weapons. Meanwhile, science as a set of practices points to the interlocking sets of ways in which science is conducted, such as the organization of laboratories and communication of scientific knowledge through professional associations.

Finally, in removing the rubble to make room for a Buddhist dialogue with science, methodological materialism must be distinguished from metaphysical materialism. It is often popularly assumed that science necessarily entails a materialist metaphysics. Both lay people and scientists alike share this assumption. While, as a systematic means of producing knowledge, science may be methodologically or even epistemologically materialist in its presuppositions, that methodological commitment should be distinguished from any particular metaphysical commitment derived from it.

Having made some distinctions in what can be meant by science, a second set of clarifications is needed. Discourse between Buddhism and science is encumbered by caricatures of Buddhism. Authentic exchange cannot take place until these misconceptions are cleared from the field of dialogue.

The first misconception that must be dealt with is the idea that

Buddhism is exclusively concerned with "the other world" or "liberation from the world of phenomena" (seen above in relation to Needham's claim that Buddhist other-worldliness was responsible for inhibiting science in China). This view, which was current at the time Needham was writing, continues to be found in much of the literature on Buddhism. However, since Needham's time, this view has been critically reexamined. This representation of Buddhism results from a confused understanding of two assertions: (1) that there is no permanent, independently existing essence (or "self," *atman*); and (2) that awakening involves extinction ("blowing out," nirvana). It has been wrongly assumed that this has meant that awakening results from the extinction of the self. This appears to have been in large part the result of a failure to discriminate between Buddhist and certain Hindu conceptions of liberation. A close examination of the tradition, however, shows that awakening is the extinction of mistaken conceptions and misplaced affections, and not the extinction of the self. While not unrelated, this description of the path to awakening is distinct from the ontological claim that there are no independently existing essences.

A second contemporary caricature of Buddhism is the assertion that it makes claims effectively identical to those of science or that Buddhism is perfectly compatible with science. This version of Buddhism grows out of the movements beginning in the second half of the nineteenth century now known collectively under the title of "Buddhist modernism." Buddhist modernists emphasized the rational character of Buddhism and the human character of Shakyamuni Buddha, Buddhism's historical founder. Buddhism here is presented as primarily a philosophy of life, a path to achieving the full potential of human existence. This humanistic portrayal of Buddhism facilitates simplistic claims concerning the relationship between Buddhism and modern science.

A third, less common caricature, one that was once prevalent in academic circles and still can be found in popular discussions of Buddhism, portrays Buddhism as an Oriental version of Occidental idealism. Here complex philosophical positions within Buddhism are misinterpreted because they are assumed to be unproblematically the same as those within Occidental philosophy. The category of idealism, with its emphasis upon a correlative relationship between "observing mind" and the "external world" is falsely seen as corresponding to Buddhist descriptions of the workings of consciousness as central to the quest for awakening. This correspondence leads to the superficial appearance that Buddhism has a relationship to science that parallels the relationship of idealism to science. One of the most important schools of Indian Buddhist thought is sometimes described as the "mind only" school, an overly literal translation of its name (Vijñaptimatrata). This formulation, "mind only," was then mistakenly taken to mean that the school taught a doctrine that only the mind exists, i.e., classic European idealism. The doctrinal claims of the school, however, are more accurately described as asserting the necessary concomitance of mind with all perception and knowledge of objective existence – a theme we will come back to in considering contemporary developments in the relation between Buddhism and the sciences.

Differing Landscapes: Buddhist and Christian

In the discourse on religion and science, religion is almost invariably equated with theistic religion, if not explicitly with Christianity. Further, much current scholarship focuses on the relation between theology and science, as distinct from religion and science. For the three Western monotheisms, and even for the theistic strains within Hinduism, this is not particularly problematic. However, the fundamental conceptions of Buddhist thought differ substantially from those of the theistic traditions. Without essentializing Buddhism, there do seem to be some basic landmarks which, if not permanent fixtures on the landscape of Buddhist history, are present through much of its historical and cultural reshaping. The difference in conceptual landscapes is not adequately recognized by a science and religion dialogue that is based on the theology of theistic traditions. Therefore, dialogue between science and Buddhism must take time to point out distinctively Buddhist landmarks.

Buddhism differs from Christianity in at least three important respects, which affect the way in which Buddhism relates to science. First, Buddhism does not have a history of antagonism with science. While the historical background to the contemporary dialogue between Christianity and science includes much consonance, it has, particularly in the last century, been marked by moments of conflict.

Second, the path toward awakening, central to Buddhism, is understood very differently from Christian soteriology, or the study of salvation. The path to awakening is not based on faith in an external transcendent deity. Nor is it a salvation that comes through external intervention in history. Rather, the path to awakening is a praxiological process of overcoming ignorance about the way the world actually is.

Third, the mythic background of Buddhism does not involve the creation, a vision of natural history that gives priority of concern to questions of origin. The absence of emphasis on creation means that dialogue between Buddhism and science should not give conceptual priority to cosmology, then astrophysics, then chemistry and then biology. Rather, Buddhism begins with the awakening of the Buddha, which involves insight into the workings of his own mind. Thus, the priorities in the religion and science discourse for Buddhism are psychology, cognitive science, and the philosophy of mind.

Rather than being based on the idea that the world was created, for Buddhist cosmology the universe as it is has simply always been this way "from beginningless time." Within traditional Buddhist cosmology there are living beings which are superhuman (gods and titans), as well as living beings which are subhuman (animals, hungry ghosts, and those dwelling in the hells). However, all of these, not only humans, animals, hungry ghosts, and hell beings, but also gods and titans, are subject to the same natural processes. Central to the Buddhist conception of these natural processes is the idea of karma, meaning action, which identifies a conception that one's actions produce results, which affect both others and oneself.

There are debates, both historically and within the contemporary interpretation of Buddhist thought, as to which actions are consequential. One interpretation is that it is only those that might be called ethical which constitute karma. Others maintain that all actions have consequences and that the category of "ethical" is itself a social creation rather than a natural category. Under either interpretation, however, there is no creator god who, in the beginning, establishes the ethical order and who then also serves as judge of individuals within that ethical order.

These fundamental distinctions between Buddhism and theistic religious traditions produce differences of orientation within a discourse with science.

A last task of ground-clearing is needed before we move to a survey of the ways in which Buddhism, through its history, may be seen to be amenable to discourse with science. This task involves distinguishing the major divisions of contemporary Buddhism: Theravada, Mahayana, and Vajrayana, also known as tantric Buddhism. In the contemporary world these are generally described in terms of geographic divisions. Theravada Buddhism is found in the countries of South and Southeast Asia: Sri Lanka, Thailand, Burma. Mahayana Buddhism is that found in China, Japan, Korea, and Vietnam. Vajrayana Buddhism is generally identified with Tibet and Mongolia.

These geographic identifications are overly simplistic and hence of very limited utility. For example, there are Vajrayana lineages in China and Japan. Similarly, the Buddhism of Tibet and Mongolia is strongly Mahayana. The situation is further complicated by the fact that many Mahayana monks take the same vows as part of their initiatory process as do Theravada monks. The typical characterizations of these divisions are as much a result of historical accident resulting from what caught the attention of different writers at different times as they are reflections of the actual situation. An additional problem with the geographic conceptions of divisions within Buddhism is that they implicitly reinforce the mistaken conception that contemporary nation states are in some sense natural entities having unique religious cultures. While it is unavoidable to speak of "Chinese Buddhism" or "Tibetan Buddhism," it should be noted that the reference here is to religious cultures, which have always interacted with one another and not to modern nation states.

During a history extending over two and a half millennia and across so many linguistic and religious cultures, there cannot possibly be a single relation between Buddhism and science. The historical background to the relation between Buddhism and science extends across the two dominant intellectual cultures of Asia, i.e., Indian and Chinese, as well as in the other, less influential intellectual cultures, such as Tibetan, Korean, and Japanese. This historical background bears on how Buddhism is portrayed in its relationship to science. The introduction of Buddhism into East Asia, for example, needs to be understood not solely in terms of religion as we understand that category in contemporary society, but also as a spreading of Indian culture into East Asia. When and if a more comprehensive history of Buddhism and science is written, it will need to reflect deeply on the specific kinds of relations existing at different times and in different places within Buddhism itself. The following section will outline three basic kinds of relations that can be identified within those historically and geographically conditioned relations. This outline will attempt to answer the question, "What evidence is there within its history that might suggest models for relating Buddhism and science?" in terms of a threefold typology. It is my hope that this typology adequately reflects Buddhism's wide and diverse tradition of relating to the various sciences.

(Preliminary) Typological Foundations: Historical Evidence for the Possibility of Constructive Relations between Buddhism and the Sciences

Having cleared some of the intellectual ground which might encumber discourse, the second step in the process of building constructive dialogue between Buddhism and science involves posing the question, What is it about the Buddhist tradition that appears to be amenable or open to dialogue with the sciences? As suggested above, the relationship between Buddhism and the sciences should not be founded on the unambiguous claims of polemical or apologetic writings. In building a solid foundation for dialogue between Buddhism and the sciences we should consider various models for the possibility of constructive interaction throughout the history of Buddhism. This history suggests that Buddhism is open to at least three types of relationship with science: *supportive*, *integral*, and *consequential*. The supportive relation is where existing science and technology has been used in support of Buddhist projects of one kind or another. In such cases, the Buddhist projects may either stimulate further development or involve the import of science and technology across cultural boundaries. The integral is characterized by the many scientific and technological assumptions and understandings actively maintained within Buddhism itself. Finally, the consequential relation is that in which Buddhist teachings and values are the impetus for scientific or technological undertakings.

Supportive: Buddhist Projects, Science, and Technology

Throughout its history one can find examples both of Buddhist projects that were supported by the science and technology of their time, and of instances in which science and technology were stimulated by Buddhist projects. In the mid-eighth century, when the temple of Todaiji was built in the capital city Nara in central Japan, scientific and technological efforts in Japan were greatly stimulated. The temple building itself is the largest wooden structure in the world, and the Great Buddha Vairocana, which is housed within, is the largest bronze statue. In addition to engineering and metalworking this also stimulated mining in Japan, as construction of the statue and ornamentation of the building drew on copper, gold, mercury, and silver mines from various locations around Japan.

Another instance of how a Buddhist project affected the science and technology of its day can be seen in the life of the priest Kukai

(774–835), founder of the school of esoteric Buddhism in Japan known as Shingon. During his studies in China he acquired not only the ritual and doctrinal knowledge of esoteric Buddhism, but also many requisite practical skills. These included linguistics, particularly Sanskrit, brushmaking, metalworking, architecture, and other technologies. These technologies were necessary for the transmission of new doctrinal and ritual texts, and for the performance of esoteric Buddhist ritual practices that require special ritual implements and altar fittings of various kinds.

Integral: Science and Technology as a Part of the Buddhist Institution

Buddhist monastic education in India included study of five fields of knowledge: linguistics, logic, speculative philosophy, medicine, and creative arts. The presence of linguistics, logic, and medicine in this curriculum indicate that Buddhism did not have an oppositional relation to the sciences. This distinguishes Buddhist monastic education from the education provided to Brahmins, which appears to have disdained secular training. One can speculate that the origin of this monastic curriculum may be the consequence of the Buddhist rejection of the caste system with its attendant division of labor according to differing social groups. This same pattern of monastic education continued in the Tibetan Buddhist context as well.

One of the central issues in any reflection on the nature of science as a source of knowledge is causality. Causality has been a central concern of Buddhism from its very inception. This concern is expressed in the foundational teachings of the four noble truths and conditioned co-arising. The four noble truths are that all things are dissatisfying, that dissatisfaction has a cause, that having a cause, dissatisfaction can be extinguished, and the path to such extinction. Conditioned co-arising is the assertion that nothing exists independently of all other things, but rather each thing arises along with all other things as the result of causes and conditions. The concern with causality is found throughout almost every form of Indian Buddhist thought. For example, the *abhidharma* – the classic scholastic system of speculative philosophy and psychology which provides the basis for all later Buddhist thought – has in its extensive literature several discussions and theories of causality. For example, Vasubandhu's *abhidharma* verses and autocommentary, which is considered by many to be the most important medieval compendium of *abhidharma* thought, identifies six kinds of causal relations.

Later in medieval India the concern with epistemology, which characterizes so much of Indian religious thought, developed into a semi-formal analysis of inference in the work of Dignaga and Dharmakirti. In common with much of Buddhist thought, these thinkers asserted the existence of only two valid sources of knowledge – perception and inference. Another source, testimony (or what we would call the appeal to authority), is also one which is discussed extensively by other Buddhist thinkers.

The inferential schemes of medieval Indian philosophy grew out of the debate tradition, rather than the mathematical tradition as was the case in Greece. Debate was an important function in the medieval Indian religious milieu since the religious affiliation of kingdoms at times depended upon the outcome of a debate. The debate tradition of medieval India continues into present-day Tibetan and Japanese Buddhism. One of the fundamental distinctions that Dignaga makes is between an argument intended to convince another, and an argument intended to determine the truth of a claim for oneself. This distinction evidences the debate background for the formation of Buddhist logic.

An argument for others has five parts, called "limbs" in Sanskrit. One of the most common examples of a five-part argument is the following:

proposal:	There is fire on the mountain,
reason:	because there is smoke on the mountain.
justification:	Wherever there is smoke, there is fire, as for example in a kitchen.
application:	Because there is smoke on the mountain,
conclusion:	there is fire on the mountain.

Upon examination, one can see that the final two parts are a restatement of the proposal and reason. It is these two parts that Dignaga eliminates as unnecessary when one is creating an inference for oneself. In the instance given here the justification is a positive one. It was also recognized that one could infer on the basis of a negative justification, such as: Where there is no fire, there is no smoke, as in a lake. Dignaga pointed out that where one has both a positive and a negative warrant, one has a more convincing argument.

This openness to logic and reason reveals a disposition within Buddhism that one can tentatively conclude suggests an amenability to dialogue with contemporary science.

Consequential: Science and Technology as the Result of Buddhist Teachings and Values

Belief in reincarnation has been considered one of the central teachings of Buddhism throughout its entire history. The desire to understand the processes of rebirth led to a concern with embryology. This concern is evidenced, for example, in both the Tibetan and Japanese traditions. Typically, the process of rebirth was divided into two periods: the period between death and conception, and the period from conception to birth. The treatment of these concerns most familiar in the West is the so-called *Tibetan Book of the Dead*, which focuses most of its attention on the period from death to conception. However, it is far from being the only Buddhist text to discuss the processes of rebirth. For example, Gampopa's *Jewel Ornament of Liberation* gives greater attention to the gestation period itself.

Several similar works are also found in the Japanese esoteric Buddhist tradition of Shingon. While the Tibetan works largely assume a negative view of the cycle of rebirth (*samsara*) as unremittingly marked by suffering, the Japanese works more consistently operate from a non-dual conception of the cycle of rebirth as identical with the awakened condition in which the sources of suffering are extinguished (*nirvana*). These Japanese works generally employ a five- or an eight-stage developmental sequence. This is usually an eight-week-long period, covering the time of conception to the time when the fetus is fully formed, i.e., a tiny human being, and not to birth as such. A key religious concept for the Shingon discussions of embryology is that of awakening in this body (*sokushin jobutsu*). This is the idea that one is already inherently awakened and can become aware of that inherent purity of mind through practice, in one's present body rather than over the course of countless lifetimes of practice. The emphasis on embodiment provided a way of giving positive religious value to conception and birth.

One of the central values for the Mahayana tradition is that of compassionate action. The ideal figure for the Mahayana is called a *bodhisattva*, or one who is committed to attaining full awakening. Bodhisattvas are characterized by both wisdom and compassion. While wisdom is seen as passive insight into the absence of any metaphysical absolute in either persons or objects, compassion is the resulting activity which arises from wisdom.

Thang-stong rGyal-po (1361–1485), a fifteenth-century Tibetan visionary and lineage founder, is a culture hero celebrated for the construction of iron chain suspension bridges in several locations in central and eastern Tibet. Travel in Tibet is very difficult as the country is marked by a large number of narrow river valleys. Even if there was a ferry across a river, passage could be subject to the whims of the ferryman. In addition, the countryside was troubled by bandits who preyed upon travellers. As a consequence of his bodhisattva compassion, Thang-stong both established monasteries and temples in locales made dangerous by bandits, and also built many iron chain suspension bridges across rivers. He is said to have discovered a mine of iron ore, which then made it possible to create the links necessary for the construction of his bridges. Here we see the Buddhist value of compassion motivating mining, iron smithing, and bridge construction.

Similarly, in the summer of 820, the priest Kukai, mentioned above, was put in charge of the reconstruction of a reservoir in his home island of Shikoku. Originally constructed almost a century before, this reservoir was needed by farmers for irrigation. Although several prior reconstruction efforts had failed, Kukai was able to complete the project within about three months. While the reservoir has needed further repairs in the intervening 1,100 years, it continues to provide water control services to this day.

Another instance of scientific and technological work being motivated by Buddhist values is the construction of an armillary sphere and an astronomical clock in eighth-century China. This was motivated by the traditional Buddhist conception that the effectiveness of the Buddhist teachings would decline in three stages, and that eventually after the end of the last stage, another Buddha would be born into this world. These ideas created a concern with calculating the temporal distance from the death of Shakyamuni Buddha in order to determine what stage one was in, and to calculate how long before the next Buddha would appear. Buddhist messianism was combined with Chinese utopianism, the goal of achieving a stable, harmonious, peaceful, and prosperous social order under the direction of an emperor whose actions are guided by being harmoniously integrated into the order of nature. Yixing (673–727) was one of the most important Buddhist monks of the Tang dynasty, and has been recognized not only for his extensive translation work and doctrinal studies, but also as one of the greatest mathematicians and astronomers of his time. While the clock that Yixing constructed drew on earlier clocks, his is the first definitely known to have employed an escapement.

An interesting side-note here involving the construction of clocks in China in the late seventh and early eighth centuries addresses one of the preconceptions regarding the effect of religion on science – the belief that a linear conception of time characteristic of Western culture was necessary for the creation of clocks. Buddhist conceptions of time, which may be described as cyclic, did not preclude a concern with time and its accurate measurement.

A stereotype frequently repeated is that religion is concerned with "the timeless" or with "eternal truths." This fundamentally Neo-platonic view of religion has been uncritically projected onto Indian religions in their entirety, including Buddhism. The implication of this projection is that religions of Indian origin are unconcerned with a more "scientific" conception of time. Buddhist science of time belies this uncritical assessment.

These three models of the historical relationship between Buddhism and science and technology – supportive, integral, and consequential – suggest that Buddhism is indeed open to contemporary discourse with science. With these models serving as conceptual background, we will assess the work of current scholars working to establish constructive dialogue between Buddhism and the sciences.

Contemporary Constructions

The foundations of Buddhist thought rest on the awakening of Shakyamuni Buddha. In the context of Indian religious culture, that awakening is itself understood as the cessation of mistaken conceptions and misplaced affections that keep us from living in the world as it actually is, i.e., as impermanent. Thus, the primary focus for Buddhism, which shapes its interaction with the sciences, concerns issues of epistemology and the nature of consciousness. The path to awakening is primarily concerned with developing an understanding of how the mind works so as to be no longer misled by our mistaken belief that permanent satisfaction is possible. It is for this reason that despite the popular fascination with possible similarities between contemporary physics (e.g., chaos theory, folded universes, black holes) and Asian religious traditions, it is neuroscience, psychology, the cognitive sciences, and philosophy of mind that I would suggest ought to have the highest priority for the discourse between Buddhism and science.

As mentioned above, in late nineteenth- and early twentieth-century scholarship, the Buddhist critique of the idea of an independently existing mind was understood in terms of the Western philosophical tradition of idealism – the idealism both of Berkeley and of Hegel. More recently, however, especially in light of some of the contemporary work in neuroscience, cognitive science, and psychology, these critiques are being reinterpreted in terms drawn from Husserlian phenomenology. For example, the phenomenological category of intentionality, i.e., the necessary relation between subject and object (not to be confused with the common usage, meaning purposefulness), provides a way of talking about Buddhist conceptions of the relation between subject and object without falling either into idealism or into the now long-discredited introspectionism. This is a theme that B. Alan Wallace has recently developed as part of a general critique of materialism and objectivity as necessary presuppositions concerning the nature of scientific knowledge.

From the Buddhist perspective developed by Wallace, the necessarily concomitant relation between the mind and the world it apprehends addresses both naive realism and scientific realism. Naive realism is the ordinary, unreflective conception that objects exist independently of our perception or knowledge of them. Critical realism extends this to include the independent existence of unobservable, theoretical objects. In this way reflections on the nature of mind motivated by the Buddhist priorities do speak directly to the philosophical presuppositions underpinning much of contemporary science.

Phenomenology, particularly that of Maurice Merleau-Ponty, has also contributed to the interface between Buddhism and cognitive science in the work of Varela, Thompson, and Rosch. They have emphasized the importance of embodiment in any understanding of consciousness. Much contemporary discussion in cognitive science concerns the question of conscious awareness. The Buddhist view that all existing things arise as the result of certain causes and conditions is congruent with many contemporary approaches to consciousness that view consciousness as the result of complex physiological interactions arising as the human body has evolved within the natural world of which it is an integral part.

Reflections such as Wallace's on the philosophy of science explore how materialist and realist metaphysical views have come to influence our own contemporary preconceptions about the nature of science and with it the nature of nature itself. At the same time this kind of reflection has also been directed toward cultural preconceptions concerning religion and how those have influenced our apprehension of the Buddhist tradition. One of the surprising outcomes of such reflection is that positivist understandings of science and Romantic conceptions of religion, two schools of thought that, on the surface, may appear to be antithetical to one another, share much more than is usually recognized. Recently, Dale Wright has noted that the conception of unmediated experience as the ground of religion is analogous to the notion that one can get at "the facts" as irreducible items of information, or, in other words, that it is possible to allow the data to speak for itself without interpretation. In both cases the knowing subject is understood as existing separately from the object of knowledge, and the process of coming to know has little or no effect on the object known. The assumption Wright identifies as being shared by both positivism and Romanticism – that the mind exists independently of the objects of which it is aware – is fundamentally different from Buddhist conceptions of the mind and how it works, and descriptions of the path to awakening, both of which emphasize the interdependence of all existence.

Conclusion

The relation between Buddhism and the sciences has largely been overlooked in modern, Western Buddhist studies. Why is this? Perhaps one important factor in the image of Buddhism as having not been involved in scientific thought results from the background training and concurrent interests of those who study Buddhism. Neither philological nor religious studies approaches to Buddhism necessarily lend themselves to examinations of those texts and traditions that contain information about the history of Buddhism and the sciences. Moreover, the presentation of Buddhism in the West by apologists and polemicists has misrepresented the relationship of Buddhism and science. Challenged by Christian missionaries in their homelands, Buddhist advocates focused, in their interactions with Western intellectual traditions, on the most immediate kinds of questions being raised, that is, religious questions. Challenged by a Western imperialism that deployed science and technology to its own benefit, many Buddhist apologists attempted to appropriate the prestige of science in their own rhetorical claims of superiority to Christianity.

How might discourse between science and religion be reconceived to consider more adequately core Buddhist concerns, and in turn attract the interest of Buddhist scholars? In this chapter I have suggested that this reconception should include at least three steps. First, we need to clear the intellectual ground upon which discourse will be established. Much of the recent work done in the area of science and religion, because of its roots in theistic traditions, fails to address Buddhist concerns. Much popular work that has addressed the relationship between science and Asian religious traditions has misrepresented Buddhist concerns as well. Hence, the establishment of solid discourse between Buddhism and contemporary science begins with a process of defining terms, making distinctions, and finding clarification.

The second step in reconceiving dialogue to account more appropriately for Buddhist concerns involves surveying models of discourse throughout Buddhist history. In posing the question, "In what ways has Buddhism been amenable to discourse with science and technology?" this chapter has articulated a threefold typology of relations: supportive, integral, and consequential.

Finally, the third step in reconceiving dialogue involves assessing current developments in Buddhism–science scholarship. This assessment reminds us that discourse between science and Buddhism remains most true to the central concerns of Buddhism when that discourse begins with questions of epistemology and the nature of consciousness, drawing on neuroscience, the cognitive sciences, psychology, and the philosophy of mind.

As noted in the introduction, that much of the contemporary discourse on science and religion is structured according to assumptions and concerns particular to the theistic traditions generally and Christian theology specifically, is understandable. This discourse finds its origins in a theistic context. However, because the fundamental concerns of Buddhist thought differ substantially from those of Christianity and other theistic traditions, basic presuppositions about the nature of science–religion interaction need to be revisited if Buddhist scholars are to be more fully involved in the future of this discourse.

The Nature of Being Human

EDUARDO CRUZ

Is there a human nature? If so, what can be said about it?

These simple questions recur throughout human history. Indeed, these questions would seem to be inherently inexhaustible. Such is the diversity of peoples, cultures, personalities, genders, ages, and experiences, one is hard pressed to conceive of a single "nature" or "essence" that might point to the unique character of human beings. Nevertheless, throughout intellectual history, particularly that strand of intellectual history which includes Christian theological traditions, the nature of this evasive human nature has been continually pursued. That is, until of late it has been pursued. In our intellectual age, with accent upon the process, flow, plurality, and relativity of perspective, talk about "essences" seems to strikes an anachronistic cord. The questioning of human nature has been called into question.

This push toward the relative has been felt in the Latin American context. The past three decades have seen the emergence of "local theologies": liberation, black, feminist, post-colonial, and, in the wake of interreligious dialogue, "theology of religions" as well. Post-modernist trends, moreover, have emphasized new awareness of cultural context, where everything is produced by human language and action, entailing the absence of any grand narratives or of a single foundation for our knowledge. The invaluable contribution of these new trends is that they have opened our eyes to the fact that any talk about "human nature or condition" has excluded up until recently the experience, suffering, and hopes of minorities and of those who are at the margin or at the "underbelly" of society. Meanwhile, however, for good or for ill, the contextualism of local theologies has troubled the traditional anthropological task. If truth is conceived locally, then claims about the human person ought to be local in content as well. The absence of a single grand narrative is nowhere felt more strongly than in the question of what it means to be a human person.

Yet, even as theology and philosophy have reminded us of the contextual nature of claims made about the human person, the natural sciences have moved against the tides of anthropological pluralism. Though the impetus for this move is diverse, it finds perhaps its greatest force in evolutionary biology, and the behavioral disciplines developed from it. The evolutionary sciences, as pointed out by Martinez Hewlett earlier in this volume, weave all of natural history – human history with it – into a single cloth. This unified history raises the anthropological question: Does biological evolution provide a single framework within which a single human nature might be identified? While theology and philosophy are threatening to abandon the quest for a single response to the question of essential human nature, the natural sciences dare to take it up.

What are we to make of these changing and, to a great extent, conflicting shifts in the pursuit of knowledge about human nature? Is one forced to choose between theological and scientific resources when reviewing the human person? I would argue that one is not. Rather, as I will suggest throughout this chapter, at the turn of the millennium a new vision of human nature is being framed, which appears to draw on both religious and scientific resources. It is my task in this chapter to outline that vision, and to point to those theological and scientific resources that best inform and support it.

A word about this reframing: the new vision, prompted by science, but informed by religion, is characterized by what I would call *strong realism*; it takes note of, but ultimately moves away from, contextualism and relativism. Core characteristics of this vision include: the conviction that there *is* indeed a human nature; that it is a fallen nature, displaying simultaneously perfection and flaw, nobility and wretchedness; that though it is bestowed on us from the past, it awaits redemption and completion; that it can be tentatively known by the powers of human reason; and, finally, that knowledge of our biological inheritance, particularly the gene–culture interface, is utterly necessary to the task of relating the scientific idea of nature with the theological idea of creation, if we are to affirm the latter without falling into some form of nature romanticism or even fideism.

My method for unpacking this new vision will involve indicating some of the developments of theological anthropology in the Christian theological tradition, from ancient sources up to the recent impact of local theologies. Without denying the importance of the latter, contextual approaches, I will also move beyond them, suggesting that recent developments in the understanding of the biological substrate of human traits and behavior require a more unified approach to the human, one that characterizes well the grandeur and misery of this uniquely endowed species which is *Homo sapiens*. Specifically, I will focus on the development of evolutionary approaches to the origin and behavior of human beings.

This two-step examination of an emerging, scientifically informed, theological anthropology will not exhaustively review theological or scientific resources. Its more limited aim will be to compel the reader's imagination in rethinking basic assumptions about human nature.

Changing Thoughts about Human Nature in Christian Theology

Within the Judeo-Christian tradition generally, and Christian theology specifically, the task of understanding the human person is indelibly caught up in the larger task of understanding God and God's relationship to creation. Biblical scriptural resources testify to this: from the first chapter of Genesis to the last promises in Revelation, we read that humans have been created in God's "image and likeness," are cherished throughout history into the fullness of time, and finally will partake of God's companionship in everlasting bliss. Moreover, in Jesus of Nazareth, the scriptural history of God's nature and human nature coincide. While we should recognize that, until recently, when ecological concerns have come to the fore, theology has been too anthropocentric, it is undeniable that human beings have a unique place in the religions of the book. In short, theology cannot escape the task of asking anthropological questions.

Certainly the coalescing of "theological anthropology" into doctrinal discipline is a recent phenomenon in the history of theology. Theological anthropology has become systematic in its inquiry into the nature of the human person, drawing carefully from both religious and secular resources. Curiously enough, this formalization has, in large part, been the positive fruit of modernity, and the rigorous critical challenges to theological conceptions of both God's and humans' nature. Yet from its inception, Christian theology has asked basic questions about the right place of humans in nature and the basic character of our nature. The so-called Gnostic controversy in the second and third centuries illustrates the centrality of anthropology in Christian thinking. Prior to even the Christological and Trinitarian challenges, the Church Fathers fought a battle over human nature, in which they struggled to make sense of the body's meaning for human identity.[1]

This fundamental anthropological inquiry within the Christian tradition is summarized in a question raised by the biblical psalmist, "What is man, that thou are mindful of him?" (Psalm 8.4). While answers to this question of human nature have been varied if not, on some levels, conflicting, theologians, throughout the history of the tradition, have agreed on several points. Central to this convergence is the belief that there is a human nature that is bestowed on us by virtue of creation. The question of how one can recognize and understand the characteristics of that nature has, however, been disputed. Most theologians have agreed that ours is a fallen creation, that creation is corrupted on some level by human sin. The hermeneutical consequence of this fallen condition is this: given this supposed corruption, how can we *know* anything whatsoever of what human nature is, or, more importantly, what human nature is intended to be?

In response to these questions, the Reformed tradition – as we find it among Presbyterians, Baptists, and others – has stressed the role of God's revelation in this quest for human nature. What is undiscoverable by means of human reason alone, God gracefully let us know through revelation, as chronicled in scripture. This means that the content and knowledge of human nature is more adequately framed in Christological, Trinitarian, and eschatological terms. That is, what we are as humans can be understood not primarily by looking to our beginnings, but rather from God's intended ends.

The Roman Catholic tradition has placed greater emphasis on what can be learned by the proper use of human reason, in distinction from the aid of God's special revelation in Jesus Christ. Influenced by Greek philosophical thought concerning human nature, this tradition acknowledges the importance of studying the natural world – our corporate past – in learning more about ourselves. Concepts such as of *natural law* and *human nature* are less bound to strictly Christological terms, and can, in part, be derived from an inquiry about natural origins. In either case, both traditions betray an optimistic outlook with regard to the possibility of understanding human nature. In fact, these basic sets of notions, with an emphasis on our ability to know human nature, were conducive to the emergence of modern science in European nations.[2]

From the seventeenth century onwards, theologians from both Roman Catholic and Protestant traditions, to a greater or lesser extent, have been influenced by developments in secular thought. From the Enlightenment, through modernity, and into the postmodern intellectual milieu, Christian anthropology has been reshaped by non-theological sources. This influence begins with challenges to the authority of ecclesiastical sources for knowledge of the human person, illustrated by Descartes's *cogito, ergo sum*, that is, the turn to the subject as a surer foundation for knowledge, even knowledge about God. From the medieval drama of salvation, framed in a macro–microcosm typified in Dante's *Divine Comedy*, humans now operate only in one cosmos, framed to human measure, reason, and will. The sole alternative to Descartes's rationalism in the seventeenth century was British empiricism, championed by Newton's followers. What they had in common, however, was of far greater significance than what separated them: a view of the world in which a single cosmos can be accounted for by the human mind.

Contemporary theological anthropology, therefore, is, by and large, the product of dialogue between traditional theological insights and modern, secular thought. European thinkers such as Pascal, Feuerbach, and Kierkegaard helped theologians to bridge intellectual worlds. From Descartes's inheritance, this dialogue has modern philosophy as its partner; from Newton's, the partners are more on the side of the sciences (with the help of philosophy following British and Scottish empiricism). Whether explicitly acknowledging it or not, most theologians have incorporated insights from these partners in their speculations about human nature.

How has this dialogue transformed the early Christian anthropological inquiry with its emphasis on a knowable human nature and the ambiguous nature of understanding a fallen world? If we follow the trajectory of theology's dialogue with philosophy into our contemporary setting, we see the strong influence of hermeneutics (philosophy of interpretation) as theology has most often allied itself with the work of so-called postmodern philosophers. As mentioned above, these past three decades have seen the development and influence of local theologies. These theologies, with other postmodern trends, emphasize local cultural context and social location, where knowledge is the product of human communities. As a result, the quest for a universal understanding of human nature is rendered problematic. The unity of theological conversation is not found in metaphysics or metanarratives; rather human unity is affirmed by a shared sense of commitment to the well-being of all human persons.

We should remember our indebtedness to these theological shifts. These new trends argue that an evaluation of human nature or the human condition has too often excluded from consideration the experiences of the most marginalized members of society. One of the most striking accounts of this exclusion is Gustavo Gutierrez's imaginary letter to Dietrich Bonhoeffer, where he shows that our concern should not any more be directed to "modern man", but rather to the "non-person," the one who is at the margin of our concerns and of society.[3]

These new local theologies have been accompanied by ethical concerns and a strong drive for action. As such, they remind theology of its practical task of addressing suffering in the world. However, in developing the anthropological foundations for their ethical work, they have too often failed to look to the insights of that second trajectory of dialogue mentioned: dialogue with the natural sciences. Indeed, while these new approaches often look to the social sciences and cultural studies, they rarely engage the insights of such disciplines as cosmology, evolutionary biology, or the neurosciences. As a result, these strands of theological discourse insulate themselves from contemporary insights into the nature of the human person. Insights from the natural sciences seem to temper contextual approaches, encouraging theology to move back toward a more universal description of the human person.[4]

Evolutionary Insights in the Understanding of Human Nature

At the very outset of any anthropological inquiry, we should recognize that many contemporary scientific advances are relevant to a new understanding of the human person (e.g., evolutionary biology, neuroscience, artificial intelligence). As such, many advances are not addressed in this chapter; such is the result of the scope of issues raised by them. Given the limitations, I will focus on the anthropological centerpiece: evolutionary biology and its social interpretations. Evolutionary biology, perhaps more than any other dimension of the natural sciences, has reshaped our understanding of the human place in the non-human natural world. This reshaping raises new questions about human meaning, reappraising the moral status of human behavior.

Since the publication Charles Darwin's *Descent of Man* (1871) scientists have been trying to explain human traits and behavior in evolutionary terms. These efforts are exemplified by work in the 1960s that used Neo-Darwinian evolutionary assumptions to develop a theoretical framework to account for traits specific to cooperative behavior. This framework was characterized by the works of William Hamilton and George Williams, who developed concepts such as "kin altruism" and "inclusive fitness"[5] and "reciprocal altruism."[6] This work, in turn, laid the foundations for the rise of contemporary disciplines such as *sociobiology* and *evolutionary psychology*, which

employ evolutionary insights to achieve a more scientifically informed interpretation of the social behavior of humans and non-
human animals.[7] Though the relative scientific success of these
disciplines is still debated, they exemplify the way in which evolutionary biology pushes anthropological inquiry. If, in fact, the history
of human life is fully integrated into the broader history of nature, we
are compelled to ask whether or not the mechanisms driving that
broader history are adequate to the task of defining human nature. In
other words, does a shared evolutionary framework provide illumi-
nation adequate to the task of identifying a shared human nature?

Regardless of how one feels about the scientific achievement of
these new evolutionary interpretations, they forcefully represent a
significant shift in our thinking about the human person. These applications of the evolutionary framework are mapping the territory for
much future talk about a universal human nature manifest in amaz-
ing plasticity.

This amounts to mixed news for traditional anthropology. On the
one hand the news looks bad: these new disciplines more often stress
the continuity than the discontinuity of humans from the rest of the
animal kingdom, a stress that is noticeably absent from much traditional anthropological work as well as local theologies. On the other
hand, the news looks good: these disciplines also stress the relative
uniformity of the human genome, consequently suggesting that there
may be something of a common basis on which cultural and other
apparent human differences are constructed. The influence of this
evolutionary approach has been felt in areas which, until recently,
may have been considered the exclusive domain of the humanities.
Work such as Jared Diamond's acclaimed *Guns, Germs and Steel*,[8] in
which large selections of human history and anthropology are reinterpreted in terms of a natural history of expansion and conquest,
seem to both bridge and blur the line between the humanities –
including theology – and science.

New Books Theologians Should Read

A summary of recent advances in these new fields of inquiry is
beyond the scope of this chapter. However, dozens of new books are
being brought into the intellectual marketplace, each one making the
claim of being the best synthesis on the subject. These attempts to use
evolutionary insight to interpret human behavior are relatively new.
Despite the plurality of voices engaged in asking these questions, a
synthetic, agreed-upon canon of thought is lacking. This lack of

synthesis does not diminish the importance of these new disciplines for our understanding of anthropology.

Because of this, it is, perhaps, valuable to single out one issue that seems to resonate throughout this body of new work and examine its relevance for a theological anthropology. Much like early Christian theology, most of this work seems to agree that there is, at least in theory, an identifiable human nature. This agreement results in what I would call the *ontologization* of scientific concepts of human nature. That is, these interpretations of human behavior through the lens of evolutionary biology may allow for scientific insight to function philosophically as an ontology of *human nature*, a scientifically informed peek into the "essence" of humanity.

Science has a long tradition of framing its concepts in empirically based terms. However, many interpreters of evolutionary biology tend to use evolutionary concepts in a way that is closer to a common-sense usage, even giving scientific terms a metaphysical ring. This foray into non-scientific language raises protests from colleagues and critics alike. Take use of the term *human nature* as an example. David Hull, a renowned philosopher of biology, has shown in his *Metaphysics of Evolution*[9] how this concept is used and misused in ways that blur the distinction between science and metaphysics. There are those, however, who think that this concept can be defined in a way that is strictly scientific. Several of the essayists who contributed to Laura Betzig's volume *Human Nature*[10] seem to hold this position. For example, William Hamilton, in his advance praise of the book, has the following to say:

> The *tabula* of human nature was never *rasa* and it is now being read. The inscription found is no dogma or world system and it bids to build no empire whose later painful collapse will sweep it away. Darwinist and self-critical, data-based from pole to tropic and from gamete to despot, the text is the science of a young and growing army.[11]

Tabula rasa here refers to the notion held by some eighteenth-century thinkers that humans, in their personality and behavior, are defined not by a human "nature," but only by the nurturing influences of their environment (i.e., culture). Hence, when it comes to answering anthropological questions, one does not need to look to anything intrinsic in the make-up of the human person, but rather, to the extrinsic environment in which that person moves. "Dogma" here refers to religious conceptions of the humans, and "world system" to either metaphysical or ideological ones. Hence, Williams is implying that science can now give us answers to questions of human nature that neither the philosophers nor the theologians could provide. While Williams's positivistic frame of mind may not be all that fashionable today, it still works as an influencing presupposition for many interpreters of evolutionary biology, even those who are religious. Science, according to this frame of mind, holds the keys which will unlock the mysteries of human nature.

The frame of mind represented by Williams's quote, however, represents something of an ironic turn, from the scientific back to the metaphysical and religious. Laura Betzig evidences this turn, from the very beginning of her argument: "It's happened. We have finally figured out where we came from, why we're here, and who we are."[12] In other words, those questions that religion and philosophy have been raising for millennia, with less than satisfactory answers, are, in her mind, finally being resolved in a more credible manner by the new science of human evolution.

Edward O. Wilson, the famous entomologist from Harvard, reveals a similar conviction in his acclaimed book *Consilience*:

> Still, I had no desire to purge religious feelings. They were bred in me; they suffused the wellsprings of my creative life. I also retained a small measure of common sense. To wit, people must belong to a tribe; they yearn to have a purpose larger than themselves. We are obliged by the deepest drives of the human spirit to make ourselves more than animated dust, and we must have a story to tell about where we came from, and why we are here. Could Holy Writ be just the first literate attempt to explain the universe and make ourselves significant within it? Perhaps science is a continuation on new and better-tested ground to attain the same end. If so, then in that sense science is religion liberated and writ large.[13]

Wilson makes it clear: when it comes to asking and answering questions pertaining to religion and human nature, he wants to be on the empirical side of the intellectual ledger (see chapter 11 of the same book, *Consilience*). Yet, he sees science as a new religion (an expansionist trait noted by his friends and foes alike[14]), stressing the need for a new human story. According to Wilson, humans are storytellers, and this has been one of the major functions of religion for millennia. Despite Wilson's reductionistic account of religion, there is here at least an implicit admission that one cannot treat science as a replacement for religion without science having to borrow some of the traits and functions (positive or negative) of religion. Most of Wilson's sociobiological colleagues would disagree with his sentiment; they do not want to take science as a new religion. We can point out, however, that convictions and preferences notwithstanding, the broader one's interpretation of human history and meaning is, the more likely it is that that interpretation will take on metaphysical overtones.

Despite confused efforts to provide a more or less technical rendering of the term *human nature* in the work of these evolutionary interpreters, a consistent dimension of the treatment of that term appears: its uniqueness. These fields are new. The agreed-upon list of universal and uniquely human characteristics is short. But an important point can be driven home: these thinkers speak of human nature in a way that allows for engagement with and assessment of traditional religious and metaphysical assertions.[15]

Two modest conclusions should be drawn at this point. First, despite the fact that work in interpreting human behavior through the lens of evolutionary biology and sociobiology is still new, and often as much philosophical as scientific, it represents a clear shift in thinking about the nature of the human person. The insights of evolutionary theory represent a counter-current to the relativistic tendencies of much postmodern philosophical and theological thought. Evolutionary theory offers us a single framework, with a limited set of interpretive tools, for understanding the human person. This single framework is producing fruit at an incredible rate; science is providing insights for revisiting the question of human nature. Second, though work in new evolutionary disciplines such as sociobiology and evolutionary psychology varies, painting an inconsistent picture of the human person, this work attempts to describe human nature in universal language. This attempt is not unlike the attempts made throughout the history of Christian thought. In short, the presumption of an identifiable human nature, even essence, is alive and well. Moreover, it is influencing the way in which science contributes to anthropology. Theology would do well to pay attention.

A word should be said here about the content of *human nature* as it is being pursued by sociobiologists and others using the insights of evolutionary biology to interpret human behavior. One can legitimately ask: Despite a similar use of the term human nature, is the resulting picture of the human person as given by these new disciplines altogether different from traditional insights? If so, is their work, despite its philosophical consonance with traditional theological inquiry, ultimately unhelpful, even harmful to the theological task? Certainly any philosophically reductionist reading of evolutionary history precludes any fruitful relationship between the work of these new disciplines and theology. If science is the only reliable means of understanding the human person, then the insights of theology are at best superfluous, at worst misleading. But one is not forced to accept reductionism in this way. In turn, one can indeed find points of consonance between the work of scholars interpreting evolutionary theory and theological anthropology. Indeed, these points of consonance represent what I referred to as the "new vision at the turn of the millennium" in the introduction.

Both of what one might think of as the positive and negative traits of human nature seem to converge in the theological and evolutionary readings of the human person. As Charles Harper has put it, "human 'fallenness,' freedom and pain are the preserve of both arenas."[16] While interpreters of science may never in their work refer to "the fall," many of the characteristics of human nature implied by that theological term seem to be shared by those interpreters. Human life is ambiguous. It is marked by significant moral achievement as well as significant more failure.

Note that the claims here are limited. Theology and interpretations of evolutionary biology do not provide one with a single picture of the human person. Rather, we should note that, given the presumption of a shared human nature, convergence around a workable picture of human nature cannot be ruled out. This possibility of convergence suggests that the difficult and tentative task of building bridges between scientific and theological understandings of the human person may by both possible and fruitful.

Conclusion

It is ironic that while philosophical and theological anthropology have been struggling to free themselves from the intellectual currents of a universal, abstract approach to the question of human nature, new developments stemming from the biological sciences have started to move precisely in the opposite direction. Philosophical and theological movement away from universal characterizations of human nature have, in part, been the result of new ethical movements seeking full recognition of the diversity of human experience. Moreover, these new trends in theological anthropology have taught us that the Western cultural and intellectual experience is not an adequate model of humanity for everyone else; the marginalized have much to teach us about our own humanity.

However, despite its ethical heart, the move toward contextualism and relativism has often left us ill-equipped to achieve the very ethical task that it calls us to. A pluralistic anthropology appears to be unable to address dramatic political conflict, concrete instances of bigotry, economic and military dominance, intolerance and prejudice, and the banal reality of violence around the world. While pluralism in anthropology has provided useful tools for dealing with post-modernism, it does not seem to provide an alternative, politically effective, constructive vision of the human person. A strong realism about human nature seems to be required, one that engages contemporary thought earnestly and honestly. On the one hand, advances in evolutionary theory allow us to say that the use of our freedom, language, and symbols do help to change and configure our nature. On the other hand, they warn us not to be too optimistic about the outcome of our conscious will, bound as it is to all sorts of constraints resulting from a haphazard evolutionary history. Curiously enough, long-standing traditions in Christianity offer a similar warning about the human condition, although framing it in terms of creatureliness, image and likeness, finiteness, and fallenness. Human nature is marked by a capacity for violence and destructiveness as well as a capacity for justice and creativity. A realistic appraisal of human history through the eyes both of evolutionary theory and of the Christian theological tradition seems to confirm this ambiguity. Perhaps this realism will more adequately equip us for the task of seeking justice in an unjust world.

To speak again of a human nature and condition, following the tracks of provisional but sound depictions of our humanity coming from interpretations of science based on a Neo-Darwinian evolutionary framework, is a salutary reminder that our hopes for human equality cannot be expected solely from a change of attitudes and habits. We have to cope with a stubborn, opportunistic, egocentric, and self-deceiving human nature. Yet it is this very "earthen vessel," our evolutionary-entrenched humanity, which carries the treasures of God's grace as we seek to unite what is divided and heal what has been wounded.

Traditional Hinduism and Modern Science

VARADARAJA V. RAMAN

I am, by training and in intellectual outlook, a physicist first, a scientist more generally. I regard the physical world as governed by inexorable laws and principles, extensively explorable through ingenious instruments, and analyzable with the aid of concepts and mathematics.

I am also a Hindu by upbringing. I have been initiated into the symbols and sacraments of this ancient religion, I have rejoiced in its feasts and festivities, I have grown sensitive to its traditions, and I am imbued with its lore and literature.

My intellectual horizons have been considerably expanded by my study of science, my outlook refined, and my perceptions of the world enhanced. The spiritual dimension of my existence, my attitude to life and love, my respect for traditions, and my reverence for creatures have all been sharpened considerably by my religious background.

I have, of course, experienced moments of dissonance between what I have been told in my religion and what I have understood from my studies of science. Like my colleagues belonging to other religious traditions, I have difficulty reconciling certain Hindu worldviews with the results of modern science. Nor do I have any sympathy with some of the beliefs and behavior of some of my co-religionists, much less with some of the social customs that have for long been associated with Hindu society.

From what I know of other religions and about other scientists, my experience of living life as a religious practitioner and as a scientist is not unique. In this dual context, some have abandoned their religious affiliation and repudiated *in toto* their religious roots. Others have sought refuge or found satisfaction in other religions. In so far as this gives them fulfillment, I understand and respect such decisions.

In the chapter that follows I will report both dissonance and consonance between modern science and traditional Hindu belief. In some instances, Hindu reflections on reality, particularly the Hindu view of nature, "anticipated" our modern scientific knowledge; in other instances, what modern science says contradicts what traditional religion-based views affirm. I find myself living in both worlds.

Cosmogenesis and Hinduism

Over the ages, the human spirit has pondered the question of cosmogenesis. When the religions of the human family gradually gained sway, their respective narratives of the Beginning became embedded in the cultures. These were slowly frozen in the collective psyches of peoples. The inquiries of modern science began to articulate views on cosmogenesis which seem to be different from ancient ones in at least two important respects. First, they arose from data amassed by empirical studies of the world. Second, unlike religious views, they regarded human beings as only incidental phenomena in the story of the universe. Yet, ironically, new scientific cosmologies sometimes extend and expand on ancient visions.

In the Hindu world, there is a famous Hymn of Creation in the First Book of the *Rig Veda*, which is the primary scripture in the tradition. This hymn is reflective and imaginative. It is also modest in affirmation, for, after declaring how the world came to be, the seer concludes with two stanzas which reflect a sophisticated skepticism:

> Who really knows, and who can swear,
> How creation arose, when or where!
> Even gods came after creation's day,
> Who really knows, who can truly say
>
> When and how did creation start?
> Did He do it? Or did He not?
> Only He up there knows, maybe;
> Or perhaps, not even He.

According to current scientific thinking, the universe arose as a result of something called symmetry-breaking: this is a technical and mathematical concept. In any case, the result of whatever triggered the Big Bang birth of the universe was that in an inconceivably small time-interval vast amounts of fundamental entities were spewed. Prior to emergence of the universe, there was nothing.

Here, it is interesting to recall that the Rig Vedic hymn on creation begins with the following verses:

Not even nothing existed then
No air yet, and no heaven.
Who encased and kept it where?
Was water in the darkness there?

Neither deathlessness nor decay
No, nor the rhythm of night and day:
The self-existent, with breath *sans* air:
That, and that alone was there.

For some years during the twentieth century, there were two competing theories to account for the world. According to one, the universe has always existed, without a beginning. This was known as
the Steady State model. It encountered some difficulties in the context
of an expanding universe in which the galaxies are moving farther
and farther away from one another. This galactic recession and other
matters are explained more successfully by what is known as the Big
Bang model according to which the universe did have a beginning in
space and time.

In a way, the Hindu view might imply a synthesis of the two. On
the one hand, it looks upon the world as having existed forever. On
the other hand, the universe is said to have a finite life-span. This is
possible because the universe is believed to be in one of its never-
ending transformations. In other words, our present universe did
have a starting point, but it has had countless previous births and
deaths. This is very much like the oscillating universe model in which
the world expands and contracts and bursts forth again, repeating the
process indefinitely. One of the merits of the oscillating universe
model is that it solves the problem of the origin of time. Time has
always been there, and it will always be.

Eschatology

One might ask: What is going to become of this world in which we
live, of our planet and sun, of stars and galaxies, indeed of the
universe in the very long run? What will become of man and microbe,
of bird and insect, in the end? What will happen to the physical world
eventually? Let us look into ancient Hindu visions on these eschatological questions.

Traditional Hindu belief is that there are four *yugas*: long and
unequal time periods. We are currently in the fourth one, and it is
called the *Kali Yuga*. It is said to have begun some five thousand years

ago, and is expected to last for a total of 432,000 years. The preceding *Dvâpara Yuga* lasted for twice as long: 864,000 years, whereas the one before that, called *Treta Yuga*, lingered on for 1,296,000 years. *Krita Yuga*, the very first *yuga*, had a span of 1,728,000 years.

The total period of time forming all the four *yugas* adds up to 4,320,000 years. This constitutes what is known as a *Mahâyuga* or Great Yuga. A thousand *Mahâyugas* make up an *Ardhakalpa* or a half day in the life of the cosmic Creator. Thus, a full day or *kalpa* for the Creator is 8.64 billion years.

Beyond all mythologies and mathematics, beyond all the poetry of physics and the tales of tradition, *Brahma* stands in the Hindu vision for the supreme abstraction of the unfathomable mystery of creation from which springs periodically the magnificent universe.

At the conclusion of the Brahmic day, there is a *laya* or dissolution. At this time, the whole universe is absorbed in the mind of *Brahma*, after which there is another *shrishti* or creation, followed by the long phase of *sthiti* or preservation which will last a *kalpa* before the next laya occurs. It may be recalled that it was only in the latter half of the nineteenth century that modern science even pictured such a physical end of our world. The idea, referred to as the heat-death of the universe, was proposed by Rudolph Clausius.

In Hindu mythopoesy, there is the abstract principle that brings to naught all that has emerged. Not just the short-lived bloom of a rose and the steady heartbeat of a healthy human, but everything ultimately comes to a total terminus. From the frail whisper of the gentle breeze to the sturdiest of rocks, from the mute interactions of leptons and hadrons to the seemingly endless existence of spectacular galaxies, everything is destined ultimately to vanish. What causes this ultimate dissolution is a mystery that the Hindu world represents as *Shiva*. *Shiva* is the dot that completes every sentence of existence, the last breath that lulls the lungs, the invisible rope that closes the curtain at the end of the cosmic show, the ultimate sigh of the grand universe itself, the final puff of the physical world. *Shiva* is the mythic symbol of what in thermodynamics is called the heat-death.

Biogenesis and Evolution

Another important question tackled by religions as well as by science relates to the origin of life: the problem of biogenesis. In the Vedas, the Creator is referred to as *Prajâpati*: Lord of the People. He is said to have created the three primordial gods: *Agni*, *Vâyu*, and *Sûrya*, and placed them in the three worlds. These names stand for Fire, Air, and

Sun. Then there were the principles of Sky and Water too. In the Book of Genesis there is a cosmic framework prior to the creation of humanity, in which Light is primary as also the sun and the stars. In Vedic imagery one detects the relevance of the sun and air and water for the emergence of life.

Beyond this, there is in the Hindu world a series of mythological accounts which speak of the divine as having come down to earth in different forms. These are known as *avatâras*: divine descents to the world. Divinity first came as Fish, then as Unicorn and next as Turtle. These were followed in the aspect of Boar, followed by manifestations that were Man-Lion and Dwarf. Finally, the divine came in full human form: appearing as the One with an Axe, then as an Embodiment of Righteousness, and finally as Wisdom Supreme. According to the tradition, a tenth *avatâra* is yet to come.

Tales of fantasy and lofty epics are associated with the various *avatâras*, and these have become intrinsic parts of the lore and legend of the Hindu world. Like any other child of Hinduism I grew up listening to the epics and mythologies that narrate these incarnations of the divine: some strange, some eerie, some grand and glorious. It is remarkable that these narratives have uncanny parallel with our current views on biological evolution, and they transcend the current scientific picture. We see in this enumeration, not just humanity but all life as a manifestation of the divine (*imago dei*). And it speaks of a gradual development of humanity from the purely aquatic to a beast state, from a small creature to a magnificent one.

I may mention in passing that one is tempted to interpret the ten *avatâras* as a propaedeutic to Darwinian evolution. Perhaps we need to be careful here. It is true that we see here, as in some other ancient thinkers, glimmers of the profound insight that various organisms are at different *levels* of sophistication in their characteristics, but from this to conclude that they are in different *stages* of an *evolutionary process* is a huge leap. One requires considerable observational studies before making that assertion.

Science unraveled the emergence of life from the oceans of the world, and its gradual transformation from beast to conscious humanity. The *avatâra* stories reflect not only biological, but also cultural evolution. Humans have been evolving from wielders of brute force, symbolized by the axe, to proponents of moral principles, and ultimately to agents of deeper truths about the world. As to the *avatâra* yet to come, it may be taken to mean that no-one can say that this is all there is: for no-one can foresee what the future holds.

I have come to see in the mythologies of bygone days much

meaning in the context of both biological and cultural evolution. In this sense, they have for me relevance in the context of modern science.

Genetics and Hinduism

Modern biology traces many human characteristics to genes. Knowledge of the structure and complexity of genes has grown considerably in recent decades. While genetics explains many human traits, we are still intrigued by why one individual is endowed with genes that make that person chronically sick, while another has genes which provide the basis for becoming an athlete of Olympic caliber. Science simply says the genetic gift arose from a play of chance: a particular sperm breaks into a particular ovum, and all is ready for the inherited strengths and weaknesses.

But we crave for clearer answers to the question of the uneven, often unfair, distribution of fate and fortune. Here the Hindu view presents a picture that has provided answers as satisfying as any. This is the *law of karma*: all our experiences, whether from genes, material gifts, good education, or whatever, come from actions that we once did, in this or in a previous life. Our current actions are consequential too: they will also bear fruits of one kind or another, in this life or in a future one.

The combination of the law of *karma* and the theory of reincarnation are intrinsic to the Hindu framework. This synthesis includes the principle of both fatalism and free will. It says that what has happened was inevitable, for its seeds had been sown before, and also that what is to happen can still be fashioned by what we do and how we behave in our current life. Furthermore, it does not point the finger at a merciless God when we suffer pain, but reminds us we alone are responsible for the good we get and for the bad we go through. Rather than genetic chance, the Hindu believes our identity and destiny are determined by law, the law of *karma*.

Scientific Objectivity in the Hindu framework

The concern of science is with *objectivity*. That is to say, science is concerned with describing as thoroughly as possible and explaining as coherently as possible all observed phenomena, without any reference to human presence in the world. In other words, science seeks to know how the world would function whether or not the human mind happens to be in it.

This key idea was expressed in the seventeenth century by René

Descartes by saying that there is *res extensa* or an extended thing, i.e., the external objective world; and *res cogitans* or a thinking thing, i.e., the human mind. Many centuries earlier, Hindu philosophers had propounded a similar dichotomy between *prakriti* or mindless nature and *purusha* or the experiencing principle. One way of picturing this model is as follows:

From abstract *Brahman* emerged *purusha*, which is the experiencing principle, and *prakriti*, or the world of matter-energy. From *prakriti* was formed both the animate and the inanimate components of the world, both of which contribute to the phenomenal world. Minds developed in some of the animate components: these are the ones with *jîvâtmans* (individual souls). They are the individual *experiencers*. The *jîvâtman* is no more than a spark of the *purusha*. The efforts of *jîvâtmans* to connect with the *purusha* and *Brahman* constitute the religious quest. Their attempts to grasp the phenomenal manifestations of *prakriti* constitute the scientific quest.

The demand for complete objectivity may be looked upon as science's attempt to picture *prakriti* without a *jîvâtman* (*purusha*).

A little reflection will reveal that such a goal cannot be attained even in principle. This is because science is hinged to concepts which are products of the human mind. Scientific theses demand certain universality of appeal based on appropriate experimentation and logical modes. By scientific objectivity one means that scientific descriptions ought to be independent of the *specific* minds which articulate and accept them. *Scientific objectivity thus becomes essentially collective subjectivity.*

Furthermore, quantum physics has brought out the intrinsic inseparability of subject and object, between the observed and the observer. At our everyday level of common experience, a clear bifurcation between subject and object is possible, and is necessary for a rational description of the world. At the microcosmic level, however, such a distinction becomes impossible in practice, and also conceptually untenable.

The interconnectedness between the conscious mind and the external world makes objectivity very difficult. It forces us to look upon physical reality as being ultimately a single unified whole. Indeed, we find that the separateness which we observe and experience depends on the level at which we function. Exploring the world at a different level of experience, the wholeness becomes clearer.

From the Hindu perspective, the substratum of physical reality may be grasped analytically via the scientific mode, with the help of concepts, mathematics, and instruments, leading to quantitative and exploitable results. But it can also be apprehended through the mystical mode via meditation, prayer, or yogic exercises. This would lead one to intensely personal and profound experiences.

In this context it may be pointed out that a number of practicing scientists, active physicists who have contributed to the development of quantum physics, have stated that aspects of our discoveries in the microcosm resonate with some ancient Hindu spiritual insights. On the other hand, other physicists have seen modern scientific insights in some of the religious insights of other religious traditions also.

Building Bridges

It should be mentioned that in the framework of *traditional* Hinduism, science and spirituality are quests for very different aspects of reality. In classical India, scientific investigators went about their business, producing practical technology, observing and calculating stellar configurations, predicting eclipses, creating mathematics, and even speculating on the nature of matter. The true spiritual seekers would have nothing of all this. These were the saints and the sages of the culture to whom the populace came, not to learn about physics or biology or cosmology, but to show their reverence for sainthood and to derive some mystical experience.

Since the advent of modern science in India, many historical forces have come into play, largely due to European intrusions and influences. One result of this is that Hindu thinkers have also adopted the apologetic approach of Western theology. Their goal is to reason out and elucidate religious doctrines, often to defend them against the iconoclastic onslaughts of modern science. Many now believe a bridge needs to be built between science and sainthood. Thus, in the Hindu tradition, as in the Judeo-Christian, efforts have been made to establish that the ancient Hindu spiritual visions are in perfect harmony with the latest findings of quantum physics and Big Bang cosmology. Such efforts are interesting at the analytical and academic levels, but in the actual practice of faith, many people such as myself, find them quite unnecessary, and sometimes even awkward.

Consciousness and Hinduism

Let me now turn to the vision of the Hindu world on the topic of consciousness: the mystery of mysteries. This is a subtle splendor that lights up the cold expanse of silent space. All the brightness or beauty, the grandeur and majesty of the universe are reflected only in the human spirit. There would be no equations for elliptical orbits, no reckoning of space or time if there was only mute matter and no measuring mind in the cosmos.

Modern science is still grappling with this fascinating phenomenon in the universe. We are probing into neurons and quantum processes, we analyze dreams and waking states, we construct robots and artificial intelligence, and hope some day to unravel what makes each of us not only self-aware but also unique.

The Hindu world has explored this too, not with the tools of modern science or in its framework, but through meditation, yoga, and other spiritual modes. They formulated elaborate theories of the origin and nature of the conscious self. In broad and current terminology, I would present it in the following terms:

The human being, as a biological entity, is a negligible entity, confined to a planetary speck in the vast stretches of the cosmos. To all appearances, this minuscule bundle of mind and matter emerged barely a few million years ago, largely as a result of physico-chemical laws, acting in harmony and at random too. If the phenomenon of life can be tracked down to molecular bonding, no calculation could have predicted the countless chance factors that brought them into play.

The human being is much more than a biological entity. There is in each of us the magic of thought and feeling, the glory of art and music, the excitement of love and the ennobling of ideals. There is also the penetrating power of the mind that can fathom the ultimate nature of the complex world, reach the very ends of the universe, and mathematize the microcosm.

This capacity for awareness and experience, for logical analysis and joyful interaction, constitutes the intangible component in the fleeting persistence of *Homo sapiens*. This is the essence of what we call the human spirit. Just as there is more to a flower than soil and tree-branch, the spirit is more than neural network, heartbeat, and vital breath, though these are what create and sustain it here below.

If there is splendor in the perceived world and pattern in its functioning, and if it can all result in the grand experiences of life and thought, then even prior to the advent of humans, there must have been a *purusha* of a vastly superior order, an Experiencer who spanned the cosmic range in space and time. This is the undergirding cosmic principle, the *Brahman* in Hindu vision. Just as the expanse of water in the seas is scattered all over land in ponds and lakes and rivers and bottles, all-embracing *Brahman* finds expression in countless life forms. We are miniature lights, one and all. We have emanated from that primordial effulgence, like photons from a glorious galactic core, destined for the terrestrial experience for a brief span on the eternal time-line, only to re-merge with that from which we sprang.

Is this poetic imagery, scientific hypothesis, or perhaps the ultimate truth? I do not know for certain. But if it is poetry, let us remember that poetry and prayer are for the human spirit what the telescope and the microscope are for human eyes. Lenses enable us to discern entities beyond our normal recognition, and profound poetry is a response of the spirit to that which is not fathomed through logic and reason. Poetry brings home to us, indeed it forces us to reckon with, the world of experience, not in terms of sense data and charts and proofs, but in subtle and holistic ways. It reveals meaning and majesty in the universe, which lie in a realm beyond the plane of rigid rationality. Poetry is mystic experience verbalized.

The Hindu spiritual vision paints individual consciousness on a cosmic canvas. It recognizes the transience of us all as separate entities, yet incorporates us into the infinity that encompasses us. It does not rule out the possibility of other manifestations of *Brahman*, sublime and subtle, carbon or silicon-based, elsewhere amidst the stellar billions. It recognizes the role of matter, and the limits of the mind, but sees subtle spirit at the core of it all. It does not speak of rewards and punishments in anthropocentric terms, nor of a He-God communicating in local languages. Yet, it regards the religious expressions of humanity as echoes of the Universal Spirit, even as volcanic outbursts reveal submerged forces of far greater magnitude.

Being Hindu in a Scientific Context

The passionate skeptic Bertrand Russell once wrote a book to explain why he was not a Christian. Others too have rejected their religions for various reasons. But there are also scientists, Christian, Jewish, Muslim, and others, who are deeply religious. Being religious and being scientific have little to do with each other. Yet, many people think that there is something dissonant in such harmony.

An atheist friend once asked me how, as a physicist, I could call myself a Hindu. I regard this as a legitimate question in that there are aspects in the worldview of scriptural Hinduism which drastically diverge from current scientific pictures. There are practices in the Hindu world – such as casteism and untouchability, endogamy and astrology – with which I have but little sympathy. Furthermore, I do not find it convincing at all to ascribe historical validity to the epics and mythologies of my tradition, the way many – including some scholars – do.

But I find in the epics and the legends much magnificent poetry. There is meaningful symbolism here, as also ideals and directives for a moral life: adherence to truth, commitment to family, discharge of responsibility to society, respect for elders, humility in the face of unfathomable mystery, and the like. There is much art and music in the culture, and beauty in the rites and rituals of the tradition: all these have enriched my life considerably.

Moreover, I cannot give up my religion because it is part of the very basis of my being. The fundamental elements that constitute me as a cultural entity are derived from the Hindu tradition. I was initiated into the sounds and symbols of the religion from my cradle days, by mother and father, siblings and teachers. Much of what I absorbed in this matter have their origins in distant times, shrouded in the mystery of antiquity. I resonate with the mantras of Hinduism, I feel its spirit is in my deepest core, there is something Hindu that courses through my veins.

Finally, even though there are respectable religious leaders who tell their followers what is right belief and what is not, and religious fundamentalists who dictate what it is that entitles one to be called a Hindu, there is no institutional authority in the Hindu world who can enforce his or her directives on me as a Hindu, nor anyone who can excommunicate or ostracize me or call me an apostate for my views and beliefs. It is this religious freedom, as well as tolerance, indeed respect for other faiths, that keeps me anchored to my religious tradition.

12

Cosmology, Evolution, and Biotechnology

GEORGE L. MURPHY

From earliest times, religious traditions have provided human beings with ways of understanding the world and their place in it. Buddhism, Christianity, Taoism, Islam, the Hindu and Confucian traditions, and other faiths have attempted to make it possible for a person to relate his or her life to what is most fundamental about reality.

Over the past four hundred years, however, the emergence of a modern science, with its success in understanding, predicting, and controlling the natural world (particularly through the technologies developed with it), has presented serious challenges to traditional religious and cultural beliefs around the globe. It would be inaccurate to represent the relationship between science and religion as one of unremitting conflict. However, it is true that many people perceive an ongoing war between them. Accompanying this misconception is the widespread belief that religion has been on the losing side of that war.

Popular perceptions, right or wrong, should be taken seriously. It is important to consider the reasons why so many people think that religion, and its explanations of the world, have been made obsolete by scientific and technological advances. This consideration begins by asking the question: In what ways have science and technology challenged traditional beliefs? The single most forceful challenge posed by the rise of modern science, perhaps, is the constriction of human understanding to the mundane reality, excluding ultimate reality.

This constriction proliferates into many challenges. Here in this chapter we will look at three of the most vexing of these: first, the modern scientific understanding of nature seems to render religious explanations superfluous; second, the long evolutionary history of bio-organisms seems to involve suffering and species extinction to such a degree that it threatens the notion of a loving creator God; and third, the growing capacity to alter human nature through genetic technology prompts a religious reassessment of what it means to be human and the need for constructing a viable ethic in response to biotechnological advances.

Among the possible religious responses to these challenges, I lift up one theme within Christianity, namely, the theology of the cross. The cross of Jesus Christ provides a lens through which people of faith can view the course of nature, seeing the presence of God in suffering and the promise of new creation.

Natural Law and Religious Explanation

The first challenge to religion has resulted from the success of science in explaining features of the natural world formerly explained by reference to divine action or other religious causes. The motions of the heavenly bodies, the weather, the development of various kinds of living things, and diseases and their cures are just a few of the phenomena that can be explained in terms of natural processes. Physics describes accurately the structure of the atom and the motions of the planets, and antibiotics seem to be much more effective than prayer rituals in stopping the spread of infections. The regularity of natural processes, and subsequently our ability to predict and control them, makes it difficult to believe that any deity is intervening in the processes that determine the functions of the world.

Because science has been so successful in its explanations, it is natural to ask why we would need to talk about *God* acting in the world at all. (I use the word "God" here for simplicity, although some religions would speak of a variety of divine beings or use other concepts and language to speak about what they understand as ultimate reality.) We do not need religious explanations in order to understand the growth of crops or the conception of children, or other natural phenomena that used to be attributed to God's action. Certainly not everything has been explained by science and perhaps our scientific knowledge never will be complete. It is unsatisfactory, however, for both science and for religion, to use the concept of God merely to explain things we do not yet understand scientifically.

The first challenge science raises for religion can be summarized in this question: With the successes of scientific explanation, why do we still need belief in divine action in the world? Interestingly, this question first appears as a result of the work of Isaac Newton, a man for whom science and religion were intimately and harmoniously related.

A Mechanical Universe

The motions of the heavenly bodies gave humanity some of its first clues to the fact that the world displays law-like regularities. Nicholaus Copernicus developed a model, made more accurate by Johannes Kepler, of the way the moon and planets move. The planets travel with varying speeds around the sun on elliptical orbits, as do satellites around planets. But why do they move in that way? The path to real understanding begins in our local neighborhood of space and time, and the knowledge gained there is gradually extrapolated to larger regions.

Newton, like others in the 1660s, was pondering this question. Just how he came to his insight is uncertain, but the idea occurred to him that the familiar force that causes objects to fall to the ground is the force that keeps the moon in its orbit. Calculations showed that for this to be the case, the force the earth exerts on any object must be inversely proportional to the square of its distance from the earth's center. Newton's law of gravitation is that every body in the universe attracts every other body with a force that is inversely proportional to the square of the distance between them, and proportional to the mass, or amount of matter, of each body.

Building on the work of Galileo Galilei and others, Newton stated mathematical laws that describe how a body of a given mass moves when forces act on it. It was then possible to describe and predict many phenomena on the earth and throughout the solar system. These laws were the result of observing and theorizing about simple phenomena, but they have very broad implications.

One issue is raised by the first law of motion, Galileo's principle of inertia: A body at rest remains at rest, and one moving with uniform velocity continues in that way, unless a force acts upon it. This contradicts Aristotle's idea that force is needed to *keep* a body moving, and that it will come to a stop if no force acts, the idea behind Thomas Aquinas's "unmoved mover" argument for the existence of God. Thus the principle of inertia raised questions about a need for some God to keep the world functioning, the first of the problems we discussed in our opening section.

Newton stated his laws in terms of the position and momentum (mass multiplied by velocity) of each body in a system. If we know these quantities at a given instant, and the forces that are acting, these laws make it possible in principle to calculate how the state of the system will develop in the future. It seemed as though the whole future development of the universe would be determined by its present state.

This led to a view of the universe as a huge machine that could run indefinitely in a predictable fashion. One might believe in a God who made the machine and started it going, but from then on the course of affairs would have been set. It was natural to ask what point there was in praying for rain if the earth's atmosphere simply evolves from its initial state in accord with the laws of motion, so that today's weather was actually determined long ago.

We now know that this picture of the world is oversimplified, for we can never know the initial positions and motions of all the bodies in a system with complete accuracy. In some cases small errors will not make any significant difference: An uncertainty of 1 percent in initial conditions will mean that the future state can always be known to within about 1 percent. But many systems are "sensitive to initial conditions," meaning that a small uncertainty at the start grows rapidly to a large uncertainty in the future state of the system.

The study of systems of the latter type is now called "chaos." Weather was one of the first phenomena for which sensitivity to initial conditions was realized. It used to be thought that eventually accurate knowledge of atmospheric and surface conditions at a given time would enable meteorologists equipped with powerful computers to forecast weather precisely for long periods in the future. But while some weather forecasting is possible, we will never be able to do it to the degree that we can predict eclipses because it is not possible to have sufficiently detailed knowledge of initial weather conditions. This is the so-called "butterfly effect": A butterfly flapping its wings today in Asia will change the weather in America a few days later.

The results of chaos theory are not simply negative. Studies made possible by modern computers have given a great deal of insight into the behaviors of complex systems. However, they have also shown that there are limits to our ability to know about such systems.

Quantum Theory and Indeterminacy

Chaos theory, however, is based on classical mechanics, and so it too, for all its unpredictability, provides a deterministic view of the world, a view that again renders divine action untenable. The idea that all future states can be predicted by analysis of present conditions is not called into question until the rise of quantum theory in the twentieth century. Quantum theory demanded changes in common-sense ideas even more radical than those required by the theory of special relativity out of which it grew. It stimulated rethinking of the most fundamental of questions: what does it means to understand the world?

By 1900 a good deal had been learned about the realm of the very small. The idea that matter was composed of atoms had worked well in chemistry, but an adequate description of atoms required a new type of mechanics. That theory, quantum mechanics, began with Max Planck's studies of the radiation emitted by heated objects. The way in which a body glows red, then orange-red, then white as its temperature increases is familiar. But attempts to understand this behavior gave the ridiculous result that the energy radiated every second by a heated object should be infinite!

Planck removed this absurdity by dropping the idea that the atoms of the radiating body could emit energy continuously. He suggested that energy could be emitted or absorbed only in discrete amounts, or *quanta*, proportional to the frequency (number of waves per second) of the waves. To explain other phenomena, Albert Einstein then proposed that light is actually composed of particle-like quanta, or photons. This is confirmed by the observation that interactions between X-rays and subatomic particles are similar to collisions between two billiard balls.

The discovery that light behaves like a stream of particles in some situations does not erase the fact that in other situations it displays wavelike properties. Light has a twofold character. Louis de Broglie extended this wave–particle duality by suggesting that things that had been considered to be particles, such as electrons, also displayed wavelike properties.

Both Newton and James Maxwell had assumed that phenomena take place in continuous ways. The introduction of quanta challenged that assumption. Neils Bohr invoked discontinuous changes to explain the interaction of radiation with atoms and the term "quantum jump" entered the popular vocabulary. Because these jumps are very small, the "jerkiness" of quantum processes is imperceptible at the level of everyday phenomena.

Quantum mechanics as a complete theory was developed in the 1920s in two different ways that were soon shown to be alternative mathematical versions of a single underlying formalism. Both can be used to calculate things like the frequencies of radiation emitted by atoms or the ways in which particles will scatter off one another in collisions, and both reduce to Newtonian mechanics as an approximation in everyday situations. Erwin Schrödinger, pursuing de Broglie's idea, developed an equation that describes the behavior of the waves associated with different physical systems. Werner Heisenberg, on the other hand, found a set of rules that look at first glance like Newton's laws, but in which quantities like energy are represented not by single numbers, but by square arrays of numbers that do not obey the familiar rules of algebra. In both forms of the theory, atoms exist with only certain energies, so that quantum jumps occur.

Heisenberg's analysis of the observation of a subatomic particle showed that there are basic limitations on what we can know. An electron's position could be determined in principle by observing it with a microscope. In order to do that, radiation must interact with the particle. To get a sharp image and pin down the electron's location, the radiation must have a very short wavelength and be very energetic, and interaction of these photons with the electron will change the electron's momentum. If we try to avoid this by using photons with negligible momentum, the waves will be so long that the image of the electron will be blurred and its position will be uncertain. The result is that the uncertainties of momentum and position cannot both be reduced to zero, and there is a lower limit to the product of those uncertainties. A similar restriction holds for energy and the time at which it is measured.

This *uncertainty principle* of Heisenberg means that the state of a system in the sense of classical mechanics cannot be determined precisely. The determinism of Newtonian mechanics is cut down at the roots. We cannot predict the future state of a system precisely because we cannot know its present state with complete accuracy. There is a basic indeterminacy in the world, a point that some writers have emphasized in discussing issues related to free will and divine action.

If we cannot know exactly where things are and how they are moving, what can we know? The answer is given by Schrödinger's form of the theory. The waves described by solutions of his equation give probabilities for various positions or motions. Where the wave's intensity is large, there is a high probability of finding a particle, and where the intensity is zero there is no chance of observing it.

The use of probability was not in itself new in physics. Statistical mechanics is used to describe the behaviors of systems that contain so many particles that the motions of all of them cannot be calculated in detail. But probabilities in quantum mechanics can refer to just a single particle, not a large number of them. A more profound difference is that quantum probabilities seem to depend on what we choose to observe. According to the uncertainty principle, we can know a particle's position with 100 percent accuracy, in which case any momentum is equally probable, or we can know the momentum with complete certainty but nothing about the position of the particle, depending upon what measurement we choose to make.

Evolution, Suffering, and Divine Beneficence

Biological evolution has caused a great deal of controversy among religious believers. The problem does not necessarily lie with the idea of evolution as such; religious texts and beliefs dealing with the ways in which God created the world can be read more or less figuratively, thus accommodating the idea that life in the universe evolved. In other words, evolution can be thought of as the method that God uses to create. It is the details of that method that trouble many believers. The problem lies in the enormous suffering and species extinction that biological evolution necessitates.

Since the work of Charles Darwin and Alfred Russell Wallace, we have understood that *natural selection* plays a major role in evolution. Simply put, given limited resources available within a particular ecosystem, only some organisms will survive to pass on traits to their offspring; others will die leaving no descendants. Competition for resources and breeding opportunities act as a kind of "filter" to select the offspring of those organisms best suited to survive in a given environment. This means that privation, loss, suffering, death, and extinction are crucial factors in the development of new species.

The second challenge science raises for religion, then, is this: if God has brought humanity into being by means of the suffering and dying of millions of generations of God's creatures, we are forced to ask what *kind* of God we are talking about. A central tenet of the Judeo-Christian traditions is that the creator God is good and loving, and that the creation God brings into being reflects that goodness. What would be the character of a God who would create through a process like natural selection? Such a God might be intelligent and powerful, but in what sense could we call that God *good*? We might fear such a God, but could we ascribe the character of *love* to a deity who would work in such an apparently pitiless fashion? It is precisely these questions that have caused many people – most likely Darwin himself – to question the existence, or at least the belief in, God.

Biological Evolution

As early as the time of Carl Linnaeus, evidence was emerging that many species that used to live on earth are now extinct. The bodies of most plants and animals are dispersed or decay soon after death, but sometimes they leave molds in the rock that forms around them, or parts of their bodies are replaced by minerals. These fossils then provide a historical record of the organism. Some species have left no traces and some fossils have been destroyed or are never found. The fossil record is like a selection of sentences from a novel, an evolutionary narrative. It is up to paleontologists and other scientists to reconstruct that novel, to translate and interpret that story.

Strata older than about 600 million years contain only remains of unicellular life forms and a few other simple organisms. The Cambrian period, from about 600 to 500 million years ago, is rich in invertebrates, including the trilobites that are related to today's insects. Life appeared on land about 420 million years ago, and extensive forests 300 million years ago left today's coal deposits. Dinosaurs appeared about 220 million years ago and dominated the land for about 150 million years. Mammals spread and diversified rapidly after the extinction of the dinosaurs. The first members of the genus *Homo* came on the scene perhaps three million years before the present.

This suggests that a radical process of change has been taking place: evolution has occurred. The same type of thing can be seen on smaller time scales in situations in which an abundant and undisturbed sequence of fossils can be found.

Other evidence besides fossils supports evolution. The geographic distributions of living plants and animals are also significant. Similarities in the structures of organisms were noted early in studies of comparative anatomy. A human arm, a whale's flipper, and the wing of a bird have the same basic bone structure that has developed with different functions. Even more impressive relationships are seen on the molecular level. One chain of human hemoglobin with 144 amino acids differs from the corresponding protein in gorillas by only one acid. There are greater differences when human blood is compared with that of horses or pigs. Such relationships are also found between the DNA of different species. Virtually all organisms use the same genetic code that relates DNA to amino acids, suggesting that they share a common ancestry.

It is sometimes asked if we can observe evolution today or make it happen. Of course we cannot breed fish into mammals, but change can be seen on a smaller scale. The development of bacterial strains which are resistant to certain antibiotics is an important public health problem, and it is possible in special cases to produce speciation artificially: the "radocabbage," a cross between a radish and a cabbage, is infertile when crossed with members of its parental generations, and thus in the technical sense is a new species.

Evolutionary ideas had been discussed prior to the work of Darwin and Wallace, but it was their independently published theories of evolution through natural selection that allowed the theory to take hold with such force. The full title of Darwin's 1859 book describes the thrust of his theory: *On the Origin of Species by Natural Selection, or the Preservation of Favoured Races in the Struggle for Life*. Though major changes have taken place in evolutionary theory since Darwin's and Wallace's publications, the basic idea underlying the Darwinian theory of evolution, now known as "Neo-Darwinian" theory, continues to be defined properly as natural selection.

An environment will generally not be able to support all organisms that are produced. (Both Darwin and Wallace were influenced by the argument of Thomas Malthus that population must grow faster than food supply.) There are variations among members of species due to chance assortment of genes, physical changes in DNA, and other factors, and some members will be better suited to survive in a given environment than others. They will be more likely to succeed in getting food, mating, escaping predation or disease, or some combination thereof. They will then be more likely to have offspring that survive and inherit their characteristics favoring survival. Change over many generations may then produce new species, while old species may become extinct.

Evolution is a statistical process that refers to populations rather than individuals. A single organism that was well suited for survival could be struck by lightning and leave no offspring. Catastrophes on a larger scale have affected whole populations, as with the asteroid impact some 65 million years ago that destroyed the dinosaurs. Natural selection should not be thought of as involving any kind of absolute fitness or superiority of the survivors over those who do not survive. Natural selection favors those who are well suited for survival and reproduction in a particular environment, but they may be poorly suited if the environment changes.

Evolutionary theory continues to evolve. Some biologists today argue that natural selection alone is unable to explain evolution. It has also been suggested that evolution occurs in brief bursts followed by long periods of relative constancy of species rather than by slow change. It will not be surprising if some challenges to traditional evolutionary ideas are substantiated, for the complexity of life is such that there may be no single explanation that describes evolution adequately throughout the whole biosphere and all the history of life.

Evolution in some form, however, will probably persist, leaving religion to deal with its challenge to the idea of a loving creator.

Genetics, Biotechnology, Ecology, and Ethics

The third challenge to religion concerns ethics. Advances in technology, particularly biotechnology, have given us an unprecedented ability to control and change nature, even human nature. Developments in biological and medical technologies present us with the possibility of affecting our own evolutionary future. This possibility is manifest on multiple levels: reproductive choices ranging from the now common practice of *in vitro* fertilization, to the extraordinary and troublesome possibilities of human cloning; gene therapies offer the potential to cure debilitating diseases while raising the specter of eugenics; choices being made about the way we die, from the termination of life support for terminally ill patients, to stem cell therapies which may alleviate the suffering of age-related illnesses. What, if any, should be the ethical limits on the uses of such technologies?

Novel scientific and technological developments are producing novel ethical questions. And religious traditions are faced with the daunting task of responding to these questions out of the resources established long before the quest to sequence the human genome began. Certainly sources such as the Sayings of Confucius or the Ten Commandments of Judaism and Christianity may give us some guidance, providing ethical parameters for answering these novel questions. But it would be unreasonable to expect ancient moral codes to give us ready-made instructions about appropriate use of transplants or genetic engineering.

Molecular Biology and Genetics

Carbon and other elements such as hydrogen, oxygen, nitrogen, and phosphorus make up a huge number of organic compounds classified as carbohydrates, fats, and proteins. The latter are important structural elements as well as catalysts that make many of the chemical processes of life possible.

Proteins are constructed by connecting together *amino acids*, of which there are about twenty varieties, in long chains. A vast number of such chains is possible, and many different proteins play roles in biological processes. They may contain other groups of atoms that enable them to play special roles, such as a group with iron in hemoglobin that enables blood to carry oxygen. Proteins may be folded into three-dimensional shapes that play a critical role in their abilities to attach to other molecules and catalyze chemical reactions.

For cells to store energy in the chemical bonds of organic compounds and then use it for the things the organism needs to do, there must be metabolic processes that get the energy from other molecules. The food we eat undergoes chemical reactions, which release energy, with proteins acting as catalysts to make these reactions proceed more rapidly than they otherwise would. A complex series of reactions enables our cells to use oxygen to release the energy in glucose, which plants have made by photosynthesis. By-products of this cycle are water and carbon dioxide, the chemicals that plants need in turn for photosynthesis to make glucose and oxygen and to continue the cycle.

Energy must be made available for processes such as muscular contraction and cell-division. Cellular processes resemble a factory in which incoming materials are moved along an assembly line, and at each station an enzyme performs a task and passes the result on to the next station. But this is not simply a linear process, for one of the things the energy is used for is to combine amino acids to make the proteins which are needed to make the metabolic cycle itself run. The factory has to keep rebuilding its own machinery! There is no perpetual motion, for energy and waste material are excreted and essential materials, some of the amino acids that the body cannot make for itself, must be supplied from the outside.

There must be directions for such intricate processes. Cells have information, which tells them how to construct various proteins so that all these processes can take place, and organisms must be able to pass this information on to their offspring at a molecular level. That brings us to the topic of genetics.

The ways in which blue or brown eye colors of children are related to those of their parents are simple, and we do not usually find mixtures of these colors. On the other hand, if one parent has black skin and the other white, their child usually has an intermediate skin color. For things like mathematical ability there often is little correlation between aptitudes of parents and those of children. There seems to be no simple pattern of inheritance.

The monk Gregor Mendel made critical steps toward understanding heredity in the nineteenth century. He studied properties of the common pea plant, such as seed color and shape, and found that the inheritance of these properties could be explained with a simple model. There is a *gene* for each trait, and each organism has two genes and contributes one to the next generation. If a gene is dominant, the trait it produces will appear even if the corresponding recessive gene is also present. For eye color brown is dominant and blue recessive. Two blue-eyed parents will have blue-eyed children, but two brown-eyed parents may have a child with blue eyes because both could be carrying the recessive gene.

Bodies called chromosomes in the nuclei of cells become visible under the microscope during cell-division. There is a characteristic number for each species, humans having forty-six, in twenty-three pairs. In normal cell-division the chromosomes split lengthwise so that each of the two daughter cells receives a full complement, but when sperm and ova are produced, each receives only one from each chromosome pair. The full complement is regained when these cells are united sexually, one from each parent. Thus the chromosomes have properties which suggest that they are associated with the theoretical genes, and further study makes it possible to relate particular genetic traits to specific sites on chromosomes.

The chromosomes contain deoxyribonucleic acid, DNA, the material that carries genetic information. James Dewey Watson and Francis Harry Compton Crick used data from X-ray studies of DNA and other clues to develop the famous double-helix model of this molecule. Each strand of the double helix contains many molecules of the four bases adenine, guanine, cytosine, and thymine, which bond to one another in a specific way, adenine only to thymine, and cytosine only to guanine. Thus the sequence of bases on one strand uniquely specifies the sequence on the other. When the strands separate, each can be matched with a new partner made identical to its original one. The information coded onto the DNA is thus preserved during cell-division.

The sequence of bases carries information for the construction of proteins. Each group of three bases specifies a particular amino acid. There are $4 \times 4 \times 4 = 64$ triple combinations of bases, more than enough to code for twenty amino acids with some duplications and special instructions such as "start" and "stop." There must also be machinery in the cell to read the instructions and carry them out. These processes involve varieties of a single-stranded nucleic acid, RNA (ribonucleic acid).

Genes do not code directly for properties like intelligence but tell cells what proteins to manufacture. In some cases it is easy to see how this results in large-scale properties. Eye color is due to pigment, and DNA can code for production of specific pigments. Sickle-cell anemia is caused by a mutation in the DNA that changed the coding for one of the amino acids in hemoglobin, giving the molecule a different shape. But other situations are not so simple.

The transfer of genetic information is a one-way process from DNA to protein, genes to body, and not the other way around. This is important for the mechanism of evolution because it means that to change the information that will be passed on to the offspring of an organism, it is necessary to modify the genetic material, and not merely the body, of the parent.

Knowledge of the genetic code and the mechanisms of protein synthesis have opened up possibilities for genetic engineering. The ability to hunt down and alter genes related to specific diseases has the potential to transform medicine, alleviating tremendous suffering. For this reason, many theologians and other religious scholars have offered up support for genetic research. This potential for tremendous good, however, carries with it a tremendous potential for abuse. The same technologies that offer cures for diseases such as cystic fibrosis, Huntington's disease, and breast cancer, may some day give us the ability to make ourselves more intelligent, more athletic, and perhaps, if behavior is found to be intimately linked to genetic heritage, kinder and more generous. What kind of society will we have if we are able to engineer a genetically "superior" class of citizens? Is this a desirable future? These possibilities force religion to reassess the question of what it means to be a human person and how it is we value human life.

The View from the Cross

As we saw in our opening section, the development of this scientific picture of the world has caused some people to question the value of all religions. People influenced in this way may adopt positions of atheism or agnosticism. Others have sought a more positive view of the relationship between science and religion, taking into account the basic beliefs of their faith communities and their own experiences. Einstein, for example, expressed his belief in a pantheism in which the universe is identified with God. There are ancient religions in which a variety of gods and goddesses are responsible for different natural processes. The counterintuitive ideas of modern physics, and especially quantum theory, have seemed to some people reminiscent of mystical traditions.

In monotheistic religions, the universe is believed to be ultimately dependent on a single God. The Christian faith is a monotheistic religion that focuses on Jesus of Nazareth, who died by crucifixion under the Roman official Pontius Pilate approximately 2,000 years ago near Jerusalem. The distinctive Christian claim is that this man who died on the cross was raised from the dead, and that he is the promised Messiah (Christ) and Son of God. In his death and resurrection we are to see both the fullest revelation of the character of God and the act by which God restores the world to its proper relationship with its creator.

Here I want to describe briefly how this religious view can respond to the issues raised by science and technology. These issues are to be understood in terms of what the sixteenth-century theologian Martin Luther called "the theology of the cross." He believed that if we are truly to know God, we must look first to Christ on the cross.

At first glance this idea seems to make little sense. Conventional thinking about God, and especially that informed by the philosophy of ancient Greece, has generally assumed that God is timeless and changeless, and cannot suffer or experience death. God is supposed to be glorious and powerful and impervious to evil. How can it make sense, then, to say that a man dying a painful and humiliating death, defeated and abandoned by his disciples, reveals God?

How could he possibly be "true God," as Christians believe? This is, however, the distinctive Christian claim. If it is to make some kind of sense, then we must start here, not with conventional beliefs about what it means to speak of God.

There are interesting parallels here with some scientific developments that we discussed in the last section. We have learned from the progress of modern science that we cannot rely on ideas about the world that are in accord with our everyday experience. Scientific progress has often been made by introducing concepts that seem at first glance to be absurd, but which turn out to give a better understanding of the world than do ideas that are more in accord with common sense.

Copernicus's idea that the earth traveled around the sun, and not the sun around the earth, seemed ridiculous to many people in the sixteenth century. Surely we would feel it if the earth were moving that fast! The birds would get left behind! But Copernicus was right. Einstein's suggestion that the speed of light is the same for all observers was impossible in terms of common-sense ideas of space and time, but it turned out that Einstein was correct and that ideas about space and time had to be changed.

Scientific theories should not to be evaluated in terms of whether or not they agree with commonly accepted beliefs. Instead, they should be judged by how well they are able to explain the things that take place in the natural world. A theory that explains and predicts phenomena successfully, such as evolution through natural selection or quantum mechanics, will require us to change the way we look at the world. We will have to try to develop a new type of "common sense."

The question, then, to be asked about the Christian claim that God is revealed in the cross and resurrection of Jesus is not whether it agrees with commonly accepted beliefs about God. We must ask instead whether it helps us to make sense of our lives and of our experience in the world. Here we are especially interested in seeing how well it can help us to make sense of scientific and technological realities.

The challenges presented by science and technology that we discussed in our first section posed problems for more or less conventional beliefs about religion and morality. The theology of the cross gives us a distinctively different approach to these issues. There should be no suggestion that this theology gives easy responses to all these challenges, or answers all the questions raised by science and technology. But it does remove some of the more obvious difficulties. Let us consider the challenges that we described earlier in the light of the cross.

The theology of the cross says that God is, in a paradoxical way, hidden, even when he reveals himself. This is because a man hanging dead on a cross, an apparent failure, seems nothing at all like what we expect a God to be. We naturally want a God who is always in complete control, who cannot be defeated, and who provides unmistakable evidence of his divinity. The Christian scriptures describe Jesus Christ in a quite different way, as one who renounces overwhelming displays of power and shows his love by taking the form of a servant.

If God is hidden even in his supreme revelation, should we perhaps expect God to be hidden in the everyday occurrences of the world? Christians, like many other religious believers, have thought that God is active in the world, maintaining the universe in its development and providing the things needed for life. We may think of God doing this by making use of the things of the world as tools, or instruments. Of course these tools, which ultimately are elementary particles and interactions obeying the laws of relativity and quantum theory, are much more delicate and subtle than hammers and saws. If God always uses these instruments in accord with rational laws, we will be able to describe what happens in the world entirely in terms of the things of the world and the laws they obey. And as we have seen, science has been quite successful in providing such a description of the world.

According to this approach, the things that we observe in the world are both the instruments that God uses and the "masks" (as Luther put it) that hide God from our direct observation. Belief that God is active in the world is an expression of faith in the God revealed in the cross, not a scientific deduction.

This argument depends critically on the idea that God limits his action in the world to what can be described by rational laws of nature. But such self-limitation is just what we see in the cross, where God does not use divine power to free himself from suffering and death. Moreover, God's limitation of his action in the world is a gift to intelligent beings, enabling us to understand the world in which we live.

That gift of being able to understand the world helps us to understand why God might work in this way: God grants to the world some integrity of its own. But the way in which God has then apparently acted to develop life is still disturbing. How is evolution to be seen in the light of the cross?

As soon as we pose that question we will realize that our approach gives us a new way of responding to the challenge of natural selection that we discussed in our first section. Here God is not understood as a deity who forces millions of generations through suffering and extinction without himself being affected by the process, but rather as a God who participates in the processes and shares in the suffering and death of the world. The price for the development of life is paid not only by God's creatures but also by God himself.

The prominence of suffering and death in the natural world is disturbing, and the cross does not make it less troubling or prove that God's use of it in evolution is justified. What the theology of the cross does do is to say that God stands with the world in suffering and death and thereby gives hope for life. Nor is "survival of the fittest" to be affirmed as a universal principle that the strong will always be victorious over the weak. The resurrection of the crucified Christ is, after all, a vindication of the one who was killed.

The resurrection of the crucified may also help to give us some new ways of thinking about the ethical dilemmas introduced by modern biomedical technology. The theology of the cross does not give us a precise moral code that tells us exactly when we should and when we should not use particular medical techniques. It does tell us that God is able to bring good out of evil and life out of death, so that there is no situation that is completely without hope. On the other hand, the hope that we are given is not simply one of holding onto life for every possible second. It is a hope that comes through and in spite of death, not simply by avoiding death.

There are, of course, many other religious issues that have been raised by modern science and technology, and we may expect to encounter other challenges as new discoveries are made. The religions of the world will all try to deal with them in terms of their own beliefs and traditions, and reflection on the different ways in which we approach these questions may help believers from various backgrounds better to understand one another. What I hope to have shown in this brief sketch is that an understanding of the Christian faith in which the cross of Christ has a central place is well equipped to deal with some of the pressing issues in the dialogue between science and religion.

Science and Ethics in Judaism: Discernment and Discourse

LAURIE ZOLOTH

The pace of scientific inquiry has increased tremendously in the last two centuries, and the hegemony of science's claim to determine truth has significantly shaped our culture. Religious systems, with their texts and communities, inevitably face challenging questions posed by science. Science as a theory and a practice makes several claims: the natural world has order, laws, and causality; such order can be apprehended and explained by human persons; and the manipulation of the nameable, quantifiable and discernable elements of that natural and tangible world can be achieved to organize human social and cultural life. In Jewish thought and tradition, both this search for understanding of the order and the reordering of the natural world are not only achievable, they are divinely commanded; they are a part of a larger imperative to heal and to repair the world. For Jewish philosophers, the freely entered Covenant that assigns these tasks to an elected people is what makes ethical norms possible.[1]

However, moral norms cannot be established without reference to a complex legal system that draws on centuries of case law and textual interpretation. For over two centuries, this system has been applied in reflection on the dilemmas of science and of modernity. Science, in particular natural science, has been vividly embraced as allowing the fullest understanding of the events and causes in the world in which the community practices its religion. Unlike faith traditions that reify the natural world as essentially sacred, Jewish thought embraces our ability to alter the natural world, seeing this ability as an opportunity to create justice and healing as acts of faith and obligation. The relationship between Jewish thought and scientific understanding varies over different historical periods. In fact, the intellectual attention of the Jewish tradition had been largely focused on the moral and social task rather than the actual achievements of science until well into the Enlightenment.[2]

The Structure of Jewish Ethics and *Halachah*

Let us first turn to the structure of the *halachic* system. Ethical norms are established via a legal system called *halachah*.[3] Bounded by this system of religio-legal behavior, the individual Jew, once past the age of thirteen[4], is responsible for the performance of *mitzvot* or divine commandments of activity and response to God and to her community. (There are 613 such commandments in the traditional reckoning, a metaphorical number that stands for the completeness of obligation.[5]) Many are concerned with the daily details of ritual and familial life, many are employed in the service of civil codes, and others set the perimeters of response to questions such as how to regard cloning, nuclear fission, and space travel. At stake in the system is not only whether the intended act is regarded as prohibited, permissible, or exemplary activity, but how the activity ought to be carried out, using what criteria for assessment. Jewish ethics is a complex negotiation with procedural questions and substantive ones.

The first procedural question that the system of Jewish ethics addresses is the problem of how to achieve good ends in a non-teleological system. Judaism answers this in a way that is the unique hallmark of the method – it is a method that, while based in law, draws on a variety of sources both to create the cases for the law, and to resist and query its assumptions. The basic procedure for the evaluation of ethical norms[6] is the mode of argumentation, commentary, debate, and discussion.

Essentially casuistic, the *halachic* system uses the encounter with the Torah text, and the encounter with the other's encounter with the text, to create a continuous discursive community. Cases are raised to illustrate points of law, and then to illustrate alternative interpretations of the law. Narrative, in a variety of literary forms (metaphor, allegory, historical reference, intertextual mirroring) called *aggadah*, are embedded in the text. While the details of the *aggadah* did not create binding laws, the form was used to grapple with and embellish the discussion of the details of the *halachah*. The casuistic account attempts to decipher the particular and specific human ways the principle has been, and could be, even theoretically, applied.[7] Judaism is both a deontological and a casuistic system, rooted in rules, duties, and normative conduct and concerned with motive and process. But it is unlike a purely deontological system because the real world, and the context and outcome of each case, count in their assessment.

Judaism is a modified casuistic deontology. Consequences, once enacted, are re-examined and debated. The real world matters: knowledge of precedence, historicity, the tactile, and the theoretical. Human reason is needed both to negotiate the system and to interpret intelligently the sensory natural world. Talmudic methodology was argument structured by text, history, and community. All these three elements, and the use of reason to decipher them, modify the deontologic method of Jewish ethics. It was *deontological* because it assumes Torah law as motivational, commanded, central, and binding; and *casuistic* because it was also inductive and case (context) modified.[8]

The central claim of Jewish ethics is that truth is found in the house of discursive study – the *bet midrash*.[9] Such a public discourse is created when we argue, face to face, about the meaning and relevance of the narrative, symbols, and referents. Embedded in the problem are issues of context, causation, agency, norm, and assessment. Each of these issues must be addressed by whoever is describing whatever methodology of ethics they use, with the assumption that methodology in ethics involves not only a general theory of morality, authority, and value, but also "middle axioms," or the middle ground between general principles and the details of policy.[10] Methodology in any integral ethical system must address both the *why* and the *how* of a "right act" if it is to have coherence and if it can be useful in the human hands and heart of the world. Jewish ethics is no exception. Jewish ethics presumes public choices; it assumes community, human sociability, and embodied dailiness, that ordinary human acts have a weight and meaning that ought to be the subject of serious discourse.

A Central Question: Is there an Ethics Independent of *Halachah*?

Jews agree that rules and laws form the basis of our ethical system (deontology). Yet, our method of application relies upon discerning nuances and creative argumentation (casuistry). Rules are rules, but in debate interpretations vary and compete.[11] The multivocity of the form itself insists on the questioning of the solidity of the text: to name as definitive one personal interpretation is a violation of the Talmudic method. For many of the proof texts there are strong countervailing premises and correspondent inimitable truths, and rabbinic decisors who will defend differing positions. Marvin Fox, writing in *Modern Jewish Ethics*, one of the central works in English in the modern period on this topic, argued that the *halachic* system itself includes an accountability to a variety of sources. His insight was that the basic method incorporates science, philosophy, and natural reality into the traditional texts. The Rabbis used exegesis and interpretation as the most important device to reconcile the basic and sacred text with the reality of exile, change, and science.

Fox further noted that the incorporation of "external to Sinaitic" sources was always a part of the discourse. He argued that Maimonides assumes math, astronomy, and "speculative realities" are better known by the Arabic world than by the Rabbinic sages and that Jews need to "accept truth from any source." Fox noted Judah HaNasi's confession that, in some arguments, the Gentile sages "vanquished the sages of Israel." This was cited in the tradition as a case of how best evidence and best argument from whatever source ought to prevail.

Saadya Gaon made this point, according to Fox, even more forcefully by insisting that reason existed both prior to and after Sinai. Further, Fox noted that interpretation has always varied widely, even at the heart of basic texts (like the Moses story, the Ruth story, the view of the Nazarite vow, and the problem of creation itself). Additionally, he pointed to the flexibility of the *aggadah* as indicative of the freedom at the heart of Jewish method itself. He reminded us that tradition has each Jew at Sinai now and for eternal generations and noted the Rabbinic *Midrash* that says each Jew hears the revelation through his/her own body and experience.

> Even at Sinai the divine voice went forth to all Israel and was assimilated by each person in accordance with his particular capacity – the elders in their own way, the youth in their own way, the children in their own way, the sucklings in their own way, the women in their own way, and also Moses in his own way . . . For this reason it is written, "the voice of the Lord is according to *the* strength" and not "according to *His* strength" to teach us that each one grasps His message according to his own particular power and capacity.[12]

Rabbi Joseph Soleveitchik, the leading contemporary halachist, has written extensively regarding the relationship between the method of ethical discernment and the scientific method itself, finding in physics a way of understanding the structure of human understanding.[13] He argues that physics and the theory of relativity teach us that truth can be viewed from many perspectives; that the universe was not a Newtonian machine, but a complex of related happenings. One's perspective, then, will determine the "true" view of the object.[14] Further, Soleveitchik understood that human perception is a function of the truth that each perceives, as each person individually views the "real" from the perspective of a particular and chosen order. What is seen as actual is a chosen fact pattern based on a system of value and belief. He posited the notion that to be religious or to be scientific, while they may be radically different worldviews, was not only to value the world differently, but to experience and to see the phenomena of the world differently as well. That notion was entirely consistent with the concept of truth understood as "plural truth" and served to explain how specific events could be seen as miracles or a function of the events of the causative natural world.[15]

Science: The Epistemic Questions

Scientific inquiry is based on the application of human observation and human reasoning to events in the observable world. As such, it might seem that it offers a primal threat to faith traditions based on unseen and un-provable truth claims. However, Jewish tradition has long been able to incorporate secular knowledge in medicine and science into ethical norms. New insights are evaluated as cases to be compared to historically precedential ones.

Scientific insights and achievements can thus be incorporated. Post-Darwinian writings reinterpreted the "six days of Creation" as occurring in "six periods," or six divine "days," and electricity became legally bound by the rules of the Sabbath by understanding it as a form of "fire-making." "Science" or secular knowledge in general was often used to represent "a vehicle for a certain cluster of liberal, democratic values" argued as central to Western, or American, values, a metaphor for the use of objectivity, impartiality, and civic order.[16] The methods of science, the use of clinical trials and controls and the use of animal models was also strongly embraced by Jews. In general, Judaism makes the assumption that the order of nature is accessible to human reason, and that nature, while offering some probable models for behavior, is not the source of moral authority.

While social conditions, exclusion from the developing academy, constraints on employment, and isolation in European ghettos left Jewish intellectuals behind in the development of science in the early modern period, the nineteenth and twentieth centuries were marked by an enthusiastic embrace of and a mastery of many fields of scientific inquiry.

Science: The Substantive Questions

Astronomy and cosmology dominated early reflections in Jewish thought because of the importance in calculations of calendars holidays, and, as Hillel Levine notes, because of the Rabbinic attention to time rather than space after the destruction of the Second Temple.[17] Levine notes that beyond the calendric calculations, Jews, in their capacity as traders between different Jewish communities, acted as interpreters of the insights from Islamic and Renaissance Christian civilizations. Medicine, as a commanded obligation of Jewish communities, was often a venue for investigation in science. Jewish physicians were often called upon to assume the relatively high-risk activity of caring for the sick, but also because they had access to the large armamentarium of knowledge. Scientific discovery came later to the large Jewish community. A complex interest in kabbalistic beliefs and rituals, an emphasis on a renewed spirituality, and compelling disputes about how to resist persecution, how to engage modernity politically, or communally dominated Jewish views on the "new science" of the Enlightenment from the sixteenth through to the eighteenth century. To the extent that science was posited as opposed to faith, it was regarded in traditional communities as suspect. It is Levine's contention that Jews in that period did not view science as "universally valid, but simply as the source of religious persecution in a new key."[18]

But the search for the truthful as the source for decisions grounds moral reasoning. By the nineteenth century, the truth claims of science had been well established. Catalogues of species and descriptive science, germ theory, and the use of instruments of observation were eagerly taken on by the Jewish intelligentsia. In the twentieth century, Jewish commentators turned their attention to the problems of intervention, prevention, and cure, as well as the search for origins. Finding little to prohibit basic research, and reasoning from principles that stressed stewardship, tending and ordering the natural world, Jews were easily able to reconcile new scientific discoveries with their sense not only that the natural world was knowable, but that it ought to be known. It may be interesting here to note that Nobel Prizes in the sciences and medicine have been won by Jews in numbers far greater than their proportion of the world population.

Halachah, too, has advanced to address new science. Science disrupts categories of being. An essential premise of the method is that events are best understood by disassembly into knowable parts – ever smaller, ever more essential. For a *halachic* system, this offers an opportunity to renegotiate the borders of permissibility at each component piece, commodity, or event. Modern *halachic* authorities such as Orthodox Rabbi Faitel Levin openly struggle with the challenge that new science brings to a textual tradition governed by law.

> Once reality was relatively constant, unchanging . . . in the objective world in which *halacha* operates. But things have changed. In today's world, reality itself is undergoing repeated, fundamental changes. Objects which have little in common with traditional objects are constantly produced . . . consequently, our contemporary world is evading the control of traditional terms and concepts. But Torah is eternal![19]

Recent controversies in the field of reproductive health and genetic medicine have often dominated the debate between religious communities and scientific investigators. In these debates one can see how the concern for healing, the obligation to repair the world, and the view that human life is fully ensouled only in developmental stages, and not at the moment of conception, has allowed for a robust acceptance of basic research in biological sciences.

The acts of practice in traditional Judaism revolved around two centralities: the first is study of text, and the second is commanded acts that create a just society. Central to Jewish texts is the recognition of the as yet unredeemed quality of the world – even the natural world as understood by science. Just as circumcision is one mark of the covenant, one mark of a human response to birth and a refinement of the natural world, so too is the notion that advanced scientific inquiry is a part of *tikkun olam*, the mandate to be an active partner in the world's repair and perfection. In the world of suffering and injustice, all research can be understood as an opportunity to address this injustice.

This justice consideration is made actual by a support for science, medical advance, and freedom of inquiry, all ways that humans work to perfect the world, and such activity can be fully embraced. While texts warn of the possibility of hubris, and there are many texts that teach of the danger of confusing the quest for learning with the temptation to control, the struggle to understand and to interpret the covenental relationship includes extending the duty to heal. In this way, Jewish thought has long turned to science as a critical way to lay the groundwork for the study and the repair of the world.

Notes

Chapter 1

1. Elizabeth A. Johnson, "Presidential Address: Turn to the Heavens and the Earth," *CTSA Proceedings* 51 (1996): 1–14.

2. Helpful textbooks and overview articles include Ian Barbour, *Religion in an Age of Science*, Gifford Lectures 1989–90 (San Francisco: Harper & Row, 1990), and *Religion and Science: Historical and Contemporary Issues* (San Francisco: HarperSanFrancisco, 1997); Ted Peters, "Theology and the Natural Sciences," in *The Modern Theologians: An Introduction to Christian Theology in the Twentieth Century*, 2nd edn., ed. David F. Ford (Cambridge, Mass.: Blackwell, 1997); Ted Peters, ed., *Science and Theology: The New Consonance* (Boulder, Colo.: Westview Press, 1998); W. Mark Richardson and Wesley J. Wildman, eds., *Religion and Science: History, Method, Dialogue* (New York: Routledge, 1996); and Christopher Southgate *et al.*, eds., *God, Humanity and the Cosmos: A Textbook in Science and Religion* (Harrisburg: Trinity Press International, 1999).

3. Textbook overviews include Barbour, *Religion and Science*, part two; John Haught, *Science and Religion: From Conflict to Conversion* (New York: Paulist Press, 1995), ch. 1; Richardson and Wildman, *Religion and Science*, part two; and Southgate *et al.*, *God, Humanity and the Cosmos*, chs. 1 and 2.

4. For other relevant typologies see Southgate *et al.*, *God, Humanity and the Cosmos*.

5. For Ian Barbour, paradigms in science and in religion display "subjective" as well as "objective" features, though the former are more prominent in religion and the latter in science. See Ian Barbour, *Myths, Models, and Paradigms: A Comparative Study in Science and Religion* (New York: Harper & Row, 1974); and *Religion in an Age of Science*.

6. Helpful analysis of such accounts can be found in Mary Hesse, "Socializing Epistemology," in *Construction and Constraint: The Shaping of Scientific Rationality*, ed. Ernan McMullin (Notre Dame: University of Notre Dame Press, 1988).

7. See McMullin, *Construction and Constraint*.

8. For additional discussion see Philip Clayton and Steven Knapp, "Is Holistic Justification Enough?" and "Rationality and Christian Self-Conception," both in Richardson and Wildman, *Religion and Science*; and Gregory Peterson, "The Scientific Status of Theology: Imre Lakatos,

Method and Demarcation," *Perspectives on Science and Christian Faith* 50.1 (March 1998).

9. One should clearly note that this is not a valuative or axiological hierarchy, such as those supporting dominance or patriarchy, but a strictly epistemological hierarchy, which supports the argument for non-reducibility.

10. For a recent critique of their views, see Kirk Wegter-McNelly, " 'He Descended into Hell': A Liberation Response to the Kenosis in *On the Moral Nature of the Universe*," *CTNS Bulletin* 19.4 (Fall 1998).

11. For additional resources on these and related issues, see Sandra Harding and Merrill B. Hintikka, eds., *Discovering Reality: Feminist Perspectives on Epistemology, Metaphysics, Methodology, and Philosophy of Science* (Dordrecht: Reidel, 1983); and Helen Longino and Ruth Doell, "Body, Bias, and Behaviour: A Comparative Analysis of Reasoning in Two Areas of Biological Science," in *Feminism and Science*, ed. Evelyn Fox Keller and Helen E. Longino (Oxford: Oxford University Press, 1996).

12. Margaret Wertheim, *Pythagoras' Trousers: God, Physics and the Gender Wars* (New York: Times Books, 1995), 9.

13. For a teaching resource, see Nancy Howell, "Ecofeminism: What One Needs to Know," *Zygon: Journal of Religion and Science* 32.2 (June 1997).

14. For a teaching resource, see William Grassie, "Postmodernism: What One Needs to Know," *Zygon: Journal of Religion and Science* 32.1 (March 1997).

15. For a particularly helpful analysis, see Southgate *et al.*, *God, Humanity and the Cosmos*, ch. 9.

16. See also the articles in vols. 11 and 12 (1995) of *The Pacific World: Journal of The Institute of Buddhist Studies*.

17. See also Vine Deloria, *God is Red: A Native View of Religion*, 2nd edn. (Golden, Colo.: North American Press, 1992); and Gregory Cajete, *Indigenous Science* (Santa Fe, N.M.: Clear Light, 2000), and the online journal *Winds of Change* (www.aises.org).

18. Claude Welch notes that the language of "conflict" was inspired in part by widely influential books by John Draper, *History of the Conflict Between Religion and Science* (London and New York: D. Appleton and Company, 1874), and Andrew Dickson White, *A History of the Warfare of Science with Theology in Christendom* (London and New York: D. Appleton and Company, 1896), which had as their main target the institutional church, particularly Pope Pius IX's *Syllabus of Errors* of 1864.

19. On the issue of the interaction between science and "external" factors with regard to the formation and choice of scientific theories, see Roy Clouser, *The Myth of Religious Neutrality: An Essay on the Hidden Role of Religious Belief in Theories* (Notre Dame: University of Notre Dame Press, 1991); Philip Clayton, *God and Contemporary Science* (Grand Rapids:

Eerdmans, 1997), 130; and Max Jammer, *The Philosophy of Quantum Mechanics: The Interpretations of Quantum Mechanics in Historical Perspective* (New York: Wiley, 1974).

20. For example, the view of nature as created *ex nihilo* implies that the universe is contingent and rational. These implications provide two of the fundamental philosophical assumptions on which modern science is based. See David C. Lindberg and Ronald L. Numbers, eds., *God and Nature: Historical Essays on the Encounter between Christianity and Science* (Berkeley: University of California Press, 1986); and Eugene M. Klaaren, *Religious Origins of Modern Science: Belief in Creation in Seventeenth-Century Thought* (Grand Rapids: Eerdmans, 1977).

21. See J. L. Heilbron, *The Dilemmas of an Upright Man: Max Planck as Spokesman for German Science* (Berkeley: University of California Press, 1986); Erwin Schrödinger, *What is Life? Mind and Matter* (Cambridge: Cambridge University Press, 1945); and Max Jammer, *Einstein and Religion* (Princeton: Princeton University Press, 1999).

Chapter 2

1. George Lindbeck, *Nature of Doctrine* (Philadelphia: Westminster Press, 1984).

2. A. R. Peacocke, *Intimations of Reality* (Notre Dame: University of Notre Dame Press, 1984); and Ian G. Barbour, *Myths, Models, and Paradigms* (New York: Harper and Row, 1974).

3. See Richard Rorty, *Philosophy and the Mirror of Nature* (Princeton: Princeton University Press, 1979).

4. Ludwig Wittgenstein, *Tractatus Logico-Philosophicus* (London: Routledge & Kegan Paul, 1922).

5. For example, C. L. Stevenson, *Ethics and Language* (New Haven: Yale University Press, 1944).

6. See Jeffrey Stout, *The Flight from Authority* (Notre Dame: University of Notre Dame Press, 1981).

7. Willard V. O. Quine, "Two Dogmas of Empiricism," *Philosophical Review* 40 (1951): 20–43.

8. Karl Popper, *Logik der Forschung* (Vienna, 1935).

9. Thomas Kuhn, *The Structure of Scientific Revolutions*, 2nd edn. (Chicago: University of Chicago Press, 1970).

10. Published posthumously: Ludwig Wittgenstein, *Philosophical Investigations* (Oxford: Oxford University Press, 1953).

11. Alasdair MacIntyre, *After Virtue* (Notre Dame: University of Notre Dame Press, 1981) may be the best example here.

12. Earlier versions of the foregoing sections appeared in *Phos: Theological Reflections* (Pentecost, 1987) and are reprinted here with permission.

13. See especially David Bloor, *Knowledge and Social Imagery* (London: Routledge & Kegan Paul, 1976); and Barry Barnes, *Interests and the Growth of Knowledge* (London: Routledge & Kegan Paul, 1977).

14. Peacocke, *Intimations*, 20.

15. Martin Rudwick, "Senses of the Natural World and Senses of God: Another Look at the Historical Relation of Science and Religion," in A. R. Peacocke, ed., *The Sciences and Theology in the Twentieth Century* (Notre Dame: University of Notre Dame Press, 1981), 253.

16. Nancey Murphy, *Theology in the Age of Scientific Reasoning* (Ithica, N.Y.: Cornell, 1990).

17. See Lakatos's "Falsification and the Methodology of Scientific Research Programmes," in his *Philosophical Papers*, vol. 1 (Cambridge: Cambridge University Press, 1978), 8–101.

18. Ronald Thiemann, *Revelation and Theology* (Notre Dame: University of Notre Dame Press, 1985).

19. I wish to express appreciation to my husband, James Wm. McClendon, Jr., Professor of Theology at the Church Divinity School of the Pacific, for many helpful discussion on modern and postmodern modes of thought.

Chapter 3

1. Helpful textbooks and overview articles include Ian Barbour, *Religion and Science: Historical and Contemporary Issues* (San Francisco: HarperSanFrancisco, 1997); Alister E. McGrath, *Science and Religion: An Introduction* (Oxford: Blackwell, 1999); Ted Peters, ed., *Science and Theology: The New Consonance* (Boulder, Colo.: Westview Press, 1998); John Polkinghorne, *Science and Theology: An Introduction* (London/ Minneapolis: SPCK/Fortress Press, 1998); W. Mark Richardson and Wesley Wildman, eds., *Religion and Science: History, Method, Dialogue* (New York: Routledge, 1996); and Christopher Southgate *et al.*, eds., *God, Humanity and the Cosmos: A Textbook in Science and Religion* (Harrisburg: Trinity Press International, 1999).

2. For an overview of special relativity, see James Trefil and Robert Hazen, *The Sciences: An Integrated Approach*, 2nd updated edn. (New York: John Wiley & Sons, 2000), ch. 13. For helpful insights see Mark Worthing, *God, Creation, and Contemporary Physics* (Minneapolis: Fortress Press, 1996), 23–6.

3. For careful analysis of the contemporary theological literature on divine action, see Owen Thomas, ed., *God's Activity in the World: The Contemporary Problem*, Studies in Religion Series/American Academy of Religion, 31 (Chico, Calif.: Scholars Press, 1983); and Owen Thomas, "Recent Thought on Divine Agency," in *Divine Action*, ed. Brian Hebblethwaite and Edward Henderson (Edinburgh: T. & T. Clark, 1990).

4. Interesting examples of conservative theologians include Charles Hodge, *Systematic Theology*, 3 vols. (New York: Scribner's Sons, 1891) and Donald Bloesch, *Holy Scripture: Revelation, Inspiration and Interpretation* (Downers' Grove: InterVarsity Press, 1994). Liberal theologians include Rudolf Bultmann, *Theology of the New Testament*, trans. Kendrick Grobel (New York: Charles Scribner's Sons, 1951); and *Jesus Christ and Mythology* (New York: Charles Scribner's Sons, 1958); and Gordon Kaufman, *Systematic Theology: A Historicist Perspective* (New York: Scribner's Sons, 1978), and "On the Meaning of 'Act of God,' " in Thomas, *God's Activity in the World*.

5. Langdon Gilkey's penetrating analysis of the failure of neo-orthodoxy suggests how crucial this problem is. See Gilkey, "Cosmology, Ontology, and the Travail of Biblical Language," *Journal of Religion* 41 (1961).

6. Since 1990 the Center for Theology and the Natural Sciences and the Vatican Observatory have sponsored a series of bi-annual research conferences aimed at gaining a clearer understanding of the relation between contemporary science and a non-interventionist approach to special, objective divine action.

7. For an introduction to thermodynamics, see Trefil and Hazen, *The Sciences*, chs. 3, 4.

8. For an introduction to chaos and complexity theory, see James Crutchfield *et al.*, "Chaos," *Scientific American* 225 (December 1986). For extended references, see Wesley Wildman and Robert Russell, "Chaos: A Mathematical Introduction with Philosophical Reflections," in *Chaos and Complexity: Scientific Perspectives on Divine Action*, ed. Robert J. Russell, Nancey C. Murphy, and Arthur R. Peacocke, Scientific Perspectives on Divine Action Series (Vatican City State; Berkeley, Calif.: Vatican Observatory Publications; Center for Theology and the Natural Sciences, 1995).

9. For an introduction to quantum mechanics, see Paul Davies, *Quantum Mechanics* (London: Routledge & Kegan Paul, 1984). For a more accessible account see Nick Herbert, *Quantum Reality: Beyond the New Physics* (Garden City, N.Y.: Anchor Press; Doubleday, 1985).

10. This approach has been criticized by a number of scholars including Arthur Peacocke and John Polkinghorne. See Peacocke, "God's Interaction with the World: The Implications of Deterministic 'Chaos' and of Interconnected and Interdependent Reality," in Russell *et al.*, *Chaos and Complexity*, 279–81; and Polkinghorne, "The metaphysics of divine action," in ibid., 152–3.

11. These include the measurement problem, non-locality/separability, and the challenge to classical ontology and critical realism.

12. For a non-technical introduction, see George F. R. Ellis and William R. Stoeger, SJ, "Introduction to General Relativity and Cosmology," in

Quantum Cosmology and the Laws of Nature: Scientific Perspectives on Divine Action, ed. Robert J. Russell, Nancey C. Murphy, and Chris J. Isham, Scientific Perspectives on Divine Action Series (Vatican City State; Berkeley, Calif.: Vatican Observatory Publications; Center for Theology and the Natural Sciences, 1993).

13. For helpful surveys of the various views see John Barrow and Frank Tipler, *The Anthropic Cosmological Principle* (Oxford: Clarendon Press, 1986); and Southgate *et al.*, *God, Humanity and the Cosmos*.

14. For a non-technical introduction, see James S. Trefil, *The Moment of Creation: Big Bang Physics from Before the First Millisecond to the Present Universe* (New York: Macmillan, 1983), ch. 10 and following. For a more technical introduction, see Chris J. Isham, "Creation of the Universe as a Quantum Process," in *Physics, Philosophy, and Theology: A Common Quest for Understanding*, ed. Robert J. Russell, William R. Stoeger, SJ, and George V. Coyne, SJ (Vatican City State: Vatican Observatory Publications, 1988); and "Quantum Theories of the Creation of the Universe," in Russell *et al.*, *Quantum Cosmology and the Laws of Nature*.

15. A similar argument has been developed by Joseph Zycinski, "Metaphysics and Epistemology in Stephen Hawking's Theory of the Creation of the Universe," *Zygon: Journal of Religion and Science* 31.2 (June 1996).

16. For a view of positions taken in the nineteenth century, see Claude Welch, *Protestant Thought in the Nineteenth Century*, vol. 2 (New Haven: Yale University Press, 1985), ch. 6; and Ian Barbour, *Issues in Science and Religion* (New York: Prentice-Hall, 1966; New York: Harper & Row, 1971), ch. 4.

17. For a helpful introduction, see Trefil and Hazen, *The Sciences*, chs. 19–25. For teaching resources, see Ursula Goodenough, "Biology: What One Needs to Know," *Zygon: Journal of Religion and Science* 31.4 (December 1996); and Francisco Ayala, "The Evolution of Life: An Overview," in *Evolutionary and Molecular Biology: Scientific Perspectives on Divine Action*, ed. Robert John Russell, William R. Stoeger, and Francisco J. Ayala (Vatican City State; Berkeley, Calif.: Vatican Observatory Publications; Center for Theology and the Natural Sciences, 1998).

18. Several conservative and evangelical theologians have also offered creative interpretations of evolution, including Alister McGrath, *Science and Religion: An Introduction*, and Howard J. van Till, *Science Held Hostage: What's Wrong with Creation Science and Evolutionism* (Downers Grove, Ill.: InterVarsity Press, 1988).

19. For an introduction to sociobiology, see E. O. Wilson, *Sociobiology: The New Synthesis* (Cambridge, Mass.: Belknap Press, Harvard University Press, 1975); and *On Human Nature* (Cambridge, Mass.: Harvard University Press, 1978); and Richard Dawkins, *The Selfish Gene* (Oxford: Oxford University Press, 1976). On cognitive and neuroscience, see

Joseph LeDoux, "Emotions: How I've Looked for Them in the Brain," in *Neuroscience and the Person: Scientific Perspectives on Divine Action*, ed. Robert John Russell, Nancey Murphy, Theo C. Meyering, and Michael A. Arbib (Vatican City State; Berkeley, Calif.: Vatican Observatory Publications; Center for Theology and the Natural Sciences, 1999); and Michael Arbib, "Towards a Neuroscience of the Person," in *Neuroscience and the Person: Scientific Perspectives on Divine Action*.

20. See, for example, Paul's use of the term σῶμα ψυχικόν in 1 Cor. 15.44. For a careful analysis of New Testament views of the person, see Joel Green, "Bodies – That Is, Human Lives," in *Whatever Happened to the Soul? Scientific and Theological Portraits of Human Nature*, ed. Warren S. Brown, Nancey Murphy, and H. Newton Malony (Minneapolis: Fortress Press, 1998).

21. Although ethical issues per se are not within the scope of this essay, human genetics is one area in particular in which ethics and theology are extraordinarily intertwined. For careful reflection on the Human Genome Project and its implications, see Ted Peters, "Genes, Theology, and Social Ethics: Are We Playing God?," in *Genetics: Issues of Social Justice*, ed. Ted Peters (Cleveland, Ohio: Pilgrim Press, 1998).

22. For an introducti n to artificial intelligence, see Anne Foerst, "Artificial Intelligence: Walking the Boundary," *Zygon: Journal of Religion and Science* 31.4 (December 1996).

23. These questions were already present in the climate of the 1930s to 1950s when Teilhard de Chardin framed his elegant synthesis of science, theology, and spirituality. See Pierre Teilhard de Chardin, *The Phenomenon of Man*, trans. Bernard Wall (New York: Harper & Row, 1975).

24. Other scholars who have written on these and similar issues include Ronald Cole-Turner, *The New Genesis: Theology and the Genetic Revolution* (Louisville: Westminster/John Knox Press, 1993); and Nancey Murphy, "Of Miracles," *CTNS Bulletin* 10.2 (Spring 1990).

Chapter 5

1. *Human Life and the New Genetics* (National Council of Churches, 1980).

2. *Manipulating Life* (World Council of Churches, 1982).

3. *Human Genetics* (Catholic Health Association of the United States, 1990).

Chapter 6

1. Theologically, my position is dualistic insofar as I believe God is essentially different from the world. For a defense of this theological posi-

tion, emergentist panentheism, see my *God and Contemporary Science* (Grand Rapids: Eerdmans, 1997). We return to this topic in the final section, below.

2. Brian Cantwell Smith, unpublished paper written for the Science and the Spiritual Quest research project www.ssq.net, 3.

3. Donald Davidson, "Mental Events," 214, cited in Jaegwon Kim, *Supervenience and Mind: Selected Philosophical Essays* (Cambrdige: Cambridge University Press, 1993), 138f.

4. Godehard Bruntrup, "The Causal Efficacy of Emergent Mental Properties," *Erkenntnis* 48 (1998): 133–45.

5. See Jaegwon Kim, "The Myth of Nonreductive Materialism," in Richard Warner and Tadeusz Szubka, eds., *The Mind–Body Problem* (Oxford: Blackwell, 1994), 242–60. More recently see Kim, *Mind in a Physical World: An Essay on the Mind–Body Problem and Mental Causation* (Cambridge, Mass.: MIT Press, 1998).

6. Kim, *Supervenience and Mind*, 138.

7. See Leslie Brothers, *Friday's Footprint: How Society Shapes the Human Mind* (New York: Oxford University Press, 1997).

8. See R. M. Hare, "Supervenience," *Aristotelian Society Supplementary Volume* 58 (1984): 1–16, quote 3.

9. Donald Davidson, "Thinking Causes," in John Heil and Alfred Mele, eds., *Mental Causation* (Oxford: Clarendon Press, 1995), 3–17, quote 3.

10. The term was developed in ongoing conversations with Arthur Peacocke; see Peacocke's essay in Robert John Russell *et al.*, eds., *Neuroscience and the Person: Scientific Perspectives on Divine Action* (Vatican City State: Vatican Observatory Publications, 1999).

11. Note that under this definition there could be both reductionist and non-reductionist versions of physicalism – a point that is often overlooked.

12. See her essay in Russell *et al.*, *Neuroscience and the Person*.

13. See Warren Brown, Nancey Murphy, and H. Newton Malony, eds., *Whatever Happened to the Soul?: Scientific and Theological Portraits of Human Nature* (Minneapolis: Fortress Press, 1998).

Chapter 7

1. The works in question are, first, James Draper's, *History of the Conflict between Religion and Science* (1874), a polemical book denouncing Christian theologians for their campaign of obscurantism against scientific truth dating back to the Church of the first century. Second, Andrew Dickson White's *History of the Warfare of Science with Theology in Christendom* (1870–96) paints a dramatic tableau of what he understood to have been a perpetual state of conflict between science and religion, plac-

ing Christianity in the villainous role of relentless saboteur of scientific progress.

2. Prominent among them are David Lindberg's and Ronald Numbers's, eds., *God and Nature: Historical Essays on the Encounter between Christianity and Science* (Berkeley: University of California Press, 1984); and its forthcoming successor *Science and the Christian Tradition: Twelve Case Histories* (Chicago: University of Chicago Press, 2001); John Brooke's *Science and Religion: Some Historical Perspectives* (Cambridge: Cambridge University Press, 1991); John Brooke and Geoffrey Cantor's *Reconstructing Nature* (Edinburgh: T. & T. Clark, 1998); Gary Ferngren's *Encyclopedia of Science and Religion in the Western Tradition* (New York and London: Garland, 2000); and Maggie Osler's *Rethinking the Scientific Revolution* (Cambridge: Cambridge University Press, 2000). Of course, the opposite extreme of constructing a counter-mythology of general harmony and cooperation between science and religion must also be scrupulously avoided.

3. There have been significant treatments of particular sections of this theme. Ernst Robert Curtius, *European Literature and the Latin Middle Ages*, trans. Willard R. Trask (New York: Pantheon Books, 1953), treats the development of the idea in the Middle Ages to the Renaissance. Among the best discussions of the Early Modern context to which I am greatly indebted is Peter Harrison, *The Bible, Protestantism, and the Rise of Modern Science* (Cambridge: Cambridge University Press, 1998). Other treatments are James J. Bono, *The Word of God and the Languages of Man: Interpreting Nature in Early Modern Science and Medicine* (Madison: University of Wisconsin Press, 1995), and Frank E. Manuel, *The Religion of Isaac Newton* (Oxford: Clarendon Press, 1974).

4. Thomas Browne, *Religio Medici*, ed. James Winney (Cambridge, 1983), part I, section 16, pp. 18–19.

5. Ibid.

6. Justin Martyr, *Second Apology*, Ch. 8.

7. Irenaeus, *Adversus haereses*, Book IV, Ch. 20.

8. Tertullian, *Adversus Marcionem*, ed. and trans. Ernest Evans (Oxford: Clarendon Press, 1972), Book V. 5, 539.

9. Chrysostom, Homily IX. 5, 162–3. *The Homilies of S. John Chrysostom, on The Statutes, to the People of Antioch*, A Library of the Fathers of the Holy Catholic Church (Oxford: Parker, 1842). See also Chrysostom *Homily* X. 3, 175: "We were enquiring how, and in what manner, before the giving of the scriptures, God ordered his dispensation toward us; and we said, that by the creature he instructed our race, stretching out the heavens; and there openly unfolding a vast volume, useful alike to the simple and the wise, to the poor and the rich, to Scythians and to barbarians, and to all in general who dwell upon the earth . . . "

10. Curtius, *European Literature and the Latin Middle Ages*, 219, 320.

11. Bonaventure, *Collationes in hexaemeron* (Darmstadt: Wissenschaftliche Buchgesellschaft, 1964), 12.14–17

12. Raimundus Sabundus, *Theologia Naturalis Seu Liber Creaturarum.* Reprint of the Sulzbach edition of 1852, with critical notes (Stuttgart-Bad Cannstatt, 1966), 35–6.

13. Clement C. J. Webb, *Studies in the History of Natural Theology* (Oxford: Clarendon Press, 1915), 295–6.

14. Sabundus, *Theologia Naturalis Seu Liber Creaturarum*, 296

15. Harrison, *The Bible, Protestantism, and the Rise of Modern Science*, 194–5.

16. Jean Calvin, *Institutes of the Christian Religion*, ed. Ford Lewis Battles (Philadelphia: Westminster Press, 1960), Book I, Ch. 6.

17. Ibid. "Not in vain, therefore, has he added the light of his Word in order that he might make himself known unto salvation, and bestowed the privilege on those whom he was pleased to bring into nearer and more familiar relation to himself . . . For as the aged, or those whose sight is defective, when any books however fair, are set before them, though they perceive that there is something written are scarcely able to make out two consecutive words, but, when aided by glasses, begin to read distinctly, so Scripture, gathering together the impressions of Deity, which, till then, lay confused in our minds, dissipates the darkness, and shows us the true God clearly."

18. *Belgic Confession*, Article 2, "By What Means God is Made Known to Us."

19. Willim Ashworth, "Catholicism and Early Modern Science," in Lindberg and Numbers, *God and Nature*, 140.

20. Richard Westfall, "The Rise of Science and the Decline of Orthodox Christianity," in Lindberg and Numbers, eds., *God and Nature* (Berkeley: University of California Press, 1984), 220. See Kepler's letter to Fabricius, 4 July 1603, in *Werke* 14.121.

21. Bacon, *The Advancement of Learning*, quoted in Marshall McLuhan, *The Gutenberg Galaxy: The Making of Typographic Man* (Toronto: University of Toronto Press, 1962), 187.

22. James Bono, *The Word of God and the Languages of Man: Interpreting Nature in Early Modern Science and Medicine* (Madison: University of Wisconsin Press, 1995), 219.

23. Galileo, *Letter to the Grand Duchess Christina*, 1615.

24. Richard Baxter, *The Reasons of the Christian Religion* (London, 1667), 193. Quoted in Barbara Shapiro, *Probability and Certainty in Seventeenth-Century England: A Study of the Relationships between Natural Science, Religion, History, Law, and Literature* (Princeton: Princeton University Press, 1983), 94, quoting John Ray. Shapiro also suggests that "the emphasis placed upon the two books varied with different authors" (291, note 65).

25. Westfall, "The Rise of Science," 232–3. Westfall's source is a manuscript in the Jewish National and University Library, Jerusalem, Yahuda MS 41, fols. 6 and 7.

26. Frank E. Manuel, *The Religion of Isaac Newton* (Oxford: Clarendon Press, 1974), 49.

27. Thomas Paine, *Age of Reason, Being an Investigation of True and Fabulous Theology* (Luxembourg, 1794), 38, 41. Other early deist works are John Toland's *Christianity Not Mysterious*, and Mathew Tindal's *Christianity As Old As the Creation*.

28. Ibid., 240, 247, 250–1.

29. Charles Babbage, *The Ninth Bridgewater Treatise, a Fragment* (London: John Murray, 1838; rpt. ed. London: Frank Cass, 1967), 138–9.

30. Ibid., 139–40.

31. Ellen G. White, *Education* (Oakland, Calif.: Pacific Press, 1903), ch. 2: "The Eden School."

32. Herbert W. Morris, *Science and the Bible, or, the Mosaic Creation and Modern Discoveries* (Philadelphia: Ziegler and McCurdy, 1871), 4–5. Championing a long geological history of the pre-Adamite earth, Morris appears to reject evolution, arguing instead that God creates successive "races" of creatures as catastrophes reshape the surface of the earth (p. 42).

33. P. A. Chadbourne, *Lectures on Natural Theology, or Nature and the Bible from the Same Author* (New York: G. P. Putnam & Son, 1870).

34. Ibid., 55, 217–18, 222, 237, 320.

35. Joseph Le Conte, *Religion and Science: A Series of Sunday Lectures on the Relation of Natural and Revealed Religion, or the Truths Revealed in Nature and Scripture* (New York: D. Appleton & Company, 1902), 117, 21.

36. Ibid., 23.

37. Ibid., 244, 245.

38. Charles Hodge, *Systematic Theology* (1873), vol. 1, rpt. edn. (London: James Clarke, 1960), ch. 4: "The Knowledge of God," 339–45.

39. J. Gresham Machen, *The Christian Faith in the Modern World* (New York: Macmillan, 1936), 20. More specifically, "God has been pleased to reveal himself in two ways. In the first place, he has been pleased to reveal himself through nature – by the wonders of the world and by his voice within, the voice of conscience – and, in the second place, He has been pleased to reveal Himself in an entirely different way that we call 'supernatural' because it is above 'nature.' " (p. 32).

40. Frederick Temple, *Nature, Man and God*, the Gifford Lectures 1932–4 (London: Macmillan, 1935), Lecture 1: "The Distinction between Natural and Revealed Religion," 5–6.

Chapter 10

1. See especially Giovanni Filoramo, *A History of Gnosticism* (Oxford: Blackwell, 1990), ch. 6.

2. Edward Grant, *The Foundations of Modern Science in the Middle Ages: Their Religious, Institutional, and Intellectual Contexts* (Cambridge: Cambridge University Press, 1996).

3. This "letter," which first appeared in *Concilium*, May 1979, was reproduced as an appendix to Gustavo Gutierrez, *The Power of the Poor in History: Selected Writings* (Maryknoll, N.Y.: Orbis Books, 1983).

4. The interested reader is referred to Paul R. Gross, Norman Levitt, and Martin W. Lewis, eds., *The Flight from Science and Reason* (New York: New York Academy of Sciences, 1997).

5. William D. Hamilton, "The Genetical Evolution of Social Behavior," *Journal of Theoretical Biology* 7 (1964):1–16.

6. George C. Williams, *Adaptation and Natural Selection: A Critique of Some Current Evolutionary Thought* (Princeton: Princeton University Press, 1966).

7. Much work in these fields is still at a preliminary stage. The strength of these disciplines lies in their ability, with the resources of evolutionary biology, to construct a coherent interpretive lens for the interpretation of human behavior. Some work in these disciplines, however, has more often applied the principle insights of evolution philosophically rather than empirically. The work of Edward Wilson, for example, though it draws on critical insights with regard to the study of the social behavior of certain non-human animals, applies these insights to human behavior via analogy. In the coming years, the value of these disciplines will be measured by how these hypotheses via analogy survive ongoing empirical studies.

8. Jared M. Diamond, *Guns, Germs, and Steel: The Fates of Human Societies* (New York: Norton, 1997).

9. David Hull, *The Metaphysics of Evolution* (Albany: SUNY Press, 1989).

10. Laura Betzig, ed., *Human Nature. A Critical Reader* (New York/Oxford: Oxford University Press, 1997).

11. Ibid., back cover.

12. Ibid., xi.

13. Edward O. Wilson, *Consilience: The Unity of Knowledge* (New York: Norton, 1998), 6. Toward the end, he summarizes the argument as follows: "The true evolutionary epic, retold as poetry, is as intrinsically ennobling as any religious epic" (p. 265).

14. See Michael Ruse, *Mystery of Mysteries: Is Evolution a Social Construction?* (Cambridge, Mass.: Harvard University Press, 1999), ch. 9.

15. As Jeffrey Schloss has aptly summarized it, "human nature is not a

static entity to fill up, but a dynamic relationship between genes and labile culture," Jeffrey Schloss, "Emerging Evolutionary Accounts of Altruism: 'Love's Creation Final Law'?" ch. 13 of *Altruism and Altruistic Love: Science, Philosophy, and Religion in Dialogue*, ed. Stephen G. Post *et al.* (Oxford: Oxford University Press, forthcoming). But this "becoming" side of the human is also characteristic of any Christian anthropology – creation takes place not only "from the past" but also "from the future," in grace and in the exercise of our freedom.

16. Charles L. Harper, "Why Science and Religion Need to Talk: Human 'Fallenness', Freedom and Pain are the Preserve of Both Arenas," *Nature* 411.17 (May 2001): 239.

Chapter 13

1. David Hartman, *A Living Covenant: The Innovative Spirit in Traditional Judaism* (New York/London: The Free Press and Collier Macmillan, 1985).

2. Hillel Levine, "Science," in *Contemporary Jewish Religious Thought*, ed. Arthur A. Cohen and Paul Mendes-Flor (London: Free Press, 1972), 856. Levine argues that despite the fact that Jews lived in urban settings where science was developed, "their contributions to the beginnings of modern science were negligible." Samuelson, "Rethinking Ethics in the Light of Jewish Thought and the Life Sciences," *Journal of Religious Ethics* (Fall 2001), argues that it was the isolation in the ghettos, and the development of Rabbinics, that employed the attention of the intellectuals of the early modern period.

3. The root of this word in Hebrew is related to the word "to walk." The same root is found in Islamic law or "sharia."

4. Twelve for women.

5. There are actually more than 613 to be found in the corpus of *halachah*. Six hundred thirteen corresponds to the number of limbs of the body, in rabbinic reckoning 248, added to the number of days of the year.

6. As well as for all other norms.

7. In fact it is essential to remember that much of the case law turns on elaborate constructs that never happened, or could never be expected to happen. Much of the law concerning the role of the court in judging a murderer can be seen in this way (which, by the way, needs to be understood wherever the text is used to understand actual historical circumstance: this is one of the major sources of confusion in some traditional interpretations of Jewish tradition by Christians, especially relative to the Christian understanding of the "trial of Jesus").

8. The terms of Greek analysis do not precisely fit the Jewish system.

9. Herb Basser, as noted on the Post-Modern Jewish Philosophy Network.

10. I want to note here that Childress and Macquarrie consider this a "misleading term", in *The Westminster Dictionary of Christian Ethics* (Philadelphia: Westminster Press, 1967), s.v. "middle axioms." Perhaps a better description would be a coined word: "middle processes."

11. During the last 150 years, four branches of Judaism have developed. All acknowledge the role of *halachah*, but each gives it different weight in the setting of normative standards for their tradition. For the Orthodox Jew, *halachah* is interpreted by his or her rabbi, who then consults with leading scholars if the issue is difficult, and that decision is considered halachically binding. For the Conservative Jew, *halachah* has a strong voice in the determination of *din* by the rabbinic community. The Conservative *minhag* (custom) is determined by the community. Jewish law is then integrated with insights from the social sciences and Western philosophic norms in making a decision. For Reform Jews, the individual is autonomously responsible for his/her own choices, in light of the "tradition" and primary ethical stance of the tradition. For the purposes of this paper, the traditional or halachically grounded position will be described; although the reader should remember that among Jews there is considerable variance. My contention is that, even for Jews not bound by its restraint, *halachah* wields a strong methodological influence.

12. *Shemot Rabbah*, vol. 9. Cf. *Mekhilta, Bahodesh 9*, ed. Horowitz-Rabin, 235, as cited in Marvin Fox, *Modern Jewish Ethics: Theory and Practice* (Columbus: Ohio State University Press, 1975), 18.

13. According to Daniel Boyarin, in a comment on this passage in the first draft of this work, Soleveitchik described this position as Kantian.

14. One can see a stream and note its beauty, its physical properties, or its ritual use, for example. All are "real" views of the same phenomena. Soleveitchik explains that the religious person would first see the ritual use.

15. Joseph Soleveitchik, *The Halachic Mind* (New York: Free Press, 1986). The entire book is an argument for the summary I have presented here. See especially the last chapter.

16. David Holliger, *Science, Jews and Secular Culture: Studies in Mid-Twentieth Century American Intellectual History* (Princeton, N.J.: Princeton University Press, 1995), x.

17. Levine, "Science," 856.

18. Ibid., 860.

19. Levin, R. Faitel, *Halacha, Medical Science and Technology* (New York: Maznaim, 1987). Levin is a traditional rabbinic *poskim*, or rabbi to whom specific legal questions are directed. His field is new technology.

Authors' Bibliographies and Further Reading

Introduction

Gaymon Bennett

Friedman, Thomas L. *The Lexus and the Olive Tree*. New York: Anchor Books, 2000.

Peters, Ted, ed. *Science and Theology: The New Consonance*. Boulder, CO: Westview Press, 1998.

Chapters 1 and 3

Robert John Russell and Kirk Wetger-McNelly

Andresen, Jensine. "Review Article: Science and Technology in Non-Western Cultures." *Zygon: Journal of Religion and Science* 34, no. 2 (June 1999).

Arbib, Michael A., and Mary B. Hesse. *The Construction of Reality*. Gifford Lectures, 1983. Cambridge: Cambridge University Press, 1986.

Ayala, Francisco J. and Theodosius Dobzhansky, eds. *Studies in the Philosophy of Biology: Reduction and Related Problems*. Berkeley: University of California Press, 1974.

Barbour, Ian G. *Myths, Models, and Paradigms: A Comparative Study in Science and Religion*. New York: Harper & Row, 1974.

——. *Religion in an Age of Science*. Gifford Lectures, 1989–1990. San Francisco: Harper & Row, 1990.

——. *Ethics in an Age of Technology*. Gifford Lectures, 1989–1991. San Francisco: HarperSanFrancisco, 1993.

——. *Religion and Science: Historical and Contemporary Issues*. San Francisco: HarperSanFrancisco, 1997.

——. *When Science Meets Religion*. San Francisco: HarperSanFrancisco, 2000.

Barrow, John D., and Frank J. Tipler. *The Anthropic Cosmological Principle*. Oxford: Clarendon Press, 1986.

Birch, Charles. *A Purpose for Everything: Religion in a Postmodern Worldview*. Mystic, CT: Twenty-Third Publications, 1990.

Birch, Charles, and John B. Cobb, Jr. *The Liberation of Life*. Cambridge:

Cambridge University Press, 1981.

Bloor, David. *Knowledge and Social Imagery*. London: Routledge & Kegan Paul, 1976.

Brooke, John H. *Science and Religion: Some Historical Perspectives*. Cambridge: Cambridge University Press, 1991.

——. *Reconstructing Nature: The Engagement of Science and Religion*. Edinburgh: T&T Clark, 1998.

Cajete, Gregory. *Indigenous Science*. Santa Fe: Clear Light Publishers, 2000.

Clayton, Philip. *Explanation from Physics to Theology: An Essay in Rationality and Religion*. New Haven, CT: Yale University Press, 1989.

——. *God and Contemporary Science*. Grand Rapids: Eerdmans, 1997.

Clifford, Anne M. "Creation." In *Systematic Theology: Roman Catholic Perspectives*. Vol. 1. Edited by Francis Schüssler Fiorenza and John P. Galvin. Minneapolis: Fortress Press, 1991.

Clouser, Roy A. *The Myth of Religious Neutrality: An Essay on the Hidden Role of Religious Belief in Theories*. Notre Dame: University of Notre Dame Press, 1991.

Cobb, John B., Jr., and David Ray Griffin. *Process Theology: An Introductory Exposition*. Philadelphia: Westminster Press, 1976.

Cole-Turner, Ronald. *The New Genesis: Theology and the Genetic Revolution*. Louisville: Westminster/John Knox Press, 1993.

Cushing, James T., and Ernan McMullin, eds. *Philosophical Consequences of Quantum Theory: Reflections on Bell's Theorem*. Notre Dame: University of Notre Dame Press, 1989.

Dawkins, Richard. *The Selfish Gene*. Oxford: Oxford University Press, 1976.

Deloria, Vine. *God is Red: A Native View of Religion*. 2nd edn. Golden, CO: North American Press, 1992.

Draper, John William. *History of the Conflict Between Religion and Science*. London/New York: D. Appleton and Company, 1874.

Drees, Willem B. *Religion, Science and Naturalism*. Cambridge: Cambridge University Press, 1996.

Dyson, Freeman. "Time Without End: Physics and Biology in an Open Universe." *Reviews of Modern Physics*, 51 (1979): 447–60.

Ellis, George F.R. *Before the Beginning: Cosmology Explained*. New York: Boyars/Bowerdean, 1993.

Foerst, Anne. "Artificial Intelligence: Walking the Boundary." *Zygon: Journal of Religion and Science* 31, no. 4 (December 1996).

Gleick, James. *Chaos: Making a New Science*. New York: Penguin Books, 1987.

Golshani, Medhi. "How I Understand the Study of Science as a Muslim." *CTNS Bulletin* 17, no.4 (Fall 1997).

——. ed. *Can Science Dispense With Religion?* Tehran: Institute for

Humanities and Cultural Studies, 1998.

Grassie, William. "Postmodernism: What One Needs to Know." *Zygon: Journal of Religion and Science* 32, no. 1 (March 1997).

Gregersen, Niels Henrik and J. Wentzel van Huyssteen Gregersen, eds. *Rethinking Theology and Science: Six Models for the Current Dialogue.* Grand Rapids: Eerdmans, 1998.

Harding, Sandra, and Merrill B. Hintikka, eds. *Discovering Reality: Feminist Perspectives on Epistemology, Metaphysics, Methodology, and Philosophy of Science.* Dordrecht, Holland: Reidel, 1983.

Hartshorne, Charles. *A Natural Theology for Our Time.* La Salle, IL: Open Court, 1967.

Haught, John F. *Science and Religion: From Conflict to Conversion.* New York: Paulist Press, 1995.

Hefner, Philip. *The Human Factor: Evolution, Culture, and Religion.* Minneapolis: Fortress Press, 1993.

Howell, Nancy R. "Ecofeminism: What One Needs to Know." *Zygon: Journal of Religion and Science* 32, no. 2 (June 1997).

Iqbal, Muzzafar. "Five Eminent Early Muslim Scientists and their Contributions to Islamic Scientific Thought." *Islamic Thought and Scientific Creativity* 3, no. 3 (September 1992).

Johnson, Elizabeth A. "Presidential Address: Turn to the Heavens and the Earth." *Catholic Theological Society of America Proceedings* 51 (1996): 1–14.

Keller, Evelyn Fox, and Helen E. Longino, eds. *Feminism and Science.* Oxford: Oxford University Press, 1996.

Lebacqz, Karen. "Fair Shares: Is the Genome Project Just?" *CTNS Bulletin* 13, no. 4 (Autumn 1993).

Lindberg, David C., and Ronald L. Numbers, eds. *God and Nature: Historical Essays on the Encounter between Christianity and Science.* Berkeley: University of California Press, 1986.

Loder, James Edwin, and Jim W. Neidhardt. *The Knight's Move: The Relational Logic of the Spirit in Theology and Science.* Colorado Springs: Helmers & Howard, 1992.

Matt, Daniel C. *God and The Big Bang: Discovering Harmony Between Science and Spirituality.* Woodstock, VT: Jewish Lights Publishing, 1996.

McFague, Sallie. *The Body of God: An Ecological Theology.* Minneapolis: Fortress Press, 1993.

McGrath, Alister E. *Science and Religion: An Introduction.* Oxford: Blackwell Publishers, 1999.

McMullin, Ernan, ed. *Construction and Constraint: The Shaping of Scientific Rationality.* Notre Dame: University of Notre Dame Press, 1988.

Merchant, Carolyn. *The Death of Nature: Women, Ecology, and the Scientific Revolution.* New York: Harper & Row, 1980.

Moltmann, Jürgen. "God in Creation: A New Theology of Creation and the Spirit of God." In *The Gifford Lectures 1984–1985.* San Francisco:

Harper & Row, 1985.

Murphy, George L. "Time, Thermodynamics, and Theology". *Zygon: Journal of Religion and Science* 26, no. 3 (September 1991).

Murphy, Nancey. *Theology in the Age of Scientific Reasoning*. Ithaca: Cornell University Press, 1990.

———. *Beyond Liberalism and Fundamentalism: How Modern and Postmodern Philosophy Set the Theological Agenda*. Valley Forge, PA: Trinity Press International, 1996.

Murphy, Nancey, and George F. R. Ellis. *On the Moral Nature of the Universe: Theology, Cosmology, and Ethics*. Minneapolis: Fortress Press, 1996.

Pannenberg, Wolfhart. *Theology and the Philosophy of Science*. Translated by Francis McDonagh. Philadelphia: Westminster Press, 1976.

Peacocke, Arthur. *God and the New Biology*. San Francisco: Harper & Row, 1986.

———. *Theology for a Scientific Age: Being and Becoming – Natural, Divine and Human*. Minneapolis: Fortress Press, 1993.

Peters, Ted, ed. *Cosmos as Creation: Theology and Science in Consonance*. Nashville: Abingdon Press, 1989.

———. *God — The World's Future: Systematic Theology for a New Era*. 2nd edn. Minneapolis: Fortress Press, 2001.

Peters, Ted, ed. *Genetics: Issues of Social Justice*. Cleveland, Ohio: Pilgrim Press, 1998.

———. Michael Welker and Robert John Russell, eds. *Resurrection: Theological and Scientific Assessments*. Grand Rapids: Eerdmans, 2002.

———. ed. *Science and Theology: The New Consonance*. Boulder, CO: Westview Press, 1998.

Polkinghorne, John C. *The Faith of a Physicist: Reflections of a Bottom-up Thinker*. Minneapolis: Fortress, 1994.

———. 1998. *Science and Theology: An Introduction*. London/Minneapolis: SPCK/Fortress Press.

Primack, Joel R. and Nancy Abrams. "In a beginning . . . : Quantum Cosmology and Kabbalah." *Tikkun* 10 (Jan-Feb 1995): 66–73.

Richardson, W. Mark, and Wesley J. Wildman, eds. *Religion and Science: History, Method, Dialogue*. New York: Routledge, 1996.

Rolston, Holmes, III. "Does nature need to be redeemed?" *Zygon: Journal of Religion and Science* 29, no. 2 (1994).

Ruether, Rosemary Radford. *Gaia and God: An Ecofeminist Theology of Earth Healing*. San Francisco: HarperCollins, 1992.

Ruse, Michael. *Taking Darwin Seriously: A Naturalistic Approach*. Oxford: Blackwell, 1986.

Russell, Robert John. "The Theological Consequences of the Thermodynamics of a Moral Universe: An Appreciative Critique and Extension of the Murphy/Ellis Project." *CTNS Bulletin* 19, no. 4 (Fall

1998).

——. "Time in Eternity." *Dialog* 39, no. 1 (March 2000).

Russell, Robert John, Nancey C. Murphy, and Arthur R. Peacocke, eds. *Chaos and Complexity: Scientific Perspectives on Divine Action*. Scientific Perspectives on Divine Action Series. Vatican City State; Berkeley: Vatican Observatory Publications; Center for Theology and the Natural Sciences, 1995.

——. William R. Stoeger, SJ, and Francisco J. Ayala, eds. *Evolutionary and Molecular Biology: Scientific Perspectives on Divine Action*. Vatican City State; Berkeley: Vatican Observatory Publications; Center for Theology and the Natural Sciences, 1998.

——. Nancey C. Murphy, Theo C. Meyering, and Michael A. Arbib, eds. *Neuroscience and the Person: Scientific Perspectives on Divine Action*. Vatican City State; Berkeley: Vatican Observatory Publications; Center for Theology and the Natural Sciences, 1999.

——. Philip Clayton, Kirk Wegter-McNelly, and John Polkinghorne, eds. *Quantum Physics: Scientific Perspectives on Divine Action*. Vatican City State; Berkeley: Vatican Observatory Publications; Center for Theology and the Natural Sciences, 2001.

——. William R. Stoeger, SJ, and George V. Coyne, SJ, eds. *Physics, Philosophy, and Theology: A Common Quest for Understanding*. Vatican City State: Vatican Observatory Publications, 1988.

Samuelson, Norbert M. *Judaism and the Doctrine of Creation*. Cambridge: Cambridge University Press, 1994.

Schrödinger, Erwin. *What is Life? Mind and Matter*. Cambridge: Cambridge University Press, 1967.

Segundo, Juan Luis. *An Evolutinary Aproach to Jesus of Nazareth*. Translated by John Drury. New York: Orbis Books, 1988.

Soskice, Janet Martin. *Metaphor and Religious Language*. Oxford: Oxford University Press, 1985.

Southgate, Christopher, *et al.*, eds. *God, Humanity and the Cosmos: A Textbook in Science and Religion*. Harrisburg: Trinity Press International, 1999.

Stenmark, Mikael. *Rationality in Science, Religion, and Everyday Life: A Critical Evaluation of Four Models of Rationality*. Notre Dame: University of Notre Dame Press, 1995.

Theissen, Gerd. *Biblical Faith: An Evolutionary Approach*. Minneapolis: Fortress Press, 1985.

Tipler, Frank J. *The Physics of Immortality: Modern Cosmology, God, and the Resurrection of the Dead*. New York: Doubleday, 1994.

Torrance, Thomas F. *Theological Science*. London: Oxford University Press, 1969.

Trefil, James S., and Robert M. Hazen. *The Sciences: An Integrated Approach*. 2nd edn. New York: John Wiley & Sons, 2000.

Van Huyssteen, J. Wentzel. *Theology and the Justification of Faith: Construct-*

ing Theories in Systematic Theology. Grand Rapids: Eerdmans, 1989.

——. *Essays in Postfoundationalist Theology.* Grand Rapids: Eerdmans, 1997.

Watts, Fraser N., ed. *Science Meets Faith: Theology and Science in Conversation.* London: SPCK, 1998.

Wegter-McNelly, Kirk. "He Descended into Hell: A Liberation Response to the Kenosis in *On the Moral Nature of the Universe.*" *CTNS Bulletin* 19, no. 4 (Fall 1998).

Welch, Claude. *Protestant Thought in the Nineteenth Century.* Vol. 2. New Haven: Yale University Press, 1985.

Wertheim, Margaret. *Pythagoras' trousers: God, Physics, and the Gender Wars.* New York: Times Books, 1995.

White, Andrew Dickson. *A History of the Warfare of Science with Theology in Christendom.* London/New York: D. Appleton and Company, 1896.

Whitehead, Alfred North. *Process and Reality.* Edited by David Ray Griffin and Donald W. Sherburne. New York: Free Press, 1978.

Wilson, E. O. *Sociobiology – The New Synthesis.* Cambridge, MA: Belknap Press, Harvard University Press, 1975.

Worthing, Mark W. *God, Creation, and Contemporary Physics.* Theology and the Sciences Series. Minneapolis: Fortress Press, 1996.

Chapter 2

Nancey Murphy

Barbour, Ian G. *Myths, Models, and Paradigms.* New York: Harper and Row, 1974.

Barnes, Barry. *Interests and the Growth of Knowledge.* London: Routledge & Kegan Paul, 1977.

Bloor, David. *Knowledge and Social Imagery.* London: Routledge & Kegan Paul, 1976.

Kuhn, Thomas. *The Structure of Scientific Revolutions,* 2nd edn. Chicago: University of Chicago Press, 1970.

Lakatos, Imre. "Falsification and the Methodology of Scientific Research Programmes." In *Philosophical Papers.* Vol. 1. Cambridge: Cambridge University Press, 1987.

Lindbeck, George. *Nature of Doctrine.* Philadelphia: Westminster Press, 1984.

MacIntyre, Alasdair. *After Virtue.* Notre Dame: University of Notre Dame Press, 1981.

Murphy, Nancey. *Theology in the Age of Scientific Reasoning.* Ithaca, NY: Cornell, 1990.

Peacocke, Arthur. R. *Intimations of Reality.* Notre Dame: University of Notre Dame Press, 1984.

Popper, Karl. *The Logic of Scientific Discovery*. New York: Routledge, 1977.

Quine, Willard V. O. "Two Dogmas of Empiricism." *Philosophical Review* 40 (1951): 20-43.

Rorty, Richard. *Philosophy and the Mirror of Nature*. Princeton: Princeton University Press, 1979.

Rudwick, Martin. "Senses of the Natural World and Senses of God: Another Look at the Historical Relation of Science and Religion." In *The Sciences and Theology in the Twentieth Century*. A. R. Peacocke, ed. Notre Dame: University of Notre Dame Press, 1981.

Stevenson, C. L. *Ethics and Language*. New Haven: Yale University Press, 1944.

Stout, Jeffrey. *The Flight from Authority*. Notre Dame: University of Notre Dame Press, 1981.

Thiemann, Ronald. *Revelation and Theology*. Notre Dame: University of Notre Dame Press, 1985.

Wittgenstein, Ludwig *Tractatus Logico-Philosophicus*. London: Routledge and Paul, 1922.

——. *Philosophical Investigations*. Oxford: Oxford University Press, 1953.

Chapter 4

Martinez J. Hewlett

Barkow, J., Leda Cosmides, and John Tooby. *The Adapted Mind: Evolutionary Psychology and the Generation of Culture*. New York: Oxford University Press, 1992.

Behe, Michael. *Darwin's Black Box: The Biochemical Challenge to Evolution*. New York: Simon and Schuster, 1996.

Dawkins, Richard. *The Blind Watchmaker: Why the Evidence of Evolution Reveals a Universe Without Design*. New York and London: W. W. Norton, 1996.

Dembski, William. *The Design Inference: Eliminating Chance Through Small Probabilities*. Cambridge: Cambridge University Press, 1998.

——. *No Free Lunch: Why Specified Complexity Cannot be Purchased Without Intelligence*. Lanham, MD: Rowman and Littlefield, 2001.

Dennett, Daniel. *Darwin's Dangerous Idea: Evolution and the Meaning of Life*. New York: Touchstone/Simon and Schuster, 1995.

Haught, John. *God After Darwin: A Theology of Evolution*. Boulder, CO: Westview Press, 2000.

Miller, Kenneth. *Finding Darwin's God: A Scientist's Search for Common Ground Between God and Evolution*. New York: Cliff Street Books/Harper Collins, 1999.

Rose, Hilary and Steven Rose. *Alas Poor Darwin: Arguments Against*

Evolutionary Psychology. London: Jonathan Cape/Random House, 2000.

Rose, Steven. *Lifelines: Biology Beyond Determinism*. New York: Oxford University Press, 1998.

Ruse, Michael. *Taking Darwin Seriously: A Naturalistic Approach to Philosophy*. New York: Prometheus Books, 1998.

Wilson, Edward. *Consilience: The Unity of Knowledge*. New York: Random House, 1998.

Chapter 5

Ted Peters

Bruce, Donald, and Ann Bruce, eds. *Engineering Genesis: The Ethics of Genetic Engineering*. London: Earthscan, 1999.

Chapman, Audrey R. *Unprecedented Choices: Religious Ethics at the Frontiers of Genetic Science*. Minneapolis: Fortress Press, 1999.

Cole-Turner, Ronald, ed. *Human Cloning: Religious Responses*. Louisville: Westminster/John Knox Press, 1997.

Cooke-Deegan, Robert. *The Gene Wars*. New York: W.W. Norton, 1996.

Davies, Kevin. *Cracking the Genome*. New York: Free Press, 2001.

Evangelical Lutheran Church in America. *Human Cloning: Papers from a Church Consultation*. Chicago: ELCA, 2000.

Hamer, Dean H., Stella Hu, Victoria L. Magnuson, Nan Hu, and Angela M. L. Pattaucci. "A Linkage Between DNA Markers on the X Chromosome and Male Sexual Orientation." *Science* 261 (16 July 1993): 321–327.

Hefner, Philip. *The Human Factor*. Minneapolis: Fortress Press, 1993.

Holland, Suzanne, Karen Lebacqz, and Laurie Zoloth, eds. *The Human Embryonic Stem Cell Debate*. Cambridge: MIT Press, 2002.

International Human Genome Sequencing Consortium. "Initial Sequencing and Analysis of the Human Genome." *Nature* 409 (15 February 2001): 860–921.

Kevles, Daniel J., and Leroy Hood, eds. *Code of Codes: Scientific and Social Issues in the Human Genome Project*. Cambridge, MA: Harvard University Press, 1992.

National Bioethics Advisory Commission. *Cloning Human Beings*, June 1997.

National Institutes of Health. *Stem Cells: Scientific Progress and Future Research Directions*, 2001.

Peters, Ted. *Playing God? Genetic Determinism and Human Freedom*. New York: Routledge, 1997.

———. *For the Love of Children: Genetic Technology and the Future of the Family*. Louisville: Westminster/John Knox Press, 1998.

———. ed. *Genetics: Issues of Social Justice*. Cleveland: Pilgrim Press,

242   *Authors' Bibliographies and Further Reading*

1998.
Shannon, Thomas A., ed. *Bioethics*. 3rd edn. New York: Paulist Press, 1987.
Shinn, Roger L. *The New Genetics: Challenges for Science, Faith, and Politics.* Wakefield, RI and London: Moyer Bell, 1996.
Venter, J. Craig, *et al.* "The Sequence of the Human Genome." *Science* 291 (16 February 2001): 1304–51.
Wilmut, Ian. "Viable Offspring Derived from Fetal and Adult Mammalian Cells," *Nature* 385 (February 1997): 810–13.

Chapter 6

Philip Clayton

Brothers, Leslie. *Friday's Footprint: How Society Shapes the Human Mind.* New York: Oxford University Press, 1997.
Brown, Warren, Nancey Murphy, and H. Newton Malony, eds. *Whatever Happened to the Soul?: Scientific and Theological Portraits of Human Nature.* Minneapolis: Fortress Press, 1998.
Bruntrup, Godehard. "The Causal Efficacy of Emergent Mental Properties," *Erkenntnis* 48 (1998).
Clayton, Philip. *God and Contemporary Science*. Grand Rapids: Eerdmans, 1997.
Davidson, Donald. "Thinking Causes." In *Mental Causation*. John Heil and Alfred Mele, eds. Oxford: Clarendon Press, 1995.
Hare, R.M. "Supervenience." *Aristotelian Society Supplementary*. Vol. 58. London: The Aristotelian Society, 1984.
Kim, Jaegwon. *Supervenience and Mind: Selected Philosophical Essays.* Cambridge: Cambridge University Press, 1993.
——. "The Myth of Nonreductive Materialism." In *The Mind–Body Problem.* Richard Warner and Tadeusz Szubka, eds. Oxford: Blackwell, 1994.
——. *Mind in a Physical World: An Essay on the Mind–Body Problem and Mental Causation*. Cambridge, MA: MIT Press, 1998.
Robert John Russell, *et al.*, eds. *Neuroscience and the Person: Scientific Perspectives on Divine Action.* Vatican City State; Berkeley, CA: Vatican Observatory Publications; The Center for Theology and the Natural Sciences, 1999.

Chapter 7

Peter M.J. Hess

Athanasius. *The Coptic Life of Anthony*. Translated by Tim Vivian. San Francisco: International Scholars Publications, 1994.
Bacon, Francis. *The Advancement of Learning*. Edited by Michael Kiernan.

Oxford: Clarendon Press, 2000.

Babbage, Charles. *The Ninth Bridgewater Treatise, a Fragment.* London: John Murray, 1838. Reprinted edition. London: Frank Cass, 1967.

Balfour, Thomas A. G. *Nature and the Bible Have One Author.* London: James Nisbet, 1861.

Baxter, Richard. "The Reasons of the Christian Religion." In *A Call to the Unconverted.* London: John Mason, 1862.

Bonaventure. *Collationes in Hexaemeron.* Darmstadt: Wissenschaftliche Buchgesellschaft, 1964.

Bono, James J. *The Word of God and the Languages of Man: Interpreting Nature in Early Modern Science and Medicine.* Madison, WI: University of Wisconsin Press, 1995.

Brennan, Martin S. *The Science of the Bible.* St Louis: B. Herder, 1898.

Browne, Thomas. *Religio Medici,* (1635). Edited by James Winney. Cambridge: Cambridge University Press, 1983.

Butler, Joseph. *Fifteen Sermons Preached at the Rolls Chapel, 1726.* Edited by T. A. Roberts. London: SPCK, 1970.

Calvin, Jean. *Institutes of the Christian religion.* Edited by John T. McNeill. Translated by Ford Lewis Battles. Philadelphia: Westminster Press, 1960.

Chadbourne, Paul A. *Lectures on Natural Theology, or Nature and the Bible from the Same Author.* New York: G. P. Putnam and Son, 1870.

Chrysostom, John. *The Homilies of S. John Chrysostom, on The Statutes, to the People of Antioch. A Library of the Father of the Holy Catholic Church,* Homily IX. Oxford: Parker, 1842.

Curtius, Ernst Robert. *European Literature and the Latin Middle Ages.* Translated by Willard R. Trask. New York: Pantheon Books, 1953.

Dante Alighieri. *The Divine Comedy: Inferno, Purgatorio, Paradiso.* Translated by Allen Mandelbaum. New York: Alfred Knopf: 1995.

Dick, Thomas. *The Christian Philosopher, or the Connexion of Science and Philosophy with Religion.* 1844.

Dove, John. *A Confutation of Atheism.* London, 1605.

Harrison, Peter. *The Bible, Protestantism, and the Rise of Modern Science.* Cambridge: Cambridge University Press, 1998.

Hodge, Charles. *Systematic Theology* (1873). Vol. 1. London: James Clarke, 1960.

Holton, Gerald. "Johannes Kepler's Universe: Its Physics and Metaphysics." *American Journal of Physics* 24 (May 1956): 340–351.

Justin Martyr. *The First and Second Apologies.* Ancient Christian Writers, no. 56. Translated by Leslie William Barnard. New York: Paulist Press, 1997.

Le Conte, Joseph. *Religion and Science: a Series of Sunday Lectures on the Relation of Natural and Revealed Religion, or the Truths Revealed in Nature and Scripture.* New York: D. Appleton and Company, 1902.

Lindberg, David C., and Ronald L. Numbers, eds. *God and Nature: Historical Essays on the Encounter between Christianity and Science.* Berkeley: University of California Press, 1984.

Machen, J. Gresham. *The Christian Faith in the Modern World.* New York: Macmillan, 1936.

Manuel, Frank E. *The Religion of Isaac Newton.* Oxford: Clarendon Press, 1974.

McLuhan, Marshall. *The Gutenberg Galaxy: The Making of Typographic Man.* Toronto: University of Toronto Press, 1962.

Morris, Herbert W. *Science and the Bible, or, the Mosaic Creation and Modern Discoverie.* Philadelphia: Ziegler and McCurdy, 1871.

Osler, Margaret J., ed. *Rethinking the Scientific Revolution.* Cambridge: Cambridge University Press, 2000.

Paine, Thomas. *Age of Reason, Being an Investigation of True and Fabulous Theology.* Luxembourg, 1794.

Raven, C. E. *Organic Design: A Study of Scientific Thought from Ray to Paley.* Oxford: Oxford University Press, 1953.

Sabunde, Raymond. *Theologia Naturalis Seu Liber Creaturarum* (1436). Reprint of the Sulzbach edition of 1852, with critical notes. Stuttgart-Bad Cannstatt, 1966.

Shapiro, Barbara. *Probability and Certainty in Seventeenth-Century England: A Study of the Relationships between Natural Science, Religion, History, Law, and Literature.* Princeton: Princeton University Press, 1983.

Temple, Frederick. *Nature, Man and God* (the Gifford Lectures 1932–34). London: Macmillan, 1935.

Tertullian. *Adversus Marcionem* Edited and translated by Ernest Evans. Oxford: Clarendon Press, 1972.

Webb, Clement C. J. *Studies in the History of Natural Theology.* Oxford: Clarendon Press, 1915.

White, Ellen G. *Education.* Oakland, CA: Pacific Press, 1903.

Chapter 8

Muzaffar Iqbal

Açikgenç, Alparsalan. *Islamic Science: Towards a Definition.* Kuala Lumpur: International Institute of Islamic Thought and Civilization, 1996.

Al-Attas, Syed Muhammad Naquib. *Islam and Secularism.* Kuala Lumpur: International Institute of Islamic Thought and Civilization, 1993.

——. *Prolegomena to the Metaphysics of Islam.* Kuala Lumpur: International Institute of Islamic Thought and Civilization, 1995.

Babar, Zaheer. *The Science of Empire.* Albany: State University Press of New York, 1996.

Bakar, Osman. *Tawhid and Science.* Kuala Lampur: Secretariat for Islamic

Philosophy and Science, 1991.

Bakar, Osman. *Classification of Knowledge in Islam*. Kuala Lumpur: Institute for Policy Research, 1992.

Burckhardt, Titus. *Mirror of the Intellect: Essays on Traditional Science and Sacred Art*. Cambridge: Quinta Essentia, 1987.

———. *Alchemy, Science of the Cosmos, Science of the Soul*. Cambridge: Quinta Essentia, 1995.

Chittick, William C. *The Sufi Path of Knowledge: Ibn Al-Arabi's Metaphysics of Imagination*. Albany: State University of New York Press, 1998.

Craig, William Lane. *The Kalam Cosmological Argument*. London: Macmillan, 1997.

Golshani, Mehdi. *The Holy Qur'an and the Sciences of Nature*. Binghamton, N Y: Institute of Global Cultural Studies, Binghamton University, 1999.

Hahn, Lewis Edwin, Randall E. Auxier, and Lucian E. Stone, Jr. *The Philosophy of Seyyed Hossein Nasr*. Chicago: Open Court, 2001.

Haq, Syed Nomanul. *Names, Nature and Things*. Dordrecht: Kluwer Academic, 1994.

Hourani, George F. ed. *Essays on Islamic Philosophy and Science*. Albany: State University of New York Press, 1975.

Iqbal, Muzaffar. *Islam and Science*. Aldershot: Ashgate, 2002.

Izutsu, T. *God and Man in the Koran: Semantics of the Koranic Weltanschauung*. Tokoyo: Keio Institute of Cultural and Linguistic Studies, 1964.

Mabud, Shaikh Abdul. *Theory of Evolution: An Assessment from the Islamic Point of View*. Cambridge: The Islamic Academy, 1991.

Nasr, Seyyed Hossein. *Science and Civilization in Islam*. Cambridge: Harvard University Press, 1968.

———. *Islamic Life and Thought*. Albany: State University of New York Press, 1981.

———. *Knowledge and the Sacred*. Edinburgh: Edinburgh University Press, 1981.

———. *An Introduction to Islamic Cosmological Doctrines*. Albany: State University of New York Press, 1993.

———. *Religion and the Order of Nature*. New York: Oxford University Press, 1996.

Netton, Ian Richard. *Allah Transcendent*. Surrey: Curzon Press, 1989.

Northbourne, Lord. *Looking Back on Progress*. London: Perennial Books, 1970.

Peters, F. E. *Aristotle and the Arabs*. New York: New York University Press, 1968.

Peters, Ted, Iqbal Muzaffar, and Syed Nomanul Haq. *God, Life and the Cosmos: Christian and Islamic Perspectives*. Aldershot: Ashgate, 2002.

Piamenta, M. *The Muslim Conception of God and Human Welfare*. Leiden: E.J. Brill, 1983.

Pines, Shlomo. *The Collected Works of Shlomo Pines.* Vol. 2. In *Studies in Arabic Versions of Greek Texts and in Medical Science.* Leiden: E. J. Brill, 1986.

Rahman, F. *Major Themes of the Qur'an.* Minneapolis: Bibliotheca Islamica, 1980.

Sabra, A. I. *Optics, Astronomy and Logic.* Hampshire: Variorum, 1994.

Saliba, George. *A History of Arabic Astronomy: Planetary Theories During the Golden Age of Islam.* New York: New York University Press, 1994.

Sardar, Ziauddin. *Explorations in Islamic Science.* London: Mansell Publishing Ltd, 1998.

———. ed. *The Touch of Midas: Science, Values and Environment in Islam and the West.* Petaling Jaya, Malaysia: Pelanduk, 1988.

Sharif, M. M. *A History of Muslim Philosophy.* Karachi: Royal Book Company, 1983.

Stenberg, L. *The Islamization of Science: Four Muslim Positions, Developing an Islamic Modernity.* Ludwig: Lund Studies in History of Religions, 1996.

Whitall, Perry N. *The Widening Breach: Evolutionism in the Mirror of Cosmology.* Cambridge: Quinta Essentia, 1995.

Chapter 9

Richard Payne

Bodde, Derk. *Chinese Thought, Society, and Science: The Intellectual and Social Background of Science and Technology in Pre-modern China.* Honolulu: University of Hawaii Press, 1991.

Cabézon, José Ignacio and Roger R. Jackson, eds. *Tibetan Literature: Studies in Genre.* Ithaca, NY: Snow Lion Publications, 1991.

Davidson, Richard J. and Anne Harrington, eds. *Visions of Compassion: Western Scientists and Tibetan Buddhists Examine Human Nature.* Oxford: Oxford University Press, 2002.

de La Vallée Poussin, Louis. *Abhidharmako abhâyam.* 4 vols. Translated by Leo M. Pruden. Berkeley: Asian Humanities Press, 1988.

Forte, Antonino. *Mingtang and Buddhist Utopias in the History of the Astronomical Clock: The Tower, Statue and Armillary Sphere Constructed by Empress Wu.* Rome: Istituto Italiano per il Medio ed Estremo Oriente, and Paris: École Française d'Extrême–Orient, 1988.

Gampopa. *The Jewel Ornament of Liberation: The Wish-Fulfilling Gem of the Noble Teachings.* Translated by Khenpo Konchog Gyaltsen, edited by Ani K. Trinlay Chödron. Ithaca, NY: Snow Lion Publications, 1998.

Gyatso, Janet. "A Literary Transmission of the Traditions of Thang-Stong rGyal-po: A Study of Visionary Buddhism in Tibet." Ph.D. dissertation. University of California, Berkeley, 1981.

Kalupahana, David J. *Causality: The Central Philosophy of Buddhism.*

Honolulu: The University Press of Hawaii, 1975.

Matilal, Bimal Krishna. *The Character of Logic in India*. Edited by Jonardon Ganeri and Heeraman Tiwari. Albany: State University of New York Press, 1998.

Needham, Joseph. *Science and Civilization in China*. Vol. 2: *History of Scientific Thought*. Cambridge: Cambridge University Press, 1956.

Perdue, Daniel E. *Debate in Tibetan Buddhism*. Ithaca, NY: Snow Lion Publications, 1992.

Ruegg, David Seyfort. *Ordre Spirituel et Ordre Temporel dans la Penseé Bouddhique de l'Inde et du Tibet*. Paris: Collège de France, 1995.

Sanford, James H. 1997. "Wind, Waters, Stupas, Mandalas: Fetal Buddhahood in Shingon." *Japanese Journal of Religious Studies* 24 (1997): 1–2.

Varela, Francisco J., Evan Thompson, and Eleanor Rosch. *The Embodied Mind: Cognitive Science and Human Experience*. Cambridge and London: MIT Press, 1991.

Wallace, B. Alan. *The Taboo of Subjectivity: Toward a New Science of Consciousness*. Oxford: Oxford University Press, 2000.

———. *Choosing Reality: A Buddhist View of Physics and the Mind*. Ithaca, NY: Snow Lion Publications, 1996.

Wallace, Vesna A. *The Inner Kalacakratantra: A Buddhist Tantric View of the Individual*. Oxford: Oxford University Press, 2001.

Wright, Dale S. *Philosophical Meditations on Zen Buddhism*. Cambridge Studies in Religious Traditions, 13. Cambridge: Cambridge University Press, 1998.

Chapter 10

Eduardo Cruz

Anderson, Ray S. "Anthropology, Christian." In *The Blackwell Encyclopedia of Modern Christian Thought*. Edited by Alister E. McGrath. Oxford: Blackwell, 1993.

Betzig, Laura, ed. *Human Nature: A Critical Reader*. New York/Oxford: Oxford University Press, 1997.

Diamond, Jared M. *Guns, Germs, and Steel: The Fates of Human Societies*. New York: W.W. Norton, 1997.

Filoramo, Giovanni. *A History of Gnosticism*. Oxford: Basil Blackwell, 1990.

Grant, Edward. *The Foundations of Modern Science in the Middle Ages:Their Religious, Institutional, and Intellectual Contexts*. Cambridge: Cambridge University Press, 1996.

Gross, Paul R., Norman Levitt, and Martin W. Lewis, eds. *The Flight from Science and Reason*. New York: New York Academy of Sciences, 1997.

Gutierrez, Gustavo. *The Power of the Poor in History: Selected Writings*.

Maryknoll, NY: Orbis, 1983.

Hamilton, William D. "The Genetical Evolution of Social Behavior." *The Journal of Theoretical Biology* 7 (1964):1–16.

Harper, Charles L. "Why Science and Religion Need to Talk: Human 'fallenness', freedom and pain are the preserve of both arenas." *Nature* 411, no. 17 (May 2001): 239–40.

Peters, Ted, ed. *Science and Theology: The New Consonance.* Boulder, CO: Westview Press, 1998.

Ruse, Michael. *Mystery of Mysteries: Is Evolution a Social Construction?* Cambridge, MA: Harvard University Press, 1999.

Schloss, Jeffrey. "Emerging Evolutionary Accounts of Altruism: 'Love's Creation Final Law'?" In *Altruism and Altruistic Love: Science, Philosophy, and Religion in Dialogue.* Edited by Stephen G. Post *et al.* Oxford: Oxford University Press.

Williams, George C. *Adaptation and Natural Selection: A Critique of Some Current Evolutionary Thought.* Princeton: Princeton University Press, 1966.

Wilson, Edward O. *Consilience: The Unity of Knowledge* New York: W.W. Norton, 1998.

Chapter 11

Varadaraja V. Raman

Danielou, Alain. *The Gods of India: Hindu Polytheism.* Rochester: Inner Traditions International, 1985.

Eck, Diana L. *Darsan: Seeing the Divine Image of India.* Chambersburg: Anima Books, 1985.

Klostermaier, K. K. *A Survey of Hinduism.* Albany: State University of New York Press, 1989.

Radhakrishnan, Sarvepali. *The Hindu View of Life.* London: Unwin Books, 1971.

Raman, Varadaraja. V. *Glimpses of Indian Heritage.* Mumbai: Popular Prakashan, 1989.

——. "Science and the Spiritual Vision: A Hindu Perspective." In *When Worlds Converge: What Science and Religion Tells Us About The Universe and Our Place in It.* Edited by Clifford N. Matthews, *et al.* La Salle, IL: Open Court, 2001.

Chapter 12

George Murphy

Asimov, Isaac. *Life and Energy.* New York: Bantam, 1965.

Bonhoeffer, Dietrich. *Letters and Papers from Prison.* New York: Macmillan,

1971.

Darwin, Charles. *On the Origin of Species*. London: J.W. Dent & Sons, 1972.

Einstein, Albert, and Leopold Infeld. *The Evolution of Physics*. New York: Simon and Schuster, 1938.

Forde, Gerhard. *On Being a Theologian of the Cross*. Grand Rapids: Eerdmans, 1997.

Glashow, Sheldon and Ben Bova. *Interactions*. New York: Warner, 1988.

Gleick, James. *Chaos: Making a New Science*. New York: Penguin, 1987.

Juengel, Eberhard. *God as the Mystery of the World*. Grand Rapids: Eerdmans 1987.

Moltmann, Jürgen. *The Crucified God*. New York: Harper & Row, 1974.

Polkinghorne, John. *The Quantum World*. Princeton: Princeton University Press, 1984.

Watson, James D. *The Double Helix*. New York: Mentor, 1969.

Weinberg, Steven. *The First Three Minutes*. New York: Basic Books, 1988.

Chapter 13

Laurie Zoloth

Childress, James F. and John Macquarrie, eds. *The Westminster Dictionary of Christian Ethics*. Philadelphia: Westminster Press, 1967.

Fox, Marvin, ed. *Modern Jewish Ethics: Theory and Practice*. Columbus: Ohio State University Press, 1975.

Hartman, David. *A Living Covenant: The Innovative Spirit in Traditional Judaism*. New York/London: The Free Press and Collier Macmillan, 1985.

Holliger, David. *Science, Jews and Secular Culture: Studies in Mid-Twentieth Century American Intellectual History*. Princeton: Princeton University Press, 1995.

Levine, Hillel. *Contemporary Jewish Religious Thought: Original Essays on Critical Concepts, Movements, and Beliefs*. Edited by Arthur A. Cohen and Paul Mendes-Flohr. London: The Free Press, 1972.

Levine, R. Faltel. *Halacha, Medical Science and Technology*. New York: Maznaim Publishing Corporation, 1987.

Samuelson, Norbert M. "Rethinking Ethics In the Light of Jewish Thought and the Life Sciences." *The Journal of Religious Ethics* 29, no. 2 (Summer 2001): 209–34.

Soleveitchik, Joseph. *The Halachic Mind*. New York: The Free Press, 1986.

Index